WHO CARES?
Women's Work, Childcare, and Welfare State Redesign

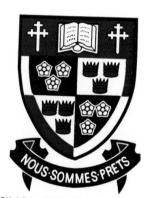

SIMON FRASER UNIVERSITY
W.A.C. BENNETT LIBRARY

Who Cares?

Women's Work, Childcare, and Welfare State Redesign

JANE JENSON and MARIETTE SINEAU

with
FRANCA BIMBI
ANNE-MARIE DAUNE-RICHARD
VINCENT DELLA SALA
RIANNE MAHON
BÉRENGÈRE MARQUES-PEREIRA
OLIVIER PAYE
GEORGE ROSS

UNIVERSITY OF TORONTO PRESS
Toronto Buffalo London

© University of Toronto Press Incorporated 2001
Toronto Buffalo London
Printed in Canada

ISBN 0-8020-4693-2

∞

Printed on acid-free paper

Canadian Cataloguing in Publication Data

Jenson, Jane, 1946–
    Who cares? : women's work, childcare, and welfare state redesign

    (Studies in comparative political economy and public policy)
    Includes bibliographical references.
    ISBN 0-8020-4693-2

    1. Child care – Government policy – Europe.   2. Mothers –
    Employment – Europe.   3. Work and family – Government policy –
    Europe.   I. Sineau Mariette.   II. Title.   III. Series.

    HQ778.7.E85J46 2001   362.71'2'094   C00-932718-5

This book has been published with the help of a grant from the Humanities
and Social Sciences Federation of Canada, using funds provided by the
Social Sciences and Humanities Research Council of Canada.

The University of Toronto Press acknowledges the financial assistance to its
publishing program of the Canada Council for the Arts and the Ontario
Arts Council.

University of Toronto Press acknowledges the financial support for its publishing activities of the government of Canada through the Book Publishing
Industry Development Program (BPIDP).

Contents

Acknowledgments

This work began as a study commissioned by the Caisses Nationales des Allocations Familiales (CNAF), the public body in France most responsible for implementing family policy and, therefore, for facing the challenges described here. We are grateful to the CNAF, especially Jeanne Fagnani and Antoine Math, for their support in the first years of the project. Much of the original research was also supported by granting agencies in Canada. Vincent Della Sala, Jane Jenson, and Rianne Mahon thank the Social Science and Humanities Research Council for research support for this project. In addition, Quebec's Fonds pour la formation de chercheurs et l'aide à la recherche (FCAR) provided major funding of supplementary research, translation, and preparation of this manuscript. Finally, we are grateful to the Social Sciences and Humanities Federation of Canada for the Aid to Scholarly Publication award.

WHO CARES?
Women's Work, Childcare, and Welfare State Redesign

Chapter One

The Care Dimension in Welfare State Redesign

Jane Jenson and Mariette Sineau

The welfare state is about the care of dependent people. The crisis of the welfare state is at least in part ... a 'crisis of the care of the dependent.'
O'Connor, 1997: 23

In the last decade, social policy in Europe has been menaced. As the politics of cutbacks, downsizing, and retrenchment has become endemic, as the invocation of globalization has become commonplace, and as the politics of neo-liberalism has taken hold, spending on social programs has been targeted as the root of our troubles. A major claim on state budgets, social programs presumably contribute to debts and deficits. Moreover, by requiring contributions from employers, they supposedly raise the cost of doing business and hinder competitiveness. Understood by many citizens to be a right, these programs stand accused of interfering with the agenda of change and adaptation to 'new times.' Critics of social spending have raised such spectres and attacked welfare states on these grounds for at least two decades.

Yet it is unwise to take these words of neo-liberals at face value. Globalization is no longer viewed as leading automatically to the demise of the welfare state (Held et al., 1999: 13–14). Nor has the wholesale destruction of welfare states occurred. There have been spending reductions, to be sure, but we now appreciate that such changes might have been more accurately described as retrenchment rather than dismantling. In his award-winning book, *Dismantling the Welfare State? Reagan, Thatcher and the Politics of Retrenchment*, Paul Pierson makes the important point that evidence about crisis in and the dismantling and demise of welfare states 'as we know them' is in short supply. His careful analysis of three sectors – old-age pensions, housing policy, and income-support policy – led him to describe 'a dominant pattern of continuity in social policy. Despite the aggressive efforts of retrenchment advocates, the welfare state remains largely intact' (1994: 179). He found that conservatives grouped behind the ideologies of Reaganism and Thatcherism had not achieved their full agenda in the United States or the United Kingdom. Nor, we argue in this book, did neoliberalism in other countries of Europe succeed in ending the commitment to social spending that characterizes the 'European model of society' – a term popularized by Jacques Delors when he was president of the Commission of the European Union (EU). According to Pierson, this non-destruction of the welfare state is due to the fact that the welfare state itself had generated a set of interests that had every reason to defend it (1995: 8–9).

In a recent publication, John Stephens, Evelyne Huber, and Leonard Ray come to a similar conclusion about the politics of retrenchment. Their quantitative analysis of expenditure data finds spending to have stalled, if not been cut back. They write: 'Our hypothesis is that this was a result of a shift of the political agenda: once it was realized that the game had fundamentally changed as a result of the sea changes in the world economy, governments found themselves with dramatically fewer options. Above all, vigorous expansion of entitlements was off the agenda. This contributed to shifting the politics of social policy to defending entitlements' (1999: 179).

Having banished the prophets of doom and destruction, however, we have little justification for the opposite view, that 'nothing has changed.' It is evident, as documented in detail in the comparative analysis of this book, that a great deal is transpiring: policies are being redesigned and rights redefined. Nor have the ideas and institutions that shaped and maintained the post-war welfare states remained unchanged. Most obviously, a new actor, with its own ideas, has come onto the scene: the European Union cannot be ignored in any consideration of social policy in Europe (Leibfried and Pierson, 1995; Hooge and Marks, 1999). New territorial politics exist, not only because of the presence of this supranational entity; national states also are rethinking their strategies for using social policy as an instrument of territorial integration, as political forces promoting regionalization or federalism gain strength in several countries.[1] Policy networks within national governments have experienced shifts in power relations, as cost-controllers in ministries of finance have gained the upper hand. Moreover, important socio-economic trends are in place, not least of which is the increase in women's labour force participation and the installation of more flexible labour market practices (Jenson, Maruani, and Laufer, 2000).

Therefore, there is still a job to be done. We need to appreciate the types of changes occurring in social programs and in welfare states' understandings of the care of dependent people. Here, the classic study of retrenchment does not always help us. While arguing that the agenda of the New Right was not met, Paul Pierson also said that 'in many cases, services have become more threadbare, benefits have been cut, and eligibility rules have been tightened.' Moreover, referring to the United States and the United Kingdom, he writes, 'income inequality increased sharply in both countries in the 1980s' (1994: 5). Despite these reductions and the rising inequalities, however, Pierson concludes that 'social policy remains the most resilient component of postwar domestic policy' (1994: 179). John Stephens and his co-authors come to a similar conclusion based on a research design of macro-quantitative analysis and brief case studies of 'institutional types.' They find 'There were very few cases in any country where benefits in the mid-1990s were more than marginally lower than they had been in 1970. Second, the basic institutional features of the different welfare states were preserved. In only two of our cases [the United Kingdom and New Zealand] could one speak of a basic transformation of the welfare state pattern that had been shaped during the golden age' (1999: 191). Such conclusions are correct, given the type of analysis conducted. Focused as they are on expenditure levels and treating eligibility, waiting periods, or reduced benefit levels as part of story of continuity, these are useful correctives to the doom and gloom scenarios or other studies. It is the case that public expenditures on social programs continue to be made; governments sometimes rename the new spending 'workfare,' a notion far from the 'social citizenship rights' of T.H. Marshall.

Our starting point is different. As the example of spending on workfare dramatically illustrates, it is precisely the details of services, the eligibility rules, the forms of delivery, and their potential consequences for fostering equality or entrenching inequalities that matter. Therefore, our research design involves more sustained attention to the details, as they affect citizens' everyday lives and their futures, than is common in the literature on welfare state restructuring. Indeed, it is only by analysing the particular trait of program spending and delivery that we can understand the ways in which new patterns of rights, access, and belonging are being created. Although these changes will not put an end to 'the welfare state' or to distinctions among its institutional subtypes, we hypothesize that they constitute more than its 'defence' as well. *We observe, and document significant alterations in the principles and practices underpinning the caring work that has been central to European welfare states.* We seek to identify in the details of policy design and delivery the new principles of citizenship, especially the second dimension of the classic French triplet of liberty, equality, and solidarity.

The claim put forward here, and addressed via a systematic, comparative analysis, is that it is precisely the changes in program design – and the social philosophies that underpin them – that are most important to understand. They signal that a fundamental restructuring of *citizenship regimes* is now occurring in many countries. Spending levels per se do not allow us to assess such shifts; the *direction and forms* of spending are what counts; they can remake citizenship regimes. Moreover, as Julia O'Connor has convincingly argued, when we talk of welfare states we must understand that we are addressing a primary issue: the care of dependent persons, whether the elderly, the disabled, or children.

Welfare States and Care

In recent years it has become common to define the welfare state as an institution designed to ensure the decommodification of labour, thereby freeing workers from the discipline of the labour market.[2] This description has historical validity, but it is also the representation of history as written by those who celebrate the successes of social democracy and a triumphant working class. Other ways of reading the same history of the welfare state are possible.[3]

For example, scholars using a gender lens to read the history of the welfare state have been critical of this focus on decommodification that makes men's experience the norm. In response, others have begun to adjust their analyses. For example, Gøsta Esping-Andersen now writes of a triangle linking family, economy, and state. He describes this triangle as destabilized by rising rates of female labour force participation as well as divorce rates. Thus, he writes: 'Family instability implies, on the one hand, that households' traditional caring capacities are eroding and, on the other hand, that poverty risks are mounting – all the while that families are asked to absorb the new risks that come from labour markets' (1999: 3). In this analysis he does pay attention to the distribution of welfare within the family. Nonetheless, by assuming that women's major – if not only – contribution in the first post-1945 decades of the welfare state was as housewives and full-time mothers, he is still failing to grasp the limitations of a history of the welfare state written in terms only of labour markets and decommodification.

Taking up another lens altogether might allow us to see more. It will allow us to understand that social movements, including the workers' movement, claimed *access to care* as a social right of citizenship. In this view, unemployment insurance loses its status as the fundamental program of the welfare state, and programs such as health care and pensions come to the fore. Indeed, a wide range of social programs address the risk of dependence and the need for care. One example is public health care: for most of the post-war period professional health care in institutions has been a social right of citizenship. In current debates about home care and how to divide the labour between the informal sector (that is, the family) and the formal sector, we see the extent to which access to health care is still a core dimension of social citizenship, albeit with quite different forms and with other consequences for equality.

We might identify three goals of social programs related to care. The first goal is to redistribute the risk of differential needs for care, for example, family policy redistributing the financial burden of raising children. The second goal is to develop programs that seek to improve the quality of care, for instance, by providing early childhood education or regulating service providers, as well as by professionalizing care. The third goal is to reduce dependence and sustain autonomy; pensions for the elderly, for example, allow individuals to care for themselves rather than sink into dependence on their families. Maternity and parental leave programs permit women to reconcile work and family responsibilities, so that they do not have to trade away their income in order to raise a family.

The programs mentioned here, and many others, have been developed as responses to the 'social question' since the nineteenth century. They reflect preoccupations with the issue of care in old age, in childhood, and in sickness, as well as with the problem of dependence on charitable or second-class care provoked by being poor, disabled, or otherwise in need. From this perspective, unemployment was a problem because it made it impossible for families to care for themselves.

Prior to 1945 in most countries, the loss of a breadwinner's salary meant he could no longer provide for his family, the doctor's bill could not be paid, the house went untended while his wife went out to work, and older children were pulled out of school in order to find jobs, thereby limiting their own potential capacity for autonomy. Unemployment insurance and other income security programs provided a way for heads of family, whether male breadwinners or single mothers, to care for their dependants with some measure of dignity. This was the victory celebrated by workers' movements and others as they claimed to have brought the welfare state into being.

Sharing this view that fears about dependence and concerns about care are central to the history of the welfare state and perhaps, even more, to its redesign, in this study we look at the changing pattern of public provision of childcare services in Belgium, France, Italy, Sweden, and the European Union. We examine the ways in which a key value of citizenship, that of equality – particularly gender equality – has been taken into account or ignored in the redesign of childcare services in these neo-liberal times.

Care and Citizenship Regimes

We can see that since at least 1945 welfare states have been concerned with the distribution of responsibility for caring work, the costs of care, and types of services. Therefore, since this is also the period during which T.H. Marshall first identified the establishment of social rights of citizenship, we are led directly towards the need for a closer examination of the notion of citizenship and its connection to care, especially caring work.[4] Indeed, it is precisely for this reason that we look at childcare programs and family policies. We treat this form of caring work as an excellent window onto the modifications occurring in the relationship between the citizen and the state as well as the balance of responsibility among state, market, and community.

In peering through this window and to make sense of the immensely rich variety of new and old programs, we will use the concept of *citizenship regime*.[5] This notion denotes the institutional arrangements, rules, and understandings that guide concurrent policy decisions and expenditures of states, problem definitions by states and citizens, and claims-making by citizens.[6]

The concept stands on two theoretical legs. One is the historical-institutionalist approach to comparative politics (Hall and Taylor,

1996). Embedded in this approach is an analytic proclivity for uncovering and attributing importance to ideas as well as to practices (Thelen and Steimo, 1992; Bradford, 1998). A citizenship regime encodes within it a set of identities, of the 'national' as well as the 'model citizen,' the 'second-class citizen,' and the non-citizen. It contributes to the definition of politics that organizes the boundaries of political debate and problem recognition in each jurisdiction. It encodes representations of the proper and legitimate social relations among and within categories and the borders of public and 'private.'

The second theoretical leg of this concept is the Regulation Approach's notion of stability and change in the patterning of social relations.[7] Without revisiting this approach to political economy in any detail, it is sufficient to say that Regulationists claim that some historical moments have sufficient stability in basic social, economic, and political relations to allow regimes to reproduce themselves. At other times, crisis provokes profound redirection. Organizing and legitimating principles break down and alternative institutional arrangements, rules, and understandings are promoted.

Standing on both theoretical legs leads us to pay attention to systems of ideas as well as to the institutions in which they are embedded and the actions of a variety of actors and their interests. In particular, the dimension of time is essential. Where stability and change are the focus, it is absolutely necessary to examine closely social and political processes as they unfold through time. Such thinking about comparison makes the method of both historical-institutionalism and the Regulationists not merely the most suitable approaches, but entirely necessary ones.

All this said, it is obligatory that we give some content to the citizenship regimes. Following T.H. Marshall (see also Kymlicka and Norman, 1995), we can define the central idea of post-1945 citizenship regimes as essentially a matter of ensuring that everyone is treated as a full and equal member of society.[8] Marshall also had a prescription for achieving that equal treatment; it was the British welfare state. For him, 'by guaranteeing civil, political, and social rights to all, the welfare state ensures that every member of society feels like a full member of society, able to participate in it and enjoy the common life of society. Where any of these rights are withheld or violated, people will be marginalized and unable to participate' (Kymlicka and Norman, 1995: 285–6). Yet, as demonstrated in the myriad studies devoted to the issues of citizenship and welfare states, there was very little agreement about the kind of rights needed, the forms of political participation and access that sustain them and that they protect, or even the feeling of belonging that results.[9] These rights, access, and belonging were the outcome of nationally specific trajectories. Nonetheless, despite the variation, equality was everywhere a central value, just as the emphasis on social rights was widespread in the welfare states created at the time.

Now, as we saw practically every day of the late 1990s, the notion that full citizenship requires a commitment to equality of social rights is much contested. Indeed, we are much more likely to hear that citizenship is about recognition of differences or access to political power than that it is about social equality (for example, Shafir, 1998: 23 ff., and the work to which he refers). Such debates and contestations about the future force us to recognize that citizenship has always been a social construction. Political controversy and competition for power produce the two major dimensions of any citizenship regime. The first dimension is the relationship between the state and the individual citizen; in particular, the rights to which citizens are entitled and the role of the state in guaranteeing these rights are crucial topics for analysis. The second is the division of labour between the state, market, and community. Indeed, the values expressed via this dimension of the citizenship regime identify matters as being rights of citizens rather than as something to be acquired through market behaviour or the consequence of enhanced community activity.

A preference for an active state, for example, will displace market mechanisms for distributing personal services and transform them into a citizens' right to a public service, with distribution decided by mechanisms of democratic control and handled by public servants. Indeed, we can define social policy as 'the use of political power to supersede, supplement or modify operations of the economic system in order to achieve results which the economic system would not achieve on its own' (Leibfried and Pierson, 1995: 3). In contrast, ideological enthusiasm for the market will provoke market-mimicking behaviour among public authorities as well as making citizens' access to services a matter of their own market capacity. In the realm of health care, for example, the first preference might well lead to a universal system, while the second probably would generate a mixed system, in which elements of public insurance would be combined with private insurance and spending from one's own private resources.

T.H. Marshall, himself, clearly understood that citizenship was a social construction, changing through time and varying across space.

He also knew it was dependent on the ideas circulating at the time as well as on the balance of political forces. He provided many illustrations, focusing on the reworking of categories. Look at one of his examples. Marshall recounted how the route to an elaborate system of social rights, which he considered to have been achieved after 1945, involved an important shift in the meaning of 'poverty.' Under England's Elizabethan Poor Laws, being poor constituted a sufficient condition for being excluded from the civil and political rights of citizenship. The dependence of the poor, measured by their inability to maintain autonomous households (indicated by their consignment to the poorhouse), was the factor that justified this exclusion. Beginning in the nineteenth century and throughout the first half of the twentieth, successful political mobilization by workers' organizations and other social reformers resulted in the 'poor' being transformed into citizens entitled to claim from the state sufficient benefits to avoid poverty and to maintain some measure of personal autonomy, free from dependence on care provided by the family, state institutions, or charitable organizations with their moralizing discourses. The categories most affected by this shift, in addition to the unemployed, were the elderly, the disabled, and women with children, that is, all those categories of the population whose relationship to the labour market was severed or maintained only with difficulty.

This story was never universal, even for the British case that Marshall examined. Rather, it is a story reminding us that definitions of citizenship are social constructions. Rights change over time, just as do definitions of routes to representation and the boundaries of the community. It also forces us to recognize that representations of citizenship are a central element of political discourse and are therefore likely to change in moments of turbulence and restructuring of the political economy. Thinking of citizenship in this way allows us to understand why such matters animate political controversy in late capitalist societies.

A single phenomenon is exceedingly instructive for appreciating this relationship between citizenship regimes and the current moment of economic and social turbulence. Our focus in this book is on the change over time in mothers' right to work under the same conditions and with the same hope of earning a reasonable salary as that of men. Economic autonomy, including the right to enter into a labour contract and earn an income by one's labour, is one of the most basic civil rights, long claimed by women's movements and their allies (Jenson, 1995). Most men gained this right with the final collapse of feudalism and its replacement by a market for labour, in eighteenth- and nineteenth-century Europe (Polanyi, 1944). Women, especially married women, gained the same individual right only after the Second World War. In many countries it was only in the mid-1960s that husbands no longer legally had the final say in their wife's decision to work (Sineau, 1992: 479–80). Well into the twentieth century, moreover, certain professions, particularly in the public sector (teaching, for example) were closed to married women.

In more recent decades, it is the distinction between formal and real equality that has come to the fore in this as in so many other domains of citizenship. Phrased simply, women's equality in the labour market is no more than formally achieved until the matter of childcare is settled. Thus, from the beginning of the second wave, feminists in many countries claimed a new social right: access to safe, reliable, and publicly financed childcare. It underpinned their civil right to enter into a labour contract.

In this book we examine how this claim has fared, as citizenship regimes have been restructured in the face of the breakdown of the post-war consensus about the role of states and markets. We examine in detail the fate of the equality agenda as well as the relative responsibility of states and markets in the provision of publicly financed and provided childcare and in encouraging private familial or commercial provision.

Childcare and Public Policy

Who will care for the young child? This question is by no means unimportant. In fact, in the last three decades almost all countries have debated the matter of public responsibility for childcare and the development of services. In part, rising commitments to gender equality help to account for the emergence of the debate (Ostner and Lewis, 1995). Thus, the EU said in its 1992 Council Recommendation on Child Care (*Official Journal.* #L 123/16, 8–5–92):

> Whereas inadequate provision of child-care services at prices affordable to parents and other initiatives to reconcile responsibility for the family and the upbringing of children with their employment, or with the education or training of parents in order to obtain employment constitutes a major barrier to women's access to and more effective participation in the labour market, on equal terms with men ...

It is recommended that Member States should take and/or progressively encourage initiatives to enable women and men to reconcile their occupational, family and upbringing responsibilities arising from the care of children.

Nonetheless, as documented in this book, framing the discussion of childcare in terms of equal opportunities or even as a response to the needs of employed women are only two of several ways of considering the issue. Childcare might be presented as an issue of social welfare (and therefore needed by poor children) or as a matter of child development (and therefore needed by all children as part of pre-school education).[10] Nonetheless, the goal of enabling mothers to reconcile their employment and their family responsibilities had generated by the 1970s, in much of Western Europe, a set of policy initiatives that resulted in state funding and delivery of new services.

The result has been the development of two major types of childcare programs. One supports the development of non-parental care and services. Traditionally, the most common forms of such services were the day nursery and family day care. In both cases a number of children are cared for in a group setting. The distinction between the two is partly in terms of size and partly in terms of the kind of pre-school program provided for the children. Recently, as documented in detail in this book, a number of countries have begun to promote and finance non-parental childcare in the family home, provided by a childminder hired by the parents. Nannies and babysitters are examples of this type of non-parental care.

A second type of childcare program stresses parental care. Parental leaves that permit a temporary absence from the job in order to care for children are an example of this kind of care.[11] Countries have made a variety of choices about the design of parental leaves. Parental leaves may be unpaid or paid, they may be paid at a low flat rate or at almost income replacement levels. Some countries have also recently created programs that give a benefit – either a direct allowance or a tax advantage – to parents who are not in the paid labour force and are caring for their own children.

Whether public policy promotes parental care or non-parental care, whether it partially or fully covers the costs of childcare, or whether it facilitates or hinders women's efforts to reconcile their working time and family time is a matter settled via political choices. There is no single way of doing things, no 'best mix' that meets the needs of all families and meets the goals of all parents. Choices are constantly being made. Therefore, a central question is: What is the basis for selecting one option over another?

In the next chapter we describe in detail the new contexts – demographic, social, and economic – that are the background to choices about childcare. We document changes in two basic measures, the birth rate and women's labour force participation. Our analysis pays particular attention to the latter, because it is often seen as the 'need' that provokes childcare policies, so as to enable mothers of young children to engage in paid work. We observe that in all four of our national cases, rates of female labour force participation, especially among mothers of young children, have risen dramatically since the 1960s.

Our argument here, however, is somewhat more complicated than one about 'needs.' While demand for childcare services may be rising, policy responses are not automatic, in terms of either level of provision or policy design. Therefore, in the rest of chapter 2 we present the institutional and policy context in which childcare policy is embedded. We describe a common pattern of decentralization of service delivery over the last two decades, as local authorities and regional governments gained greater responsibilities in several policy realms. In addition, national standards were frequently made more flexible, as subnational governments were charged with finding the money to deliver services. Of course, these changes were occurring as the European Union took on greater responsibility for social issues, including childcare. Finally, we examine the story of labour market and family policy, uncovering not only the pressures towards cost containment but also the myriad efforts for dealing with seemingly intractably high unemployment rates as national economies faced the challenges of globalization and neo-liberalism.

The premise of this study is that even attention to policy contexts and the ideology of political competition is insufficient to account for the selection of policy options. Therefore, in chapters 3 through 7 we provide five detailed case studies. Each subscribes to the historical-institutionalist approach that teaches us that we must analyse institutions, interests, and ideas (Thelen and Steimo, 1992). Actors have competing and changing interests. Families with a single breadwinner do not have the same childcare needs as single-parent families or dual-earner families. Thus, as labour force practices alter, one would expect to find families pressuring governments for new programs. Representatives of workers, whether left-wing political parties or trade unions, likewise weigh into such discussions. States also have their own interests in such matters, of course. Some see among their responsibilities the promotion of equality, including gender equality. Some have developed concerns about early childhood education and the well-being of future generations. Such interests will lead policy-makers to promote, establish and pay for day nurseries or other public pre-school services. When states consider these areas to be the sole responsibility of parents, they are less likely to provide high-quality developmental services.

In this book we examine the interests in conflict as childcare policies have been made, and then reformed, over time. As a comparative analysis, we also present an examination of the ways that institutions, such as political parties, family movements, unions, and state agencies, intervene in and shape the policy process. For example, Christian Democratic political parties, as institutions, may carry and sustain traditional Roman Catholic ideas about families and subsidiarity. They might then push for different childcare services than would Social Democratic parties, concerned about promoting equality across classes and between women and men.[12] Therefore, which parties are in office and who their allies are in civil society will affect how caring in general and childcare in particular are incorporated into citizenship regimes.

Nor do all state agencies and institutions, even those in a single country, have the same interests. For instance, some are most concerned with labour market functioning, while others have long-standing interests in family well-being.[13] If the centre of decision-making authority were to shift from social service and family bureaucracies to those responsible for employment, for example, we would expect to observe changes in the policy packages proposed. More emphasis might be placed on solving the dilemmas of workers and employers (e.g., job creation and reducing unemployment) than on the problems of poor families or single-parent families. Alternatively, if ministries of finance become involved in policy networks, one might expect cost cutting to become an important goal and tax systems the mode of delivery.

Yet, as these sketched examples illustrate, neither institutions nor interests can be understood apart from the ideas underpinning them.[14] Therefore, a key factor identified in this book to account for different policy choices about childcare provision is the model of gender relations and the representations of women's employment embedded within each citizenship regime. Policy-makers, like policy advocates, share certain assumptions about the role of women, about relations between women and men, about the role of the family, and so on. These assumptions generate a set of representations of working mothers. Their labour force participation, for example, may be described as good or bad. Their participation in the paid labour force may be described as necessary or not, comparable to that of men or different, a right or a choice.

These representations, and the model of gender relations they give rise to, provide the starting point for our policy analysis in each case study. Each chapter proceeds in a similar fashion. After a brief summary of the immediate post-war decades, the authors analyse in detail the policy debates beginning in the 1970s and through to the 1990s. They examine the ways in which policy-makers – including legislators, executives, and bureaucrats, as well as family movements, political parties, and sometimes trade unions – struggle over representations as they make policy choices about childcare. They also pay close attention to debates about alternatives, seeking to account for the options that were not selected as well as the choices that were made.

In the final two chapters an overview is provided of the results of these debates and therefore of the ways in which work and family responsibilities are currently managed. In chapter 8 the policy practices across the cases are compared. Levels of services, forms of delivery, and financial arrangements are mapped, distinguishing publicly financed and provided services from those that are privately provided, whether publicly financed or not. Finding a good deal of commonality despite the diversity of these programs, we move from a static comparison across space in chapter 8 to a more dynamic analysis in the next chapter.

In chapter 9 we summarize the changes in citizenship regimes over time and ultimately identify convergence in the five cases towards a set of basic principles in childcare provision: less costly services, decentralization of service provision from the central government to local authorities, increased diversification in programs available and conditions of access to them, greater flexibility in the use of childcare, and individualization of choice.

We end the book, then, as we began. A comparison of childcare programs is developed across time as well as space to create a window into the redefinition of citizenship regimes associated with welfare state redesign. States are altering their systems of social protection in the face of the demography of ageing societies. The challenge is not only one of caring for the dependent elderly; it is also about the need to maintain birth rates so that there will be sufficient workers to pay for social policy in the future. Childcare issues, like care issues in general, are central to such policy considerations. Similarly, states struggle to address unemployment and the regulation of labour markets. In this environment, mothers' employment has become a hot-button issue. As policy-makers observe the correlation – and it is nothing more than a correlation – between rates of female labour force participation and unemployment figures, childcare discussions find a place in debates about the 'future of work' as well as about gender relations. Finally, as states rethink their relationship to citizens and the mix between public and private responsibilities, childcare has come to be a key testing ground for new thinking about equity. Maximizing 'choice,' implementing a diversity of services, and financing non-public provision are policy options frequently adopted in this neo-liberal era. Childcare has been the testing ground for these shifts in design as well as in fundamental principles of citizenship regimes.

NOTES

1 We agree with Keith Banting that insufficient attention has been paid to the territorial dimensions of welfare state politics (1995: 270).
2 The standard formulation of this concept is by Gøsta Esping-Andersen (1990). For a feminist critique see Ann Orloff's classic article (1993).
3 This section is based on Jenson (1997b).
4 T.H. Marshall's much-cited text was written immediately after the Second World War and was first published in 1949.
5 The concept was developed in Jenson and Phillips (1996), particularly to address the issues of access to political institutions and processes of intermediation. It has also been applied to social policy restructuring in Jenson (1997a) and Boismenu and Jenson (1998).
6 This is an intervention in the ballooning literature on citizenship. Kymlicka and Norman (1995) first identified the 'explosion of interest' in citizenship. Since then, interest continues unabated.
7 On the Regulation Approach, in English, see Jenson (1989) and Noël (1987).
8 Even in the liberal welfare state of Canada, the emphasis was on equity and on the goal of overcoming structural blockages to fair, and even equal, participation (Jenson and Phillips, 1996).
9 For instance, as G. Shafir writes in his introduction to a reader on citizenship: 'Citizenship, then, is an intellectual and moral tradition that has been

repeatedly revisited and updated and, therefore, consists of a string of citizenship discourses' (1998: 2).

10 In Canada, for example, publicly provided childcare was funded by the Canada Assistance Plan (CAP), and therefore was a service targeted to low-income families. See, for example, Lero and Kyle (1991) for a discussion of the difficulties of transforming it into a program to meet the needs of all working parents.

11 Maternity leaves are sometimes included in this category. It is important to distinguish, however, the *health* issues related to childbirth (and therefore specific to the natural mother), which historically have been addressed by maternity leave, and *childcare* issues, which are longer term and may involve both parents.

12 Such differences might account for one of the major findings of the Stephens et al. study that partisan differences no longer correlate with expenditure levels (1999:179). If, as we will find in the cases of Belgium and France, both right-wing and left-wing governments are paying mothers to care for their own children, the usual expectation about left-wing parties and spending practices is not confirmed.

13 For an example of the policy consequences of certain policy configurations, or what they call 'needles' eyes,' see Ostner and Lewis (1995).

14 Here, we are clearly taking issue with Pierson, who explicitly rejects the notion that ideas are important (1994: 177), and siding with those who consider ideas an important explanatory variable. For an excellent presentation of the literature on the latter see Bradford (1998: chapter 1).

Chapter Two

New Contexts, New Policies

Jane Jenson and Mariette Sineau

During the past three decades both socio-economic structures and state policies have rapidly changed, thus putting pressure on post-war citizenship regimes. By the mid-1970s it was becoming ever clearer that the post-1945 patterns of economic boom and high growth rates were no more. Nonetheless, policy-makers did not, nor could they, respond in one fell swoop to the crisis. Indeed, for a number of years the balance of political forces, ideas, and policy networks was such that the second-phase construction of the welfare state, begun in the 1960s, continued according to the pattern of existing citizenship regimes. Most concretely, this meant that the pressure that social movements had been putting on governments, insisting that they add gender equality to their commitment to cross-class equality, was still generating positive results into the 1970s.

By the 1980s, however, this equality agenda was challenged by other visions, dominated by different ideas about combating unemployment, responding to employers' demands for greater flexibility in labour markets, and re-launching the competitiveness of European economies. These challenges were felt by all four of the countries focused on in this book, and the extension of the European Community, our fifth case, is partly a response to them. Adjustment could not stop at 'Europeanization'; domestic policies in each country also were redesigned to face up to what were increasingly described as the 'new realities' of economic restructuring and globalization and their consequences for the social rights of citizenship.

The result was a fragmentation of post-war paradigms. The dominant ideas of the post-war period were discredited and policy proclivities reshaped. Both underpinning these changes and fostered by them was a series of significant alterations in the social and economic behaviour of European women. Their actions have created pressures for new childcare programs. In simplest terms, despite falling birth rates, the number of children needing some form of non-parental care has increased because more women are in the paid labour force. Rising rates of female labour force participation also created another policy dilemma. Unemployment rates skyrocketed in the years of restructuring, and many of the unemployed were women with young children. Therefore, as we will see, policy-makers began to be tempted by the idea of again encouraging mothers to provide their own childcare. Over time, in other words, childcare policy became increasingly linked to employment policy, both as a possible source of employment (via non-parental care) and as a way of addressing high rates of unemployment (parental leaves in some countries).

The contextualization provided in this chapter is based on a specific way of understanding any policy. Childcare programs have their own specificity, to be sure, but they never develop in isolation; they always fit within larger policy domains, each characterized by its own ideas, institutions, and policy networks. The story line presented in this part – and followed up in the subsequent more detailed studies – is that there has been a tendency to bring childcare programs into line with the needs of employment policy.

In order to tell the story, in the first section of this chapter we examine the major socio-demographic changes and in the labour force activity of women, especially mothers of young children. We then provide a brief presentation of two policy realms, labour market and family, again in a comparative mode across time and space. Finally, we map the major institutional changes that underpin the ways all four countries and the European Union now address the policy challenges of family and labour market policies. After completing these three contextual analyses, we are prepared to proceed to the detailed study of five cases.

A New Demographic and Sociological Context

The first three post-war decades have frequently been characterized as ones of 'boom,' giving rise to talk of modernity, growth, and progress, as well as citizenship regimes seeking cross-class and, somewhat later, cross-gender equality. Too often, however, it has been only high rates of economic growth, full employment, rising incomes, and multiplying state services that have received political and analytic attention. During these years a second boom occurred: the post-war baby boom. It comforted demographers and pro-natalists as well as contributing to the consumption capacity of post-war Fordist economies.

In the 1970s European countries experienced two important downturns, which shook them in major ways and began a redesign of citizenship regimes. First, demographic trends began to move downward, causing policy-makers to worry about the capacity of subsequent generations to sustain the infrastructure of social protection as well as the strength of the nation. Second, economic crisis and restructuring had begun to menace economic growth, state spending, and employment. This socio-economic context of mounting female labour force participation, as well as rising unemployment rates and threats to policies of social protection, deserves attention. The eventual result, as we will see, was new representations of the links connecting employment (and unemployment), demography, and mothers' work.

The Baby Boom Ends

About 1965 in several countries of what is now the European Union, including the four studied here, demographers started to notice a change. Families were shrinking. Immediately after the Second World War all demographic indicators had risen sharply. Two decades later they were starting – although some more quickly than others – to turn down. By the mid-1990s, in all four countries, measures of fertility had fallen below the symbolic bar of 2, the rate necessary to reproduce the population. In the 1960s, as shown in table 2.1, the rate had been well above 2.

This major change in the statistics reflects two significant shifts in behaviour. First, almost all women had children but, on average, fewer children than earlier generations. Thus, the rate of childless women was decreasing steadily at the same time as was the number of children born to each woman.[1] The result is that the average family is now significantly smaller. The 'large family,' defined statistically as well as popularly as a family with three or more children, is much less prevalent today than it was previously (Rostgaard and Fridberg, 1998: 27). In Italy, for instance, 35 per cent of total births in 1960 were third children, whereas they represented only 15 per cent of the births in 1992. The Belgian and French statistics show the same pattern (Eurostat, 1995a: 66).[2] Second, European women are having their children later in life.

TABLE 2.1
Fertility rates, 1960–94

	1960	1970	1980	1990	1994
Belgium	2.6	2.2	1.7	1.6	1.5*
France	2.7	2.5	1.9	1.7	1.6
Italy	2.4	2.4	1.0	1.2	1.2*
Sweden	2.2	2.0	1.6	2.1	1.8
Europe**	2.6	2.4	1.8	1.5	1.4*

*Estimated
**Average 1960–80, for the twelve Member States; average
after 1990, for the fifteen Member States
Sources: 1960–80 – *Economie et Statistique*, vol. 220, 1989;
1990–94 – Eurostat, *Statistiques démographiques*, 1996.

The drop in birth rates has paralleled an increase in the average age at which women give birth to a first child (Eurostat, 1995a: 61).

It is important to note, however, that the fall in fertility rates is not the same everywhere, as shown in table 2.1. Despite being among the lowest of industrialized countries from the 1960s to the beginning of the 1980s, by 1990 the Swedish birth rate was comparatively very high (although it again began to fall in the mid-1990s). Fertility rates in France and in Belgium remain above the European average, while Italy's rate is clearly far below it. Moreover, while the first two countries had stable fertility rates by the 1980s, Italy's rate continued to drop. Indeed, as evident in the table, there was a significant difference between Italy and the other three countries. While rates in the latter are stabilizing at a relatively high level, Italy's drop has been steeper and may be continuing. Each generation of Italian women is having substantially fewer children, on average, than its predecessor (Bégeot and Fernandez-Gordon, 1997: 42).

The result of these trends is that the total of children under the age of 3 is in decline, except in Sweden. In France, for example, the number of under-3s was 1.78 million in 1968 and only 1.63 million in 1990, constituting 3.5 per cent of the total population in 1968 but only 2.8 per cent in 1990 (INSEE, 1992: 13). Of course, the fact that the number of young children is dropping does not in any way mean that the need for childcare services is declining. On the contrary, demand is on the increase as mothers' labour force participation climbs.

The End of Full Employment

In 1973–4 almost every country in the industrialized world experienced economic crisis, provoked by falling rates of productivity, new
patterns of production and trade internationally, and the first oil
shock. The combination of these factors is usually grouped under the
rubric 'the breakdown of Fordism.' [3] All four of the countries examined here experienced a significant increase in unemployment,
although not necessarily following the same time line. The general
unemployment rate, presented in table 2.2, shows three things. First,
there was a huge uprising between 1975 and the mid-1980s. In France
and Sweden the unemployment rate more than doubled, and in Italy
it tripled. Second, in Italy and France the increase continued thor-
ough the 1980s and 1990s. Even in Belgium, where the unemployment rate declined somewhat, it never returned to the low levels of
the first post-war decades. Third, Sweden's experience after the first
years was different from than of the other countries. It managed to
drive back down the unemployment rate, only to see it rocket in the
1990s, reaching levels comparable to the other Member States of the
European Union.

Throughout the European Union, just as in Belgium, France, and
Italy, unemployment is higher among women than among men (table
2.2). Sweden, however, is a clear exception to this pattern. From the
1960s until the 1990s unemployment rates were gender neutral. Then,
in the mid-1990s the men's rate surpassed that of women. This table
also shows that unemployment was a particular problem for young
people; their rates have been – without exception – higher than the
national averages. In all four countries, moreover, young women experienced significantly more unemployment than young men, with the
exception of only the 1994 statistics in Sweden. Women are also found
among the long-term unemployed. For instance, in Belgium and Italy
in the mid-1990s more than one-third of unemployed women had been
seeking a job for at least two years (Eurostat, 1995a: 163).

The last unemployment pattern that is important to note, given the
focus of this book, is that it disproportionately affects women with
children, women with young children, and single mothers with young
children. In the countries of the European Union in the early 1990s, for
example, the unemployment rate of women with children under 5 and
living with their spouse was 13.8 per cent; it jumped to 24 per cent for
single mothers with young children (Eurostat, 1995a: 169).

TABLE 2.2
Labour force participation and unemployment rates by sex and age, 1968–94 (percentage)

		Participation rate*		Unemployment rate*		Unemployment, 15–24**		
		Men	Women	Men	Women	Men	Women	Unemployment*
Belgium	1983	76.6	44.5	8.1	17.8	19.3	28.9	11.7
	1989	72.0	45.7	5.3	13.0	11.4	20.2	8.3
	1993	71.8	50.6	6.2	10.8	17.4	19.6	8.1
France	1968	88.1	49.3	1.5	2.5	2.7	4.0	1.9
	1975	84.9	53.0	2.5	5.3	5.9	10.2	3.7
	1983	79.3	55.6	6.2	10.6	15.0	25.5	8.0
	1989	76.2	57.4	7.2	12.6	14.7	24.2	9.5
	1994	74.5	59.6	10.8	14.3	24.2	31.6	12.4
Italy	1968	83.7	29.4	3.3	4.1	10.7	10.3	3.5
	1975	79.2	29.8	2.8	4.6	12.5	13.2	3.3
	1983	78.5	39.6	6.3	15.5	25.5	36.5	9.4
	1989	76.5	43.8	8.1	18.8	27.8	40.4	12.1
	1994	73.5	42.5	8.8	15.7	29.1	36.5	11.3
Sweden	1968	92.0	57.8	2.3	2.2	3.7	4.5	2.3
	1975	91.0	68.9	1.3	2.0	2.8	4.8	1.6
	1983	87.7	78.3	3.4	3.6	7.8	8.3	3.5
	1989	88.1	82.5	1.4	1.5	3.2	3.2	1.5
	1994	82.2	76.4	8.9	6.7	18.9	14.7	7.8

*15 and older in France and Belgium; 14 and older in Italy; 16 and older in Sweden
**14–24 in Italy; 16–24 in Sweden
Source: OECD, Labour Force Statistics. Those for 1968 are taken from the 1965–85 collection, the rest from the 1973–93 collection.

Yet Women Are Staying in the Labour Force

Since the beginning of the crisis, women's labour force participation has constantly climbed,[4] often to the great surprise of economists and policymakers, while that of men has declined over the same time, sometimes by almost as much as the women's increase (table 2.2).[5] The French case illustrates this pattern. In the decade and a half after 1975, 3.3 million people joined the labour force, of which 3 million were women and only 300,000 men (Maruani and Reynaud, 1993: 19). Recently, there has been a slight drop-off in women's labour force participation in Italy and Sweden. This decline may due to the fact that young people are delaying their entry into the labour force by remaining in school (men's participation rates have also declined), or it may be due to changing structures of employment. It is still too early to say. Nonetheless, even this slight reduction cannot halt the general trend towards increase.

It is not surprising that the increase in women's labour force participation has been most pronounced in countries where rates were initially low, such as Italy. Despite such catching up, however, none of the other three countries rivals Sweden, which continues to have the highest rate of women's labour force participation: the difference between women and men's participation rate was only 5.8 percentage points in 1994 (table 2.2). France ranks next, with both a higher overall female rate and a gender difference of only 14.9 points, followed by Belgium with a participation rate of only 50.6 per cent and a gap between the sexes of 21.2 points. Italy has one of the lowest female labour force participation rates in Europe, while among our four countries it has the largest gender gap, a difference of 31 percentage points.

Although there has been a strong general increase in women's labour force participation since the mid-1960s, there are still important differences in the extent to which the labour force is feminized (table 2.3). In 1993 women represented 48 per cent of the Swedish labour force, but in Italy they accounted for only 37 per cent. Belgium and France were in the middle: 42 per cent of their workforces were female. Such high rates of feminization of the labour force follow, in large part, from recent patterns of job creation. Between 1985 and 1990 women took fully two-thirds of any new jobs in the European Community (*Cahiers de Femmes d'Europe*, 1992: 3).

Behind these general increases in women's labour force participation and the feminization of labour forces there is one absolutely crucial

TABLE 2.3
Feminization of the labour force (percentage of the
labour force that is female)

	1968	1982	1993*
Belgium	31.3	38.4	42.3
France	34.4	40.4	42.2
Italy	28.5	33.5	36.9
Sweden	38.0	46.2	48.0

*1992 for Italy
Source: OECD, *Labour Force Statistics*

sociological fact. The labour force behaviour of women of prime child-bearing age (25–49) accounts for much of this change (Maruani, 2000: 14ff). Between 1983 and 1993, for example, the number of women in this age cohort entering the labour force rose significantly. In Belgium, there was an increase of more than 12 percentage points, reaching 71.3 per cent of the cohort. In France, the rate of increase was only 9.9 points, but the percentage of the group employed is higher, at 77.3 per cent. In Italy, 55.3 per cent of women between 25 and 49 were employed in 1993 and the increase over the previous decade was 7 percentage points.[6] The Swedish patterns are slightly different but nonetheless fully confirm that this age cohort of women is employed. First, the participation rate of the 25–49 age group was very high, at 87.1 per cent in 1993. Second, the increase happened earlier and faster, with a rise of 30 percentage points between 1967 and 1983. The rate has tended to be stable since then.

Another way to understand the changes in patterns of participation is to observe labour force participation by age group and over time. In Sweden, women's labour force participation is almost as continuous as men's and is approaching male levels. Participation rates in France now resemble those in Sweden. In the last twenty years there have been two major changes in France. The participation rate for women aged 25 to 49 has climbed, and it drops only at retirement age. Belgium and Italy, however, do not display the same patterns. In Belgium the labour force participation rate climbed sharply for those aged 25 to 34 (reaching the male rate in the 1990s) but then drops off dramatically for older age categories. Nor has this pattern shifted over time. The Italian pattern is similar, although the details are different. There the rate of

TABLE 2.4
Labour force participation rates, 1992, women, 20–39,
by number of children (percentage)

	Number of children			
	None	One	Two	Three +
Belgium	89.1	80.1	73.1	50.5
France	83.8	81.8	76.4	45.9
Italy	70.9	57.3	46.7	35.7
Europe	84.8	68.3	61.1	44.8

Source: Eurostat, *Labour Force Study*, 1995

rise in participation rates has been even steeper for the group of 25- to 39-year-olds. However, as in Belgium, the next age cohorts have much lower rates of participation.

These cross-national differences may reflect timing. In all the cases it is young women, in the 25–34 age cohort and of prime child-bearing age, whose participation rates are highest. Thus, experts have concluded that since the beginning of the 1980s all patterns are moving toward similarity, reflecting continuous participation over the life-cycle. In the words of Margaret Maruani: 'The same tendency can be observed in all European countries. The labour force participation rates of women between the ages of 25 and 49 have increased significantly, regularly, and systematically for the last ten years. In the past, this age cohort was the "empty set" of the labour force. Today, it has a rate of labour force participation that is very high, sometimes even exceeding that of other age groups' (2000: 8).

Such changes in women's labour force behaviour should never let us forget, however, that having a young child is still an obstacle to a mother's employment. It is no longer as it was in the 1950s and 1960s, of course, when it was rare for a woman to keep a job once she became a mother (Maruani, 2000: 15). However, having a young child can still cause a withdrawal from the labour market.[7] Again, we observe that the consequences of having children vary cross-nationally as well as over time. The number of children has a major impact throughout Europe, as shown in table 2.4.[8] In every country, women's labour force participation falls as the number of children increases and rises when the children are older (table 2.5).[9] It is only in Italy, however, that

TABLE 2.5
Labour force participation rates, 1990,
women, 20–59, by age of youngest
children (percentage)

	2 and under	2–7
Belgium	63.9	68.9
France	61.5	69.4
Italy	49.5	51.1
Sweden	67.0	n/a

Source: Hantrais and Letablier (1995: 71)

labour force participation plummets as soon as one child is born,
whereas in France and in Belgium the dramatic decline occurs only
with the arrival of a third child. Nonetheless, even in the latter two
cases, the presence of a child, and certainly a second child, results in a
rate of labour force participation that is significantly lower than that of
childless women.

Again, it is in Sweden that having young children seems to have the
least effect on mothers' rates of labour force participation. Nonetheless,
it is important to distinguish between employment and participation
rates in order to understand the actual situation. Among mothers of
children under 6, the employment rate (that is, the number actually
holding a job) is a full 30 percentage points lower than their participation rates (Jonung and Persson, 1993: 261). The gap is explained by the
fact that many of them are on parental leave, but are still being counted
statistically as being in the active labour force.

The last distinction, as in the other patterns already observed, makes
it not unreasonable to argue that having publicly provided or financed
childcare programs is an important factor in determining whether or
not women can retain their jobs after having a child. But it is not wise
to jump too quickly to conclusions. Indeed, as documented in table 2.4,
the participation rates of women with no children, and who therefore
suffer no handicap linked to the availability of childcare services, are
also differentiated cross-nationally. Fewer young or childless Italian
women participate in the paid labour force than do Belgian or French
women in the same age cohort. The situation is more complex, then,
than simply availability of childcare services. The structures of the
labour market must also be taken into account.

TABLE 2.6
Part-time work, 1973–95, by sex

		Percentage of workers who are part-time			Female percentage of part-timers
		Total	Men	Women	
Belgium	1973	3.8	1.0	10.2	82.4
	1983	8.1	2.0	19.7	83.9
	1995	13.6	2.8	29.8	87.5
France	1973	5.9	1.7	12.9	82.3
	1983	9.6	2.5	20.1	84.3
	1995	15.6	5.0	28.9	82.0
Italy	1973	6.4	3.7	14.0	58.3
	1983	4.6	2.4	9.4	64.8
	1995	6.4	2.9	12.7	70.6
Sweden	1979	23.6	5.4	46.0	87.5
	1983	24.8	6.3	45.9	86.6
	1995	24.3	9.4	40.3	80.1

Source: OECD, *Perspectives de l'emploi* (1996)

New Patterns of Employment

If women's and men's rates of labour force participation are drawing closer, this is certainly not the case for their conditions of employment. In recent years, as restructuring has gone forward, the gap between the kinds of jobs held by women and by men has, if anything, widened. Policies permitting the creation of more 'flexible' labour forces, via changes to working time (such as part time and flexi-hours or temporary and contingent labour contracts) have affected women's employment in significant ways.

The trend towards variable working hours and its consequences for women workers is overwhelmingly clear. In 1996 in the fifteen-member European Community 32 per cent of women but only 6 per cent of men worked part time (Maruani, 2000: 81). This single statistic hides important differences among countries. As documented in table 2.6, while fully 40 per cent of Swedish women worked only part time in 1995, merely 9 per cent of men did the same. The corresponding statistics for France are 29 per cent and 5 per cent, but for Italy they are only 13 per cent and 3 per cent. Part-time work for women in Sweden, which has been very popular since the 1960s, has almost become the 'Swedish tradition' (Daune-Richard, 1995: 115). Nonetheless, the rate has fallen since the 1970s, as shown in table 2.6. Moreover, part-time employees are working longer hours. Thus, differences between the two kinds of working time are actually diminishing (Björnberg, 1997).

In our other countries the history is quite different. First, the move towards part-time employment was part of the response to the pressures from economic crisis and for restructuring (see the next section). Examples of this pattern may be seen in France and Belgium. Until the early 1980s less than 10 per cent of the labour force and fewer than one in five employed women held a part-time job (table 2.6). Then, a steep rise in rates of part-time work created a major gender distinction in the heart of the labour force. By 1995 in these two countries, 30 per cent of women (only 10 per cent less than in Sweden) held only a part-time job, and more than four of every five part-timers were female. Much of this increase can be accounted for by the fact that more young women and women of prime child-bearing age now work part time.

The latter are precisely the same group whose dramatic increase in labour force participation we just described. Putting these two findings together, we observe that while female labour force participation rates are indeed rising, women's employment patterns, especially their working time (and therefore earning power), are not the same as those of men.[10]

It is very common to find mothers employed part time. In 1992, in the European Community only 13.4 per cent of childless women worked part time but the percentage jumped to 32.4 per cent for those with at least one child. In Italy, the part-time rate of mothers is more than three times higher than that of childless women, while in Belgium and France, it is double (Eurostat, 1995c: 152).[11] Unfortunately, these data are not available by the age of the child, but it seems reasonable to think that mothers who 'choose' to work part time are probably those with young children.[12]

Of course, the effective definition of 'part-time work' varies across the four countries. As documented in table 2.7, Swedish women working part time are, on average, working the most hours, while the Belgians are working, on average, fully three hours a week less. Indeed, nearly three of every five Swedish women and two of every five French women classified as part time are employed at least twenty-five hours per week. On the other hand, 63 per cent of Belgian and 58 per

TABLE 2.7
Women working part-time, 1995, by number of hours normally worked per week

	1–10	11–20	21–24	25–30	31+	Weekly average of hours
Belgium = 100	5.1	57.8	11.2	18.1	7.8	21.4
France = 100	10.4	39.6	9.5	22.9	17.6	22.6
Italy = 100	7.4	50.1	13.1	15.9	13.3	22.5
Sweden = 100	10.3	23.3	8.6	38.3	19.6	24.4

Source: Eurostat, *Labour Force Study,* 1995

cent of Italian female part-timers are employed for less than twenty-one hours per week. These differences have obvious consequences for their earning power.

Another distinction relates to when the part time job is done. In many cases, part-time employees work during weekends. In Belgium, France, and Italy, more women than men work on Saturday. In addition, the percentage of women who usually work on Saturday is very high in Italy (43 per cent), close to the European average in France (27 per cent), and below it in Belgium and Sweden (21 per cent in each country) (Eurostat, 1995b: table 63). Of course, what is 'flexibility' for the employer is often not compatible with efforts to balance work and family life, unless one imagines that such reconciliation involves parents' alternating childcare – mothers during the regular work week and fathers on weekends. The effect on family life may be quite negative.

European women are also more likely than men to be found among those whose employment contract is atypical. In 1992, for example, 11.9 per cent of women had limited-term employment contracts, whereas only 9.8 per cent of men were in the same situation (Eurostat, 1995a: 153). In Belgium, France, and Italy, more women than men had such limited-term contracts, although none of the three countries has an above-average use of such contracts for the labour force as a whole. Sweden differs from the other three countries, because between 1987 and 1993 the number of limited-term contracts actually fell faster among women than among men (Commission Européenne, 1995: 59).

One might have thought that homework was a thing of the past. Yet today it is booming, especially in the service industries, which employ so many women. Often, working at home is proposed as a way to balance work and family life. Belgium has the highest proportion of the labour force working at home (over 10 per cent); Sweden comes next with 8 per cent, while France and Italy are lower at 5 per cent. In every country, except in Sweden, there are more women than men working at home (Eurostat, 1995a: 155; 1995b: table 63).

Part-time jobs, limited-term contracts, and homework are features of the flexible employment portrayed in the statistical portraits of the four countries that we have briefly sketched. Is it women who are seeking this flexibility? Do they see it as a way to reconcile work and family life? We know that in France, for example, mothers provide more of their own childcare when they are working part time than they do when working full time (Leprince, 1987: 513). Are women choosing flexible employment so they can care for their own children, or is this flexibility imposed by employers who provide a choice between working part time or being unemployed?

Any answers to these questions must be carefully constructed. On the one hand, it is certainly true that a significant number of women forced to work in atypical ways wish that they could find more traditional employment. On the other hand, opinion polls uncover increasing numbers of people hoping to work part time. In 1993 among French people working full time approximately 30 per cent of women said that they would not mind working fewer hours, even if it meant a pay cut. Only 18 per cent of men willingly contemplated doing the same. Even if part-time jobs do not always allow parents perfectly to balance work and family life, having young children significantly increases women's expressed demand for part-time jobs, particularly among employed mothers with children under six years. A full 40 per cent of them would like to work part time (INSEE, 1995: 134–5). Researchers also find that a large number of unemployed women, especially those older than 25, are seeking a part-time job. Fully 25 per cent of European women in this age cohort want part-time work, but only 4 per cent of men do. Looking cross-nationally, we see that 27 per cent of unemployed Italian women, approximately 20 per cent of French women, and 17 per cent of Belgian and Swedish women would welcome such a job (Eurostat, 1995b: table 106). Again, however, we cannot distinguish between those who would truly like part-time work as a lifestyle choice, those who see it as the only way to reduce the stress they experience, and those who are forced to choose part-time jobs.

In this section we have mapped the sociological context in which increased – and different – demands for childcare services have emerged, despite the demographic downturns since the post-war baby boom. The end of that other boom, the post-war boom of Fordism, also created pressures for change, as mothers entered the labour force, faced unemployment, and began to working in atypical ways. We turn in the next sections to the policy and institutional contexts that underpin these sociological shifts. Most particularly, we will document the fact that the patterns of employment and unemployment, atypical work, and precarious employment are not simply the result of individual women's or families' choices. They are directly shaped by the economic and family policies that are also adjusting to the restructuring conditions of these years.

Employment Policy: Confronting 'Flexibility' and Unemployment

Through the decades of economic and political change covered in this book, one of the most dramatic alterations has been in the area of labour market policy. In the 1960s macroeconomic policy was shaped by a commitment to full employment, and employment policy was a tool, supposedly available for making good use of human resources. Supposedly, economic growth would thereby be fostered.[13] By the 1980s the goals were radically different. Overall, states focused most on getting their public finances in order. They treated labour market policy as a tool useful for eliminating labour market rigidities and targeting the categories of the labour force most difficult to insert into employment, that is, the long-term unemployed and young workers (OECD, 1990b: 14; Stevens and Michalski, 1994: 20). In this context the very notion of employment changed. Instead of the 'typical work' norm being full time, five days per week, with weekends off and a long-term contract, it became much more precarious, irregular, and contingent. As we saw in the previous section, such jobs are not equally distributed throughout the population; they are heavily feminized.

In this section we present two dimensions of change, both of which profoundly shape the way policy-makers address women's work. One is the move towards flexibility in labour market regulations, instituted at the behest of employers, and in response to the search by governments, including the European Union, for competitive advantage (Meulders, 2000). The other is unemployment policy, which increasingly has targeted particular categories of the population and developed special programs to promote their employment, even in atypical employment. As we documented above, the unemployed, the long-term unemployed, and young workers seeking a job are disproportionately female.

Moving towards Flexibility

There are three principal dimensions of deregulation of labour markets that fall under the heading 'flexibility': salary setting, regulations for hiring and firing, and working time (OECD, 1990b: 22). The express goal of these policies is to return to employers some of the control over decisions that had been shared with unions, and sometimes states, in the Fordist years. Thus, deregulation often occurs in a political context in which unions' bargaining power is weak or weakening, as in Italy and France, or one in which national-level peak bargaining is losing its regulatory capacity, as in Sweden or Belgium. These changes are part of the decentralization to the market and the dispersal of authority to regionally based decision-makers, as well as to the supra-national EU, that we will discuss below.

With respect to laying off workers, in all four cases there has been an easing of the conditions. In France and Italy, legislative changes were involved, while in Sweden and Belgium the peak-level labour-management agreements that have regulated the labour market for decades came under pressure for more 'give' by the unions. Salary setting also became much more decentralized in the three cases that had been characterized (with France being the exception) by central wage bargaining in previous decades (Hellman, 1997: 388–9; Stevens and Michalski, 1994: 21).

Efforts also were made to move atypical employment into the mainstream, regularizing it and providing a wider range of protections. In Belgium, for example, a new office was set up within the Employment Service to oversee temporary and fixed-term work and a regulatory framework for home work was put in place (OECD, 1990b: 27; Ditch et al., 1996: 54). France's efforts to regularize atypical contracts have born fruit: in 1995 one in every eleven workers had such a contract, and for young people it had become an almost obligatory rite of passage into the labour force (Letablier, 1996: 101). Both Sweden and Italy resisted the move towards destandardization and temporary work contracts were severely limited, but by 1993 the second was also forced to cede (OECD, 1996: 80).

Flexibility in working hours is another important dimension of the move away from standard working conditions. There has been a veritable explosion of new working times – evenings, weekends, night work – which have become ordinary rather than being the 'extraordinary' working times that merit bonuses, time and a half, and so on. As greater numbers of people, particularly in services, are called on to work on weekends and evenings, the management of family time and childcare inevitably becomes even more complex.

The Struggle against Unemployment

Employers justify flexibility and deregulation in the language of 'competitiveness,' but governments have been more likely to turn to non-standard work as a way of fighting unemployment. Despite all the efforts, however, unemployment and underemployment are widespread. Nor, as we saw in the previous section, is unemployment gender neutral. Women are very well represented, indeed, usually overrepresented, in these statistics. In general, three policy directions are identifiable.

One policy is to reduce the working time of some categories of the population, with the hope that new hirings will be made to replace those who are working less or who have withdrawn from the labour force. Typical programs encourage early retirement, part-time work, parental leave, or other forms of career breaks. This is a major point of intersection of employment policy and family policy. Sweden was the leader in this area, albeit for other reasons. As early as the 1970s the policy link was made between part-time work and family policy (Mahon, 1996): parents of young children have a right to work part time. Since then, other countries have moved in the same direction, but often have been motivated by an interest in job creation as much as balancing work and family. In the early 1990s France revised its paid and unpaid parental leaves to allow parents to combine them with part-time employment, spread not only over the week but also over the month and year. Italy has little part-time employment, as we saw above, in part because unions and employers were very reluctant to include it in collective bargaining (Del Re, 1996:69). Since 1994, however, new rights have been negotiated, although it still remains an expensive option for private sector employers (Ditch, Bradshaw, and Eardley, 1996: 67–8). Belgium instituted a general Career Break, available for any reason, but expected it to serve as the functional equivalent of a paid parental leave (OECD, 1994: 62).

The second direction of policy change is to relieve employers of some of the costs associated with employing someone. This policy of reducing the cost of labour has been widely used to target the needs of the long-term unemployed and young workers (Sterdyniak et al., 1994:

46ff.; OECD, 1994: 60; 1996: 80; Letablier, 1996: 101). Employers receive a variety of inducements, including exemption from paying social security benefits, when they hire from among the targeted groups. The European Union's structural funds have also been used to target certain groups in need of employment, with explicit mention of women as well as young people and the long-term unemployed. As we will see in the case studies, this policy of reducing employers' costs has been extended to the childcare sector in some countries.

A third direction of state policy to combat unemployment is to cultivate the service sector, particularly private personal services (Foucauld, 1994: 59; Stevens and Michalski, 1994: 18–19). Even in Sweden, where the private service sector has been stunted until now, the government is now encouraging both enlargement of the market in private services and market-mimicking forms of public provision. This strategy allows private services to substitute for public services as the public sector cuts back or seeks to appear more efficient (see below). Two labour market results can be anticipated. One is the expansion of jobs in services that are less well paid and less protected than public-sector employment. Such services are most often provided both to individuals and to governments by small or medium firms. Any active labour market policy, which has always depended on peak-level agreement among social partners, will be more difficult to sustain as the number of actors and the spaces for firm-level variations multiply, as the national system of corporatist regulation collapses (Thörnqvist, 1999). In France, policy is also increasingly focused on the development of personal services, encouraging, in particular, the non-profit sector to begin to provide home care and childcare (Pitrou and Dandurand, 1997: 13). The non-profit, third sector in Belgium has also been promoted as a provider of services as the welfare state contracts and traditional public services are reduced (Poulet, 1994; Ouali and Rea, 1994: 103ff.).

None of these dimensions is neutral in its effects on class and gender relations. Promoted in the name of 'choice' for those who are consumers of services and social 'solidarity' with those at risk of being excluded from mainstream society, these programs rarely deploy a discourse of equal social citizenship. They seek less to generate social equality across classes or gender equality between women and men than to limit state spending on public services and to reduce the social costs of long-term unemployment and non-employment. A job, any job, is the watchword. There is little concern about whether the job will ghettoize certain people in low-paid, precarious employment with few prospects for the future. There is less concern – and even Sweden's growing enthusiasm for private markets in services reveals this – with combating the social inequalities that can be associated with individuals' personally hiring others than there is with increasing choice (Rostgaard and Fridberg, 1998: 171).[14] The consequences of such choices about how to fight unemployment will become clearer as we examine in more detail the way childcare provision is changing.

Family Policies Caught up in Welfare State Redesign

The crisis of Fordism and recent adjustments to citizenship regimes involved a major rethinking of the role of the state, particularly its spending on social policy. Governments faced falling revenues at the same time as claims on social programs, due to higher levels of unemployment, rose. The fiscal crunch became severe as governments turned increasingly to the policy of exempting employers from paying social security contributions, supposedly in order to generate higher levels of employment.

At the same time, the demographic vice was tightening. Falling birth rates meant that in the not too distant future large cohorts of an ageing and retired population would be supported, through income transfers via social programs such as pensions and health, by fewer young workers. As baby boomers moved inexorably towards retirement, there were fewer potential workers to make contributions to public pension funds. Contemplating the coming crunch, policy-makers began to treat demography as part of social policy, while intergenerational issues came to the fore (Dumon, 1996: 31–2).

Such concerns generated a common cross-national pattern. Although absolute spending on family policy rose, it lost ground relative to other social policies (Fagnani, 1996: 30). In particular, unemployment insurance and old-age and survivor benefits took a higher share of public spending (see tables 2.8 and 2.9). No matter whether countries are generous or stingy towards family policy, it is losing ground everywhere except in Sweden. In Belgium, France, and Italy its portion has fallen more than 3 percentage points, placing the three countries below the average of the twelve other Member States of the European Union (table 2.9)

Despite these similarities observed in simple financial measures, the actual policy changes have not been the same everywhere. Borrowing

TABLE 2.8
Spending on social programs as percentage of GNP, 1970–94

	1970	1980	1985	1990	1994	Percentage change
Belgium	18.7	28.0	29.3	26.9	27.0	+8.3
France	19.8	25.4	28.8	27.6	30.5	+11.6
Italy	14.4	19.4	22.6	23.6	25.3	+10.9
Sweden	18.6	31.9	30.7	34.0	–	+15.4
Europe (12)*	17.3	24.3	26.0	25.2	27.6	+10.3

*Before the reunification of Germany
Source: Montalembert (1997: 161)

TABLE 2.9
Spending on particular social policies, as percentage of all social spending

	Belgium	France	Italy	Sweden	Europe (12)
Sickness, disability, workers' comp.	35.4	34.0	29.9	35.1	35.5
Old-age, survivors' benefits	44.2	43.7	64.0	40.9	44.6
Family, maternity	8.1	9.6	3.6	16.5	7.6
Unemployment, labour market	11.0	8.1	2.5	6.9	8.4
Other	1.3	4.7	0	–	3.9
Change in spending on family, maternity 1980–94	−3.2	−3.1	−3.9	0	−2.9

Source: Montalembert (1997: 161)

the typology developed by Agnès Pitrou and Renée B.-Dandurand, we can identify three vectors of adjustment in family policy.[15] Will it be universal or targeted? How important will population policy be? How will family policy address issues of reconciling work and family life (Pitrou and B.-Dandurand, 1997: 6–7)?

The first vector addresses the matter of the types of family eligible to receive benefits and income redistribution. In France and Sweden, all families, whether single parent or 'traditional,' have a right to benefits. In Belgium, 'atypical families,' whether single parent or cohabiting, also have guaranteed rights.[16] Since 1975 in Italy, unmarried parents who have acknowledged their children have rights and responsibilities comparable to those of legally married couples (Ditch, Bradshaw, and Eardley, 1996: 118).

With respect to income redistribution, calculations show that it is Sweden that uses family benefits most to achieve redistributive ends. Family benefits add fully 51 per cent extra to the income of a standard family (a couple with two school-age children), whereas France adds only 20 per cent. Moreover, the Swedish system provides a progressive redistribution, designed both to benefit poorer families and to reduce the income gap. The same cannot be said of France and Belgium. The goal of Italy is a progressive redistribution, but it is far less active than the other three countries (Bradshaw et al., 1996: 36–7).

As for the population policy vector, family policy can address it explicitly or only indirectly. This dimension brought the European Union into the picture. It quickly realized the implications of allowing population numbers to decline for the sustainability of intergenerational sharing through social spending. Therefore, the EU began to worry about population policy, despite its lack of any treaty-based responsibility for the matter. Among the four national cases, France has always been the pro-natalist, with this discourse being legitimate as much among the forces of the left as among those of the right (Jenson and Sineau, 1995: chapter 8). In Belgium, which previously had focused on population size in ways quite similar to those of France, there has been a decline in such concerns in recent years. Sweden has always formally left such decisions in the private sphere, although historically (and even these days) its family policy has not been innocent of certain pro-natalist gestures. The case of Italy is, at first glance, the most peculiar. The country does not appear on Anne Gauthier's list of twenty-one jurisdictions where population policy is on the political agenda (1996: 132–3). Yet its birth rate, as we have seen, is very low. The only way to understand this reticence is to put it in the context of the still negative reactions to Mussolini's inter-war aggressive initiatives to support the Italian family and of the high post-war birth rates in the South.

The third vector is that of reconciling work and family life; it receives the most attention in the next chapters. For the moment suffice it to say that the EU has been active in this area, making an explicit link between gender equality and the availability of adequate services for young children. Sweden has also made equality of the sexes a central goal of its family policy, even if the results have not always been all that was hoped (Arve-Parès, 1996; Hantrais and Letablier, 1995a: 95).

France and Belgium, on the other hand, have not placed as much emphasis on the equality theme, even though their services have actually been quite generous. The policy logic was other than gender equality, putting more stress on social equality and child development as well as other matters (Vielle, 1994: 101). Finally, it is only recently that Italy has even begun to make a policy link between family programs, such as services for young children, and the matter of gender equality (Ditch, Bradshaw, and Eardley, 1996: 68).

Each of these vectors has been affected in slightly different ways by the crisis of the welfare state. For example, when it is understood as a need for more services, the discourse on reconciling work and family can impose new costs on states as well as employers. Indeed, the latter may be called upon to rethink liberalism's long-standing distinctions between 'public' and 'private' and to begin to address their employees' family concerns (Laufer, 1996: 60–1). For public policy-makers, there is a growing need for cross-domain coordination. In France, there has been an effort to coordinate across policy dimensions. Thus, promotion of personal services has been informed by discourses and policy practices related to fighting social exclusion and to neo-liberalism's enthusiasm for 'choice.' In Sweden, a private market in services is proposed as a way to reduce the burden of expensive public services in a high-end welfare state. It would also provide an institutional underpinning for the rise in salary differentials that the end of solidaristic wage bargaining will set off. In general, a move towards more 'choice' and greater flexibility in labour markets is vaunted as simultaneously meeting the needs of employers, governments' goals for fighting unemployment, and parents' childcare dilemmas.

Each of the cases examined in this book has mixed and matched responses to these three issues of family policy. In doing so, they have manifested certain continuities with their past citizenship regimes. Belgium, France, and Sweden continue to be interventionist and to devote a significant portion of state spending to family policy, while Italy remains a laggard.[17] Nonetheless, as we document in detail in the next chapters, the details of these interventions, their policy logic, and their consequences for gender relations are not always the same. Nor are the variations sufficiently well captured simply by examining levels of spending. There are important changes within cases across time as well as differences among cases. In large part, these significant adjustments follow from the foundering of post-war citizenship regimes as well as new institutions of policy-making and delivery.

Changing Institutions: Decentralizing the State and Offloading to the Market

After 1945 all four countries made a commitment, explicit or implicit, to what has come to be labelled a 'post-war compromise.' There were clear variations across cases, including the extent to which the organizations of the working class accepted or were permitted to participate in the 'compromise.' Indeed in post-war France and Italy, the major organizations of the working class were excluded (Ross, 1982; Hellman, 1997). Nonetheless, even in these two cases it is fully legitimate, using the following textbook summary, to say that there was a common trend 'toward a consensus on the value of state regulation of market forces ... The state regulated the market economy by intervening to reduce conflicts of interest between labour and capital. The key shift was that the state persuaded organized labour to moderate its demands for substantial wage gains, autonomy, and control of the workplace in exchange for substantial benefits, including full employment, stable prices, welfare programs, and automatic wage increases' (Kesselman et al., 1997: 21). From this compromise emerged policies, institutions, and political formations whose goals were to reduce differences and foster equity across space as well as across social groups. These were the basic principles of the post-war citizenship regimes, leading to specific practices with respect to relations between state and market.

After 1945 state activity accelerated. If all countries did not make social programs universally available to citizens, all did substantially extend coverage. The resulting expansion of the public sector, as well as the growth of services in general, brought an expansion in women's employment, especially in the state sector. The 1980s and 1990s, in contrast, have been decades of retrenchment and redesign of state intervention. One result is that the last two decades may well mark the end of the era of state-building and a powerful central state authority. Instead of continuing to build capacity, national governments have begun to 'hollow out,' allowing some control over social and economic policy to move 'upward' towards the European Union, which disciplines policy choices of its Member States, and some control to move 'downward' to local authorities (Della Sala, 1997). In addition, in the last decade the EU has made its own contribution to the involvement of subnational political authorities by the way it has organized its regional policies.

Along with this re-mapping of governmental decision-making authority, there has been a strengthening of other institutions that distribute resources, especially markets. This has sometimes been done in the name of maximizing variety and assuring choice. Enthusiasm for market-based distribution has also brought privatization of some services. More than that, it has been invoked as the rationale for governments to mimic markets, putting the stress more on efficiency, cost-saving and variable service than on the values of universality and equality, which often served as the rationale for public provision in the post-war decades. Local government authorities, providing or regulating many of the childcare services in which we are interested, have been particularly touched by such discursive shifts and new practices in thinking about citizenship.

Two major factors accelerating these patterns of state restructuring were, of course, the economic crisis and international economic competition. Both generated fiscal problems for national governments. Nonetheless, it is also important to recognize that the impetus was much more than economic. Calls for more democracy and autonomy were especially important in the reconfiguration of governmental authority via displacement of decision-making towards subnational governments. In all four countries social forces sought decentralization in the name of democratization, in order to accommodate diversity and variety. Sometimes the claim was that the institutions of the post-war compromise were too distant from citizens, too rigid, and too bureaucratic. At other times, the argument was that centralized, national-level programs and institutions were insensitive to class, cultural, or national differences. By the 1980s and 1990s central governments were demonstrating greater willingness to cooperate in granting such autonomy, as they began to appreciate the possibilities of divesting themselves of costly social programs and handing off political responsibility for hard choices.

The examination of these changes over time proceeds case by case in this section, beginning with the Belgian federation and moving to present-day Italy, France, and Sweden. It ends with a sketch of the European Union's contribution to these processes of governmental decentralization as well as the shift to the market as a mechanism for decision-making.

Belgium: Moving towards Federalism

Belgium emerged from the Second World War with its politics organized on the basis of consensus-seeking within a deeply divided society of segmented pluralism (Marques-Pereira, 1990). Ideological and philosophical cleavages shaped classes and language groups into a system of 'pillars' that ordered Belgian society into three 'worlds' – Roman Catholic, Socialist, and liberal. These divisions date from the nineteenth century, and their influence was so great that all social as well as political institutions were separated into three subsets. Each world had its own hospitals, nursery schools, cultural institutions, unions, women and youth movements, as well as political parties.

Management of segmented pluralism depended on a set of specific and countrywide political institutions. Conflict resolution was achieved less by democratic decision-making than by negotiations across the three pillars. Thus, within each of the worlds the terms of compromise were set out, and representatives then negotiated across pillars to develop a stable set of agreements. The compromise would be formalized by a 'package deal' in which each camp would receive both access to some resources and some positions of authority, as well as satisfaction of some of its basic ideological principles, even if it were not part of the governmental majority.

The institutions of this segmented pluralism have been in crisis for at least two decades. Their legitimacy as well as capacity to function effectively has been questioned. Therefore, institutional 'givens' have foundered. It is no longer accepted as normal that the associations of the three civil societies receive major infusions of funds from the state, or that all nominations to positions of responsibility be made in the light of quotas and individuals' attachment to one of the three worlds. Political management of the cleavages has altered. 'Non-traditional' political parties transgress the frontiers, promising to represent regions, environmentalists, or the extreme right rather than the usual Catholic, Socialist, or liberal camps. At the same time, emergent federal institutions have subdivided the worlds by language and territory.

The Liberation in 1944 brought Belgium prosperity as well as a collective agreement involving significant increases in salary and a new Social Security system (Dumont, 1991: 86–7). The political foundation was the Social Pact concluded among representatives of unions and business associations as well as senior civil servants. It was a typical compromise of these years, involving tripartite negotiations, and its implications for social policy included major new family programs (Marques-Pereira, 1990). Institutions representing the interests of families were given a place. Today, these bodies are the Family League

(Francophone) and the League of Large and Young Families (Flemish), both of which are incorporated, along with unions, employers, and other sociocultural associations, in the process of making family policy.

This accord did not challenge traditional Belgian pluralism in any significant way. The educational pact (*Pacte scolaire*) of November 1958, however, was more significant in this regard. It resulted from a certain rapprochement between the Socialist and Catholic worlds, which set in motion a process that would eventually realign the three worlds, as the religious distinction blurred in favour of a socio-economic one. Beginning in the early 1960s, liberals began to find more common ground with Social-Christians, against whom they had battled since the creation of the country in 1830, than with Socialists, because they had come to be less concerned with the philosophical-religious cleavage than the socio-economic one. Then the Socialists called, beginning in 1969, for an alliance among all progressive forces, regardless of their philosophical provenance. For example, by 1979 the Flemish Socialists were seeking to make a breakthrough among Catholic intellectuals and workers.

This socio-economic realignment occurred in the context of another major institutional change. A complicated and multi-tiered federal state was being created. Four major episodes of reform – in 1970, 1980, 1988, and 1993 – put paid to the unitary and centralized state form (Devillé et al., 1995: 27). The roots of the reform were economic as well as cultural. At the start, in the 1960s, the goal was to reconcile the Flemish claim to greater cultural recognition and autonomy with the Walloons' concerns for their economic future, as their economy based on old and traditional industries floundered (Dumont, 1991: 105). According to article 1 of the 1993 constitution, Belgium is a federal state. In addition to the central government, it is composed of three Communities, divided by language. These are the Francophone, Flemish-speaking, and German-speaking Communities. Because the third group is very small, however, to all intents and purposes there are only two Communities. A second division is geographical. The constitutional reform of 1980 created three Regional governments, one for Flanders, one for Wallonia, and one for a capital region, Bruxelles-Capitale. All of these reforms required a new division of powers, distributing responsibility among seven governments (Dagastino, 1995: 38–9).

In 1980 (article 5 of the Special Law of August 8) the Communities gained responsibility for matters related to individuals (*matières personnalisables*). This means that any benefit delivered directly to individuals falls within the jurisdiction of the Communities. Nonetheless, the central government retained control over the Social Security regime and taxation; it still controls family allowances and tax credits related to families. Regions, for their part, have some areas of exclusive responsibility, such as housing policy. They also share some jurisdictions with the central government. Particularly relevant for our purposes is the fact that they share responsibility for employment and economic policy. After the constitutional reform of 1988 the Communities and Regions gained control over 30 per cent of the federal budget.

Until 1980 there was one national-level Family Department. Now each Community has assigned, whether explicitly or implicitly, responsibility for family policy to one of its ministers. In the Francophone Community, family policy is under the Department of Social Affairs and Health, while in the Flemish-speaking Community it is under the Department of Welfare and the Family. This decentralization of responsibility to subnational institutions goes further, as well. Provinces and municipal governments have some responsibility for family policy.

Overall, the result is that, with the reforms of 1980 and 1988, the role of the central government has declined in a major way. It no longer plays a significant role in shaping the actions of subnational institutions, and it no longer can establish national standards for social programs. The constitutional reforms have created plenty of space for regionally and community-based variation. The result has been a significant fragmentation in the design of family policy, which follows different ideological principles depending on jurisdiction. It has also brought variations in the investment in family, and especially childcare, programs, depending on the resources of the community.

Italy: Regions Take Their Place

The Italian polity in some ways resembles post-war Belgium's consensus-seeking democracy. After 1945 it, too, was characterized by decision-making structures designed to accommodate deep partisan and ideological differences. As in Belgium today, also, some political forces advocate major constitutional reforms. The Northern League, for example, talks of separation. Many business interests and some politicians seek the discipline of the EU as a safeguard against a state that has exhibited little capacity to reduce spending.

The anomaly of post-1945 Italian democracy was that, despite (or perhaps because of) the exile of its largest opposition party from executive power until 1996, politics was characterized by a search for consensus. Although never in government in the years covered by our study, the Italian Communist Party (PCI) was nonetheless able to insist that its constituency and its policy interests be taken into account. Italy's post-war compromise reflected this anomaly, as did the institutions of policy-making. The Communists' historic strength in the 'red zones' gave the party economic power and control over regional governments. At the same time, the central institutions in Rome, especially after the mobilizations of the late 1960s, increasingly reflected what can be termed the accommodative 'spirit of the Constitution.' The result was that coherence of political and policy-making goals took second place to system maintenance (Amato, 1980). Institutions followed the rule of *garantismo* (guarantee-ism), in which all social forces were to be included and the personalized power associated with centralization avoided (Mény, 1993: 427).

The practices of *garantismo* minimized transparency. Decision-making was dispersed, shared among Parliament, the president, regional governments, the Constitutional Court, and referenda. The boundary between government and opposition was effectively blurred. Many policy choices were made behind closed doors, in parliamentary committees where parties could more easily compromise. Such fragmented decision-making structures enabled accommodation, albeit far from the public eye. As in Belgium, policy-making in Italy depended more on elite negotiation than on efforts to generate popular support for specific policies.

Concerns about regime stability also meant that Italy's post-war compromise was politically fragile. The 'economic miracle' of the 1950s and 1960s was a haphazard affair: 'Italy's achievement was more to have set loose healthy forces that dragged the economy along rather than to follow a carefully thought-out plan' (Hellman, 1997: 376). The lack of capacity to direct economic development meant that state expenditures continued to grow through the 1980s. By the mid-1980s the budget deficit was 12 per cent of GDP, a record for Europe (Hellman, 1997: 385). Only in the early 1990s, especially after the 1992 financial crisis forced Italy out of the European Monetary System (EMS), did tax reform, tax increases, budget cuts, and pension reform begin. Elites had taken to using the 'constraint' of Europe to force reluctant elected officials to reduce spending and to privatize. Thus, the hollowing out of the Italian state occurred via privatization, altered pensions and health service, introduction of market principles to public service, and plans to transfer more powers to regional government (Ferrara, 1995; Macchiato, 1996; Cazzola, 1996).

Geographical devolution of political power generated potential for diversification and fragmentation in service levels. The 1948 constitution had provided for regional governments, but it wasn't until the onset of the social unrest of the late 1960s that enabling legislation was enacted.[18] In 1970 directly elected regional Councils were mandated. In 1978 formal devolution occurred and regional governments took up their constitutional powers in areas such as urban planning, tourism, and health care, including childcare. For a time, Rome dragged its feet, thereby hindering regional action. Eventually the Constitutional Court found that policy 'principles' could be identified in the body of existing legislation and that Regions need not wait for a framework law. Indeed, the central government seemed to prefer to leave decisions to the courts, rather than impose any national standards (Mény, 1993: 237; 435).

Therefore, very few structures are available to ensure coordination and compatibility between the central government and the Regions, or among the Regions themselves. Instead, in their own operations the regional governments tend to reproduce Italy's long-standing distinctions.[19] Differences across regions are likely only to increase in the future.[20] As the left-right divide evaporates in post-Cold-War Italy, space for cross-class regional identities widens (Hellman, 1997: 389). Political pressure is increasing for a true federal system (Mény, 1993: 432–3). Neo-liberal politics also continues to foster a displacement of national state capacity not only to markets, via privatization, but also to the EU. The result for childcare is a patchwork of policies with an immense range of variation.

French Jacobinism Adapts

No one would accuse the long-centralized French state of lacking capacity to direct the economy after 1945. France's post-war compromise was state led and designed. Direct state involvement in economic and social development, organized by government ministries, especially the central planners of the office of the Plan, was crucial to the first three post-war decades of boom (Fourastié, 1979). Accompanying the identification of national champions and subsidies for the select was much close supervision of markets (such as labour markets) via regulations.

This model changed dramatically with the Socialist government's 1983 abrupt turn away from its own program. This brought a 'regime-defining choice' that scaled back state expenditures, raised taxes, halted nationalizations, and devalued the franc (Cameron, 1996). The new economic and social policy strategy involved privatization, deregulation, and liberalization, as well as a new fiscal policy direction. The latter eventually meshed neatly with the Maastricht convergence criteria produced by the EU. Nevertheless, it would be wrong to conclude that the French state no longer shapes the economy. Rather than withdrawing, it has undertaken to supervize industrial restructuring and downsizing, and to develop policies to smooth the transition to new labour markets and production techniques (Kesselman, 1997: 172–3).

The capacity of the French state to direct its own downsizing is found in the institutional arrangements of the Fifth Republic. Since 1958 'there is a greater degree of executive dominance within the French political system than in that of virtually any other democratic nation' (Kesselman, 1997: 180). Some of this dominance derives from the direct election of the president and the powers granted the presidency by the constitution (Duhamel, 1995: 180). Presidents have used their constitutional powers to accumulate even greater political resources. Thus, the president has the autonomous capacity to direct policy, even if he comes to office with the help of a strong political party.[21] In the case of François Mitterrand, for example, there was not 'a single instance when the Socialist party leaders, or its parliamentary group, imposed a policy decision on the government' (Duhamel, 1988: 197).

The bureaucracy is part of this dominant executive and is especially important because of the embedded tradition of state direction. As is the case in all four countries, responsibility for 'the family' is dispersed across a wide range of ministries and governmental agencies. In addition, as is true in Belgium, a national-level para-state institution (the *Caisse nationale d'allocations familiales* – CNAF) and a countrywide representative association (the *Union nationale des associations familiales* – UNAF – recognized as the 'family parliament' by the state) were incorporated into the policy process (Commaille, 1996a: 280). Whereas the post-war compromise in many countries, of which Sweden is our best example, concentrated representation in the hands of organizations of labour and business, France's policy process after 1945 included another social partner, the family movement.

The capacity of these post-war creations, as well as that of Paris, to dominate policy-making was weakened, however, by the Socialists' decision to decentralize state authority to local authorities in the 1980s. Change had been prefigured in the 1960s and 1970s by enthusiasm for things 'local,' promoted by those who believed that the local authorities and associations were closer to the real needs of citizens. The Defferre Laws of 1982, 1983, and 1986 both lessened the power of the centre and altered the cast of actors involved and the logics of decision-making (Debordeaux, 1995: 3). It was also a mechanism for reducing costs, since it allowed Paris to move from open-ended to rationed funding of the local authorities' expenditures (Rocaboy, 1999: 547ff.)

These reforms had some unintended consequences. Because they took place in a context of mounting neo-liberalism, there was a tendency to pay homage to the 'political market' and to 'let the chips fall as they will.' Those local authorities with the capacity to innovate and to seek out resources prospered in the new situation, while the others lagged. The result was mounting regional disparities. Go-ahead areas benefited fully from the new possibilities, while others simply did nothing (Mény, 1993: 447).

Social policy was particularly affected by the reforms. What began as a desire to decentralize, so that decision making would be closer to the service recipient, soon became an excuse for 'offloading' responsibility for dealing with the effects of economic restructuring and crisis of the welfare state (Aballéa, 1995: 9). Local governments found themselves holding the bag. At the same time, Paris declined to coordinate the response to mounting social problems. The result, according to one observer, is that 'one might ask whether the central government was not handing over to the local authorities responsibility for managing the unmanageable' (Gaudin, 1995: 35) and thereby effectively washing its hands of responsibility.

Sweden Decentralizes

The post-war compromise created in Sweden after 1945 was a societal model constructed by the most dynamic sectors of capital, organized labour, and the state. From the perspective of the Social Democrats (SAP) and their ally, the labour movement, a full-employment welfare state was the core of the compromise. By the early 1950s expansion of economic and social policies had created a 'high-end' welfare state. It depended on economic growth's being sustained, which was achieved via solidaristic wage restraint and active labour market policy. The former resulted from peak-level agreements between employers and unions, within which the unions pursued solidaristic wage bargaining, to improve the relative position of low-wage workers.[22]

Thus, in order to understand post-1945 Sweden it is necessary to consider more than the formal political institutions. Strategic choices made by the long-governing Social Democrats about their alliances with other parties and about relations with their ally, the unions, were crucial to policy outcomes. Unions and employers have been more than actors in civil society; they have been decision-makers whose actions have had substantial direct consequences for the design of labour market and social policy. One result was that family policy and other social policies always were closely linked to employment policies; they had little autonomy. Moreover, the voice for policy change was located within the political parties and unions, where, for example, the women's movement was most developed, and from which it launched its calls for redesign of family programs (Jenson and Mahon, 1993: 85ff.).

Throughout the 1980s, unions made strategic adjustments within the compromise, under pressure from employers as well as from their own base (Mahon, 1999: 137–40). Nevertheless, the compromise could not hold, since employers went on the offensive, refusing to maintain peak-level bargaining and seeking ways of organizing work and wages that were much less solidaristic. In the process, the commitment to centralization disappeared (Pontusson and Swenson, 1996: 228). The institutions of Swedish corporatism began to break down (Thörnqvist, 1999). Wage bargaining was decentralized. The electoral base of the SAP fragmented, although it remained the largest party (Mahon, 1991). The government was forced to intervene unilaterally with an income policy. With the election of the bourgeois coalition government in 1991 and continuing even after the return of the SAP in 1994, all the elements of the post-war compromise were called into question: public commitment to full employment; active labour market policy; solidaristic bargaining; peak-level agreements; a social security system built on the replacement principle; commitment to high quality and comprehensive public services.

Sweden's post-war compromise generated more than new social relations of production; it also shaped the state and its agencies. Despite opposition, the central government had amalgamated municipalities in the post-war years (Olsson, 1990: 121). Amalgamation was modelled both on mass-production industries, with the idea that productivity could be best achieved by a large scale, and, in part, on the philosophy of universalism. The goal was to achieve uniform provision and standardization (Petersson, 1994b: 124).

Because Stockholm intervened via 'heavy-handed management techniques,' criticisms mounted. Gains in efficiency were seen as being at the cost of democracy and 'even as early as the 1970s the term decentralization was on everyone's lips' (Petersson, 1994b: 125). Objections to bureaucratization and lack of local input led to what Sven Olsson calls 'administrative decentralization,' at first via a program that set up free zones for administrative experimentation (Olsson, 1990; 275–8). In addition, the 'autonomous sector' of associations in civil society called for alternative services, including childcare, provided by cooperatives or other self-help organizations. Government financial support was soon forthcoming for this move away from public provision (Olsson, 1990: 279). Such reforms mean that the variety of services has increased and the range of choices has widened; they now depend more than before on class position and place of residence.

Not only administrative decentralization was taking place. The major source of income for local authorities remains local taxes. Nonetheless, the grant from the central government has an important second place.[23] As the central government's financial difficulties increased and austerity policies were implemented in the 1980s, 'fiscal decentralization' also was initiated.

The SAP government elected in 1984 decided to cut transfers to local governments, 'thereby putting the pressure on local politicians' (Olsson, 1990: 274).[24] As Stockholm cut the funds transferred to local authorities, it also changed the form. Instead of detailed, even item-by-item, specifications of how the money is to be spent, since 1993 the transfer has been in the form of a block grant, with the aim of providing greater freedom of choice (Petersson, 1994b: 135). Local authorities also gained autonomy in designing public services, including deciding how to cut them, as well as autonomy in the use of their taxes (Petersson, 1994a: 136).[25]

Local politicians have reacted to this increase in autonomy by instituting new management models stressing competition and privatization. They have transformed local governments into purchasers of services rather than providers of service. Tasks previously performed by local governments are contracted out to private entrepreneurs, and they provide vouchers that citizens use to 'purchase' their own services (Petersson, 1994a: 121).

The result is greater diversification in services, depending on variables such as local tax bases, the political character and commitment of local governments to certain types of services, and the choices made by local authorities about spending. This is no longer a model of uniform provision and standardization and perhaps, therefore, no longer one motivated by the principle of universalism.

The European Union Arrives

When the Treaty of Rome was signed in 1958, national-level institutions were at the height of their authority. It is not surprising, then, that the treaty made the smallest of bows to regional development, reflecting only the long-standing but seemingly unique problems experienced by Italy' south.[26] Although a small regional development fund was established in the 1970s, it took the incorporation of less developed European countries – Ireland in 1973, Greece in 1982, Spain and Portugal in 1986 – to create pressure for new forms of territorial solidarity. The Single European Act of 1986 introduced articles making economic and social cohesion a new common policy. In 1987 the Commission of the European Union instituted a reform of the structural funds. It proposed doubling the financial base between 1988 and 1992, and then implemented a second doubling between 1992 and 1999. This made the structural funds Europe's second largest budgetary item.

Planning for specific use of the structural funds involves negotiations between the Commission of the European Union and Member States, which are required to consult regional and local authorities. Commission-designed Community Support Frameworks then set out the rules for using and dispersing the funds. The programs most frequently put in place target infrastructure (modernization of transport, telecommunications, energy), small- and medium-size business, and occupational training. In addition to entrepreneurs, the groups targeted are the long-term unemployed, youth, and women.

While it is too early to make a final evaluation of the impact of the structural funds on regional development, it is clear that they have helped to discourage any 'race-to-the-bottom' strategy of offering low wages and low levels of social protection in order to attract development. 'A bonus for the Commission is that regional levels of governments ... are acquiring stakes in European integration, adding to the support for Europeanization more generally' (Ross, 1997: 618).

In this chapter we have documented the changes in sociological, labour market, policy, and political institutions that are a common background to changes in family policy and childcare services in each particular case study. Despite the fact that all four countries and the European Union have – in general – experienced the same socio-economic and demographic changes and have adapted their general policies and institutions in quite similar ways, we will observe, in the chapters that follow, that differences do remain. Indeed, the patterns of adaptation in childcare depend on more than such large-scale sociological tendencies or political trends. They follow more particularly from the interaction between them and the existing model of gender relations inscribed in each citizenship regime over the last decades and the political debates about these relations. Therefore, in the next chapters we turn to detailed and nuanced analyses of such models, locating them in their respective national traditions. The goal is to account for the patterns of provision of childcare found and described in each case.

NOTES

1 In France, for example, from 1900 to 1945 the number of childless women decreased steadily. Although 25 per cent of women born in 1900 remained childless, only 10 per cent of women born in 1945 did the same (INSEE, 1995: 28).

2 The upturn in the Swedish birth rate in the 1980s increased the number of women with three or more children (Hoem, 1993: 103).

3 This is the position of economists who use the 'regulation approach.' According to them, the situation of crisis that has prevailed since the early 1970s is not temporary but, rather, marks the end of a mode of regulation and is the manifestation of a crisis in the regime of accumulation (see, for example, Boyer, 1995).

4 A number of changes in the way labour force participation is measured have forced us to use OECD statistics for the years before 1983, with the result that there are no statistics for Belgium. For the years after 1983 we have usually used Eurostat's statistics, which means that we do not have statistics on Sweden before 1996. It became a member of the European Union only in 1995. On such problems of measurement, see Hantrais and Letablier (1995a: 64).

5 This increase was all the more spectacular because the labour force participation rate of the 15–24 age group actually has declined. Young women are staying in school longer.

6 These data are from Maruani and Reynaud (1993: 21). In Italy, between 1991

and 1993 there was actually a decline in labour force participation in this age group.

7 According to a recent Eurobarometer survey, 60 per cent of those questioned believed that children were obstacles to women's labour force participation. In contrast, only 4.5 per cent of women and 8.6 per cent of men considered children to be obstacles to men's labour force participation (Malpas and Lambert, 1993).

8 In 1992 there were almost 17 percentage points of difference between the labour force participation rates of women aged 20–39 without children and those of women with one child. This gap between the former category and women with three children was fully 40 per cent (Eurostat, 1995a: 132).

9 In Belgium and Italy, the labour force participation rate of women who have a young child (two or younger) is higher than it is among the childless, because the latter category encompasses the 20–25 age cohort, composed mainly of students, who now tend to stay in school longer.

10 The Italian pattern is again quite different. In Italy, as in Belgium and France, there is no long-standing tradition of part-time jobs for women. Nor has this type of working time become popular. Indeed, during the 1970s part-time employment actually decreased as a percentage of total employment. Therefore, although part time jobs in Italy are, as elsewhere, heavily feminized, there are simply fewer of them going around.

11 In France, however, the increase in the number of women's part-time jobs seems to be linked less to child-bearing than to the working conditions imposed on young people by the labour market. For them, we might describe such part-time employment as underemployment, or 'start-up part time.'

12 Such numbers have been read as requiring mothers to reduce their labour force participation to less than they might otherwise wish. According to Chantal Nicole, in France, only 40 per cent of mothers with two children are employed full time. The figure drops to 10 per cent in the case of mothers of three children (cited by de Singly, 1991: 147).

13 For several countries the active labour market policies of Sweden were the model.

14 This turn to private services has generated debate in Europe. In addition to the Swedish controversies, documented in chapter 6, see Fraisse (2000) and Lallement (2000).

15 Many analysts stress that family policy has been adjusted rather than blindly cut. Anne Gauthier, for example, describes the rise at both the national and the European levels of a new interest in family policy in the 1980s (1996: 158).

16 Single-parent families are numerous in Belgium; Eurostat ranks this country second in terms of the number of single-parent families and third when those headed by the mother are calculated (Paye, 1997b).

17 Bradshaw et al. (1996: 39–40) rank these three countries very high on their measures of generosity. Among the seventeen industrialized countries in the ranking, Belgium, France, and Sweden appear in the top five. Italy, on the other hand, is only eleventh or twelfth, depending on the measure.

18 The Christian-Democratic-dominated government feared that the Communists would succeed in controlling the regions.

19 'By almost all relevant measures – from how efficiently they deliver services to whether they even manage to spend the funds that have been earmarked for their use – the South lags behind the rest of the country, while the red regions and the northern industrialized areas show the most initiative' (Hellman, 1997: 413).

20 Distinctions already exist between the five special status Regions which have greater powers and the fifteen ordinary Regions (Mény, 1993: 236).

21 Periods of cohabitation are the only – partial – exception to this generalization.

22 The virtuous circle worked this way: 'While unions in growth sectors accepted wage restraint in return for policies that promoted the expansion of these sectors and avoided subsidizing inefficient production, unions in declining sectors accepted the phase out of jobs in return for higher wages and active state intervention to help workers adjust to the process of industrial change' (Pontusson, 1992b: 448).

23 Fully 30 per cent of public revenue comes from local taxes (Petersson, 1994a: 135).

24 This choice followed from the SDP's attack on the Conservative government's cuts to household transfers, criticisms that had contributed to the Social Democrats' re-election in 1984 (Olsson, 1990: 274).

25 It is important to note, however, that this autonomy is not complete. The central government can limit – even freeze – municipal tax rates and intervenes if a local authority runs a deficit.

26 This section is drawn directly from Ross (1997: 616–18).

Chapter Three

Belgium: The Vices and Virtues of Pragmatism*

Bérengère Marques-Pereira and Olivier Paye

Belgium's 'Social Pact' was the major political event of the first post-war decades. Secretly concluded during the war by senior bureaucrats, employers, and unions, it was ratified at the Liberation by the National Union government (Vantemsche, 1994; Arcq and Blaise, 1999). The was a social democratic compromise, but one that delegated to the social partners decisions about the distribution of the fruits of economic growth (via wage policies) as well as management of the Social Security system created at that time (Marques-Pereira, 1990; Alaluf, 1999). The post-war Social Pact, in other words, was squarely in the tradition of the pluralist societal paradigm that had structured Belgium society since the end of the nineteenth century (Dumont, 1996).

Rather than constructing a truly republican nation, the Belgian state continued to support a civil society divided into three 'worlds.' The citizenship regime followed from an institutionalization of the Christian, Socialist, and liberal worlds, the latter two forming what we might call a lay world. Each had its own values and social projects; each was structured by its own organizations. In addition to unions and youth, and women's and popular education movements, each had its own mutual societies, hospitals, newspapers, schools, and even banks, insurance companies and cooperatives (Devillé et al., 1995; Paye, 1997b). The role of politics was primarily to manage the points of contact among these worlds, while guaranteeing to each the means to develop freely, according to its relative weight in society (Delwit, De Waele, and Magnette, 1999). Political parties, as an extension of these worlds, played a crucial – indeed, often hegemonic – role.

*Translated by Brent Bauer and Jane Jenson

The state's capacity to make policy was, however, doubly constrained. A first limit came from the fact that '*grands accords*' (high-level pacts) were concluded at the initiative of the social partners. A second was that a whole set of public services and other tasks were subcontracted to the organizations representing the three worlds. This system is termed 'subsidized liberty.'

In 1945 the familialist model of gender relations that had characterized the inter-war years still held sway (*Cent ans* ..., 1987; Keymolen and Coenen, 1991; Peemans-Poullet, 1991; 1994). It entailed a certain ideal-typical gendered division of labour. The wife and mother looked after child-rearing, housekeeping, and other household tasks, whereas the husband worked to provide an income to satisfy the needs of the family. This model was incorporated into policy thinking and program design of both the Social Security system and the family policies of post-war governments. For example, although the same Social Security deductions were taken from the salaries of female and male workers, the former did not receive the same amounts of unemployment insurance or sickness and disability benefits. Access to benefits was even more restrictive if the woman's salary was not the household's principal source of income. By contrast, male workers with a stay-at-home spouse received higher unemployment, sickness, and disability benefits and retirement pensions than did other workers. Moreover, without making additional payments, they could provide their spouse with 'derived rights.' These rights gave the stay-at-home wife access to the Social Security system's health benefits and a survivor's pension at the death of her husband.

Family policy primarily targeted large families, that is, those with three or more children, because of fears about the birth rate, which had plummeted during the war. Level of family allowance benefits depended upon birth order, so that the amount paid was higher for later born than for earlier children. Moreover, families received the same allowance, whether both parents or only one paid into Social Security. Income tax credits varied according to the number of 'dependent persons' (including a wife at home as well as children). There were also reduced prices for public transport for large families, and young men supporting their own families were excused from compulsory military service (Dumon, 1987; Delvaux, 1987).

In this model, it was assumed that women's labour force participation hindered the achievement of a satisfactory rate of population growth. The position expressed in a 1929 study remained a basic principle into the post-war years: 'A wise social, family and population policy must do whatever it can to impede the employment of the woman and, above all, the married woman working outside the home' (quoted by Peemans-Poullet, 1994: 50). Therefore, in 1949 the Social-Christian-Liberal government created a 'housewife allowance.' This payment increased with each child, and the allowance was paid, regardless of the family's income, to any woman who did not engage in paid work.

As these programs were coming into force, however, families and individuals were abandoning many of the behaviours that had sustained the familialist model. The early 1960s were years of transition; sociologists of the family began to observe new trend lines as early as 1963–64. Both the fertility rate of women of childbearing age and the marriage rate among single people were falling, while the proportion of the population that was divorced, single, living together without being married, or living in recomposed families was rising (Rezsohazy, 1991: 16–22; Bawin-Legros, 1988: 77). These shifts in behaviour coincided with the birth-control pill's arrival on the market and the massive entry of women into the paid labour force. Such changes in social and economic behaviours helped to erode support for the traditional familialist model among policy-makers.

Even at the end of the 1950s there were signs of a shift towards an egalitarian model. In this new ideal-type, gender relations were supposed to be founded upon autonomy and equality among women and men. For example, the principle that married women were minors before the law (found in the Napoleonic Civil Code) was eliminated and in 1958 was replaced by the principle that marriage did not alter one's standing before the law. Nonetheless, elements of the familialist model continued to temper the change under way. For example, the law still tolerated a series of inequalities in marriage, to the detriment of women. They touched on issues such as the management of property, the choice of the family's residence, and the exercise of parental authority. Even though the return of the Socialists to power put an end to the housewife allowance, it did not prevent a 1962 reform that calculated tax levels according to family rather individual income. Such a measure disadvantages dual-earner couples and favours those with a stay-at-home partner or one low income due, for example, to part-time employment.

Discussions of the birth rate also revealed contradictory principles. For example, in 1962 an official report appeared (the *Delpérée Report,* named for the secretary general of the Welfare Ministry), which distinguished for the first time between a population policy, intended to maintain population size, and a family policy, designed to assure a satisfactory standard of living for families. Nonetheless, another official report, the *Sauvy Report* (named for the French demographer Alfred Sauvy and submitted by the Walloon Economic Council) still favoured a pro-natalist policy to promote a high birth rate. The report reflected traditional representations of the importance of a stay-at-home wife and mother (Dubois, 1991: 18–19).

Egalitarian Citizenship at the Height of the Welfare State

By the end of the 1960s there was no denying that change was under way. A range of new social programs consolidated the welfare state. Social Security benefits were increased and extended. For example, family allowances rose in value, women's access to unemployment insurance was improved, and payments made under the several different Social Security regimes became more uniform. At the same time, the state began to weave a social safety net, providing a minimal level of protection to persons not covered by any Social Security regime. As well, a guaranteed income program for the elderly was set up in 1969, and in 1971 a system of guaranteed family benefits was created. A guaranteed minimum income program (*le minimex*) was initiated in 1974.

A new era in gender relations also began (*Cent ans ...*, 1987; Keymolen and Coenen, 1991; Peemans-Poullet, 1991; Devillé and Paye, 1995). In 1969 and 1972 divorce by mutual consent became more readily available, and in 1974 it became possible to obtain a divorce simply on the basis of years lived apart (reduced in 1982 from ten years to five years). Differential treatment and gender inequalities in unemployment legislation were removed in 1971, the same year in which a law protecting pregnant workers was introduced. After 1973 it was no longer illegal to advertise contraceptive products and methods and family planning centres gained official recognition. The right of wives to divorce 'for cause' was made the same as that of husbands in 1974,[1] and in 1976 marriage law became gender neutral. A 1978 law guaranteed equal treatment in employment.

Family policy also changed. It is important to note, however, that new programs supplemented rather than displaced existing ones. A 'new familialism' took hold, adding a different representation of gender relations than was found in traditional familialism. This new model was less sensitive to pro-natalist concerns and more egalitarian. It focused on the well-being of families, spawning information campaigns about, for instance, marriage and married life, subsidies for marriage and family counselling, and grants to centres set up to combat family violence. Public services took over some of the work previously carried out within the family, usually by women. For example, programs for childcare, elder care, and care of the disabled were put into place (Dumon, 1987; Delvaux, 1987).

Public financing of the services and infrastructure for care of young children was an integral part of this new family policy (Dubois, 1991; Dubois et al., 1994; Humblet, 1996). At its origin in the 1920s childcare addressed simply the needs of the poorest children, particularly those whose mothers were forced to go out to work. It was organized by social welfare institutions. As a result, the Œuvre nationale de l'enfance (ONE; created in 1919) financed only those spaces in day nurseries used by families with very limited incomes. In 1960 in Belgium there were, at most, 500 childcare spaces more than there had been at the end of the war; that is, there were only about 3,000 for a population of 480,000 children under the age of two. By 1965 the number had climbed to only 5,200.

Between 1965 and 1970 a first wave of new childcare services appeared, although it hardly touched the established institutions. Rather, the expansion came in kindergartens (écoles maternelles). Its goals were educational rather than welfare-based (Humblet, 1996: 116). Spaces for young, pre-school children were created in prégardiennats (which we will call school-based childcare centres). It was primarily middle-class parents who used this form of care. Then, a second wave of reform modified the established system by altering the way subsidies were paid to childcare facilities. After 1971 public subsidies were calculated according to the number of children using the facility rather than on the basis of users' family income. The shift required an infusion of new funds to the ONE, which remained the principal source of financing for childcare facilities. At the same time, rates paid by parents were set on a sliding scale, fixed proportionally to their own income. New regulations also established higher standards for personnel employed by childcare facilities. Overall, the spaces available in both school-based childcare and other facilities rose by a factor of 3.5 between 1965 and 1980.

An important factor in this change was the involvement of a new institution, the Fonds d'équipments et de services collectifs (FESC), created within the *Office national d'allocations familiales pour travailleurs salariés* (ONAFTS) in 1971. The FESC supports facilities whose priority is day-care for the children of salaried workers. In practice, this means that the FESC will subsidize a facility if at least 60 per cent of the children's parents are salaried. The FESC makes reduced-interest loans to stimulate the construction or extension of childcare facilities, and covers costs not included in ONE subsidies (for example, the salaries of the cleaning staff or cooks) or by fees paid by parents.

From the late 1960s through the 1970s there was considerable change, while a number of important innovations continued. It is clear that policy-makers and others were aware that female employment patterns were altering mothers' behaviour and that pressures for more equal gender relations were mounting. Yet, no single, agreed-upon model of gender relations existed. Although an emerging egalitarian model challenged traditional familialism, it was also facing competition from a modernized familialism. During these years it was also demonstrated that the pluralist paradigm was still in place. The three worlds – Christian, Socialist, and liberal – had not lost their relevance. The egalitarian model and the new familialist model each had its origins in a different world. The political task still was to arbitrate among competing models.

The egalitarian model of gender representation developed primarily within the Socialist, and perhaps the larger lay, world.[2] The first objective of this model was to enable mothers to enter the paid labour force, this being seen as the key to their economic and personal autonomy. A second was to reduce gender inequalities in the workplace, in hiring, promotion, pensions, and so on. In terms of policy, both goals translated into the call for new programs, including infrastructure and services that would move the care of young children, traditionally the responsibility of mothers, into the public domain.

The Christian world was updating traditional familialism, giving a more family-based reading to gender equality. Without dismissing the legitimacy of women's desire for greater autonomy, it nonetheless defended the institution of the family and a gender division of roles, as long as the latter was 'freely' negotiated between spouses. Therefore, there was preference for sticking to existing programs, for bigger family allowances, and for a new program, the *'allocation socio-pédagogique'* (ASP; a child-rearing allowance). The latter benefit would be paid to mothers (above all, in the poorest families) who 'chose' to remain at home to raise their young children.

The pact concluded by the Social-Christian-Socialist coalition in 1968 reflected, in a very typical manner, the long-standing logic of compromise so central to Belgium's pluralist paradigm. The coalition promised to develop, simultaneously, 'more public services for the family' and to recognize the 'child-rearing role of the mother.' Two new measures were created in these years, promoting seemingly contradictory goals. Publicly provided childcare was expanded to enable, and therefore promote, mothers' labour force participation, whereas an allowance to be paid to mothers who cared for their own children discouraged their labour force participation. Despite the lack of coherence, Parliament passed the two programs. In the terms of Belgium's pluralist societal paradigm they were less contradictory than at first glance.

The Difficult Birth of the FESC

Detailed analysis of the creation of the FESC and then the ASP reveals the gymnastics involved in tracing a path through the pluralist paradigm. From 1968 on the ONAFTS, the institution providing family allowances to salaried workers, was well in the black, thanks to both rising wages and a growing pool of salaried jobs (especially those held by women). The organizations represented on the Management Committee of the ONAFTS[3] were divided over what to do with these unexpected surpluses.[4] Their debates reveal the confrontation of two models of gender and family relations and the ways that organizations from different worlds worked to make sense of changing socio-economic conditions.

In a debate about whether ONAFTS funds should be used for something other than family allowances, Socialists wanted to give priority to investments in *'crèches'* (day nurseries). The representatives of the Socialist unions said, for example:

> Making more day nurseries available to mothers of young children ... would allow them to remain in the work world. These nurseries would not be used by working mothers exclusively. Mothers whose partner is the one employed but who themselves are ill for a time could also use them. This would speed-up their recovery, by freeing them from childcare and household tasks.
>
> One of the reasons for making this proposal ... is found in the Third Plan of the National Committee of Economic Expansion, which seeks to

slow down immigration of foreign workers by encouraging the employment of women. In order to permit young girls as well as mothers of young children to work, programs for children must exist. To entrust these children even to people of good will during the work day is a very bad solution. From a child development perspective it is not a good idea that day after day children are left with their grandparents who, for the most part, are not equipped to fulfil this onerous task. A community that calls on mothers to join the labour force must provide facilities for young children. As the community has heretofore failed to do so, the ONAFTS should take the initiative to construct day nurseries ... and do so everywhere the need exists ...

The association of Socialist women thought it preferable to offer services to parents rather than allocating them a supplementary – and probably derisory – sum of money through family allowances. In presenting its arguments, the group identified the factors hindering the full integration of women into economic life and the achievement of equal rights and responsibilities. The Socialist women emphasized three points:

- that there has been a fundamental change in family structures. Young parents can no longer turn to their parents for childcare; more and more the 'young' grandmother herself is still at work;
- that there is a lack of guaranteed and secure solutions of success, as much for young children as for the tranquillity of mothers;
- that the failure to recognize that maternity is a social good has translated into an unacceptably low number of available facilities. Having enough would allow mothers to find the necessary balance between their professional and family responsibilities, at the same time as it would permit children to integrate very early into a stimulating environment ...

In addition, using ONAFTS surpluses to support day nurseries would correct inequities; working mothers paid into the system but received no extra benefits.

Although they did not reject the idea of supporting day nurseries, other organizations in the Management Committee of the ONAFTS (representatives of confessional groups, the League of Families, the liberal unions, and business) preferred that the government and Parliament address this need, rather than the *Office*. They felt that the

ONAFTS should not spend its money on day nurseries as long as there were still needs that could be met by more generous family allowances. For the League of Families, moreover, 'the goal of the family allowance regime is certainly not an economic one and does not stretch to enabling more mothers to work.'

According to the Social-Christian women, a certain scepticism was in order. They said that one might 'ask whether it would be still appropriate to provide family allowances to children for whom the regime were now paying maintenance (via the financing of day nurseries). The children now placed in childcare centres come from families with very low salaries, particularly foreigners, or from families with high salaries, with two parents working in intellectual professions. In the latter case, the financial contribution of the ONAFTS to the construction of day nurseries would contribute directly to their [capacity to earn] high incomes.'

As for the representatives of the confessional unions, they certainly felt that 'each woman must be free to decide if she will remain at home or if she will go out to work. A lack of day nurseries could render this choice impossible.' Nonetheless, they feared that it would be discriminatory for the ONAFTS to finance construction of such facilities, because all families could not benefit from them. Only those with an employed mother or those living in large urban centres (where childcare spaces were more numerous) would have access to facilities financed out of the *Office*'s surplus. When the representatives of these organizations turned to the matter of family allowances, they proposed a significant increase (with the exception of the employers who wanted their contributions reduced). They advocated raising the allowance by an amount equivalent to a half-month's payment,[5] arguing that this was necessary because the allowances still did not cover all the costs of raising a child. Members of the Management Committee from the Socialist world rejected this suggestion. As a Socialist unionist underscored, 'the family allowance benefit must not cover the full costs of supporting a child. Parents must continue to assume a part of the responsibility for the expenditures necessary for raising children. In effect, children belong to their parents and not to the state' (ONAFTS, P17, 19/5/1970).

When various compromise solutions failed to elicit agreement, the minister of welfare, a Flemish Social-Christian, made the decision, as he was empowered to do. He instituted additional family allowance payments, at a cost of 1 billion Belgian francs (BF) (ONAFTS, RA 1970:

2). Concurrently, however, he invited the Management Committee to draw up a draft bill establishing an endowment of 400 million BF for a 'special fund financing public services and infrastructure' destined to meet salaried workers' needs for childcare facilities. When discussion dragged on and the Management Committee failed to reach agreement on a bill to set up the FESC, the minister himself wrote the text.[6]

The bill was finally sent to Parliament, where it was passed.[7] The mandate of the FESC was to finance 'public services and equipment' for families of salaried workers, and it received an endowment from the ONAFTS to do so.[8] Although the House approved the bill without discussion, some Social-Christian senators, part of the majority, voted against the text because they wanted to create, alongside the FESC, a *Fonds d'allocation socio-pédagogique* (Fund for Child-Rearing Allowances) similarly endowed. They claimed: 'It is imperative to respect fully parents' liberty of conscience. They must be able to decide whether they will use a day nursery or they will raise their children themselves. This liberty of conscience would not be guaranteed if certain advantages were only offered to one side' (DS627, 8/7/1971: 3). Entrenched as it was in the new familialism, their discourse was not hostile in principle to either publicly provided childcare or mothers' employment.[9]

The FESC was created in 1971 but it could not begin to function until a new minister of welfare, a Flemish Social-Christian of the new Social-Christian-Liberal government, actually promulgated the necessary royal decrees in 1974. In the name of balance, he simultaneously launched another ASP trial balloon.

The Aborted Child-Rearing Allowance

In 1971, when the ONAFTS Management Committee first received a proposal from the Flemish Social-Christians to establish a child-rearing allowance (DS534, 17/6/1971), it unanimously rejected the idea. The committee found the proposed amount of the benefit completely unrealistic. The suggested allowance of 8,000 BF would have made the allowance higher than the monthly before-tax revenue of close to three-quarters of women workers (A77, 5/10/1971). Four years and several draft bills later, the Management Committee again rejected a Social-Christian text, but this time by only a very narrow majority. The debate about the ASP (*allocation socio-pédagogique*) at that time reveals the same divisions we saw with respect to the FESC.

On one side, the Socialist organizations insisted that priority go to public services, while they objected in principle to any ASP. Thus, the representatives of the Socialist unions argued that an ASP would only hinder women's full and equal integration into the work world. Rather than helping women re-enter the labour force after childbirth, such an allowance would prolong their absence while reinforcing traditional gender roles at home and at work. The Socialist women's organization mounted the following criticisms:

- the cultural, social and economic roles of the mother is not necessarily recognized or valued by paying an ASP. The father and the mother fulfil concomitant roles in child-rearing, and it is therefore appropriate to speak of the cultural, social, and pedagogical role of the family, and more precisely of the parents [rather than only the mother];
- if these parental roles are to be recognized properly when mothers enter the labour force, adequate working conditions must exist ...
- paying an ASP would be like reintroducing the housewife allowance. It provides no measures that permit mothers, once their children are older, to enter or re-enter the paid labour force;
- paying an ASP is no guarantee that the mother will have a free choice between employment and ... devoting herself exclusively to home-making tasks and raising young children. Such a choice is the result of many factors, among which are need and the desire to go out to work. Moreover, there is a risk that the ASP will divert attention from other programs that would make such a choice a real one. (A77, 5/10/1971)

While arguing that would be more logical to finance any new program from general revenues or the Social Security system (and that recipients should not be restricted to the spouses of salaried workers), the other organizations on the Management Committee (except the employers) supported the idea of an ASP. Nonetheless, the proposition did not carry in the committee.

Despite opposition and the lack of a recommendation in 1976,[10] the government decided to create a fund for an ASP (based on 0.25 per cent of employers' payments into the ONAFTS). The new allowance would be available to those families of salaried workers who already qualified for family allowances (DC680/1, 28/10/1975: 4, 38). It was left to the government to set the amount of the allowance and to define eligibility conditions, including income ceilings and age limits.

In contrast to the debate surrounding the FESC, parliamentary discussions of the ASP were long and detailed. They pitted Social-Christian parliamentarians, who supported it, against Socialists and Communists who opposed it. The exchanges focused on two basic issues: the link between the ASP and the traditional model of gender relations; and the kind of public action that would guarantee a 'free choice' to mothers either to raise their infant children themselves or to place them in childcare facilities.

Characterizing the ASP as 'socially backward,' its opponents judged it to be

> antipathetic to anyone who sincerely wants to address ... the need to [achieve] real equality between men and women ... absolutely contradictory [to the objective of the emancipation of women] ... discriminatory ... doubtful ... totally against the current of sociological trends, which are, happily, improving ...
>
> Justification of [such a limitation on the equality between men and women] is really found in traditional ideology, in the classic notions of patriarchal ideology, notions that are reproduced socially in women's roles, in men's roles, in the definition of women's work – it is only for pin money, not a real job – in child-rearing – it is the special role of mothers – and so on. Such traditional notions mean that when we face a basic problem such as ... the current economic crisis ... choices are limited. At such times there is a return to the idea of sending women back to the home ... because it is their special place because ... they are the pillar of the family, the family that paradoxically creates the psychological conditions for women's subordination. (AC, 12/12/1975: 1273–4; also AS, 31/12/1975: 1146–7)

Supporters of the ASP defended themselves from the charge that they sought to relegate women to the domestic sphere as well as to revive traditional familialism. The prime minister and the minister of welfare, both Flemish Social-Christians, insisted that the bill made no 'distinction between whether the mother or the father, a woman or a man, assumed responsibility for child rearing. It is not impossible that a father caring for a child in a household with an employed mother might receive an ASP' (AC, 12/12/1975: 1274; AS, 2/1/1976: 1179).

The principal argument of the ASP supporters, already deployed during the FESC debate, was that state funds must not be used to favour one form of care over another; it must not discriminate among families according to the kind of care selected. Defining parents using day nurseries as 'privileged' (AS, 2/1/1976: 1179), given that the state subsidized facilities up to an amount of 100,000BF per child, supporters of the ASP considered 'it only reasonable that the state should contribute when a mother or father is caring for a child' (AC, 12/12/1975: 1274). Marshalling the major arguments in favour of the child-rearing allowance, a Social-Christian deputy provided this summary:

> [the ASP] must be able to permit one of the parents, if he or she really wishes, to withdraw temporarily from the labour force. It could be used to extend a maternity leave, but also to pay for the care of a child and lighten domestic tasks or to augment the household's belongings. Its strong point is its recognition of parental responsibility and its [contribution to] improving the quality of their involvement with their children. It must be accompanied by other measures to improve the conditions and hours of work. One can never stress too much the importance of the first three years of a child's life for healthy development. Mothers who work outside the home receive insufficient help in confronting their dual responsibilities. (AC, 10/12/1975: 1020)

Opponents of the allowance rejected such arguments. They were sceptical of both the gender-neutral discourse and the idea of choice. 'Do you know many fathers who are going to choose to stay at home to raise their children?' a Socialist deputy asked ironically (AC, 12/12/1975: 1274). Another wondered:

> What does the oft-repeated slogan 'woman's freedom of choice' really mean? It implies that the woman who has children must be free to choose either to be employed or to devote herself exclusively to household tasks and child-rearing. The argument is made that, thanks to a child-rearing allowance, women who today are obliged to work will be able to choose to remain at home. For us, this is the wrong way to present the issue ... Isn't the choice of staying home in large part the result of limits found in the traditional schooling for girls? It gives girls, especially those coming from working-class families, very few chances to learn an interesting and responsible job. As a result, staying home most often means an escape rather than a free choice ... Moreover, in the guise of scientific findings, women are told that a constant maternal presence is necessary. There is unrelenting emphasis on their responsibilities in their roles as mother, wife and guardian of the family and on their family duties. The feeling of guilt drilled into their heads – that a woman who works outside the home

shirks her responsibilities – makes mothers' choice[s] very far from anything that we might call 'free.' (AS, 31/12/1975: 1147)

The ASP debate clearly distinguished two ideological positions. On
one side were those who, convinced that participation in the paid
labour force was *the key to the emancipation of women*, criticized the idea
of 'choice' and the notion that the state actions should be 'neutral.' For
these proponents of the egalitarian model, gender relations remained
unequal precisely because the traditional model still reigned supreme
in the minds of many. Therefore, in order to achieve real equality
between women and men, the state would have to promote publicly
provided childcare and discourage family-based care. On the other
side were the new familialists, who invoked the freedom of parents to
decide how to share family responsibilities. Moreover, making parents
available to their children was the *key to successful rearing of young children*. Thus, they attached the label 'discriminatory' to any program
supporting public provision if it was not matched by equivalent support for family-based care.

These discourses follow the classic opposition between left-wing
and liberal visions of the principles of liberty, of the distinction
between 'real' and 'formal' equality, and of whether or not the role of
the state was to promote change. In the background are even larger
questions, such as the relation between culture and nature and
between progress and tradition. With respect to gender relations the
debate is between universalist and differentialist positions.[11] Whereas
universalists seek to transform women into individuals equal to men
(particularly through employment), differentialists celebrate what they
describe as typically feminine characteristics, which enable women
better to undertake certain roles (for example, mothering and caring
for young children).

If universalism underpins the egalitarian model and the traditional
familialist model adopts the differentialist perspective, the new familialist model seems to bridge the two. It both accepts women's right to
lead a life, especially a work life, equal to that of men, and seeks to protect women's right to continue certain traditional activities, such as
devoting themselves to child-rearing when their children are young.
This modernized familialism provides a middle ground between the
progressive egalitarian model and the conservative traditional one. It
also fits very well into the terms of Belgium's pluralism, where the role
of the state is to foster the material conditions that allow people to live

their lives in accordance with their personal convictions. According to pluralist principles, state subsidies to both non-parental care (FESC) and family-based care (ASP) were not contradictions. They were, in contrast, simply a coherent expression of foundational values and, in particular, the notion of 'subsidized liberty.'

The compromise arrived at by 1975 could hold only if there were good economic times. The oil shocks of the 1970s and the ensuing economic restructuring altered the situation. The government, invoking businesses' mounting difficulties and the costs of fighting unemployment, quickly amended its own draft bill so that the fund no longer had a guaranteed income (DC680/7, 12/11/1975).[12] From that point on the ASP remained on the books but was never implemented.

The Egalitarian Model Tested by the Economic Crisis

By the end of the 1970s Belgian politics were shaped by two phenomena. One issue was skyrocketing unemployment and government debt (up to 140 per cent of GNP at the beginning of the 1990s), which were putting pressure on social spending. The other was federalization. In 1980 a new division of powers gave new responsibilities, including family and childcare, to the Communities (French speaking, Flemish speaking, and German speaking) while employment policy went to the Regions (Bruxelles-Capital, Wallonia, and Flanders). The result was not a modification of pluralism per se, but certainly the ways it is applied in policy making and the broader political realm changed (Lentzen and Mabille, 1995).

A very different situation than that of the post-1945 years is emerging. First, the traditional division of Belgian society into its three 'worlds' is being challenged. Each is now subdivided by language, into either Flemish speaking or Francophone. If in the 1960s the division had been sociological, by the 1970s it was political and by the 1980s and 1990s institutional. The result is that the weight or importance of each world is measured no longer at the national level but regionally (Leton and Miroir, 1999).[13] Furthermore, new political parties have appeared. The regionalist parties of the late 1950s and 1960s were followed at the beginning of the 1980s by ecologists and extreme-right parties, including Vlaams Blok, the neo-fascist Flemish nationalist party. The issue was how to incorporate these parties into existing ideological structures, concretized by the 1973 Cultural Pact as well as the long-standing system of subsidized liberty (Delwit and De Waele, 1999).

As a result, the post-war citizenship regime underwent profound changes, especially as the three worlds started to shrink (*Mitoyens* ..., 1990; Molitor, 1992; Seiler, 1999). Unions became more distant from 'their' political parties. The practices of partisan nominations lost legitimacy, as did the idea of 'watering' the associations of each world with public funds. In an even more basic sense, the rise of individualism undermined citizens' links to intermediary organizations, while the younger generations began to engage in '*zapping.*' This means that they chose institutional affiliations – unions, mutual societies, women's groups, and so on – less on the basis of their identification with a particular world than according to the concrete benefits that membership and participation might bring.

The state also faces new challenges and has developed new practices, including those in social spending. Confronted by budget shortfalls, the central government has sought to reduce spending by taking back powers previously 'subcontracted' to civil society organizations. Wage policy and management of the Social Security system are clear examples of this 'repatriation.' Moreover, the government has begun to set limits within which negotiations among the social partners have to occur. If they fail to reach agreement within the imposed constraints, the government then imposes a settlement. Finally, regional and communal institutions have begun to develop their own policies, which sometimes diverge from those of the central government. The result is that the system of subsidized liberty has begun to fragment.

In order to appreciate fully the impact of such changes on childcare policies and the representation of gender relations we would need to analyse each level of government, particularly that of the three Communities. Since we are unable to do so here, this analysis is limited to the central government and its fiscal and employment policies as they affect childcare. We do so by providing a broad-brush portrait of new orientations in economic and social policies, particularly the family policy dimensions (Alaluf, 1999; Nagels, 1999).

When the Liberals joined the government in 1981 and formed a coalition, until 1988, with the Social-Christians, understanding of the economic crisis and how the state might act to end it, changed in a major way. After 1981 any 'solutions' to economic crisis would come from supply-side policies, which were supposed to return businesses to profitability. These policies tended to be focused on fiscal incentives, such as reduced taxes and lower deductions for social programs, as well as deregulation that would supposedly eliminate the 'rigidities' of the labour market. There was an explicit rejection of any demand-side policies that would stimulate consumption, such as public spending – whether Keynesian or welfarist – and regulation of labour markets. Ratification of the Treaty of Maastricht reinforced such orientations, making them appear to be treaty-imposed constraints.

The Social Security system also experienced major changes. The accent was on eliminating deficits and new management practices (Arcq and Blaise, 1999). The family allowance system underwent extensive remodelling. Surpluses were used to sop up problems in other sectors (such as sickness and disability insurance), while, except for certain categories of the poor (children of the unemployed, for example), family allowances were drastically reduced. Several major reforms also occurred in unemployment insurance. In 1980 three categories of the unemployed were created: heads of families (single-parent families or those with only one employed spouse), people living alone (*isolés*), and two people living together (*cohabitants*). The latter, approximately 70 per cent of whom were women, had their benefits reduced several times and were the only ones who could be excluded from the system if they were unemployed too long. From 1991 to 1995 some 20,000 unemployed per year, about 90 per cent of whom were women, were thus taken off the roles.

Tax Reform and Childcare

Begun by the Social-Christian-Liberal coalition, and legislated by the Social-Christian-Socialist government, the 1988 tax reform included a much-touted 'family dimension.'[14] The overall objective was 'to lighten the fiscal burden on employment income and, at the same time, to make the personal income tax regime more favourable to the married and to families with children, without losing sight of the situation of single people ... It signals the end of discrimination between married and non-married couples and the enlarged freedom of choice in the organization of work and family life' (DS440/1, 26/9/1988: 1–2). The draft bill included a measure long sought by many women's organizations. Up to 80 per cent of the costs of childcare for the under-threes could be deducted from employment income or its (taxable) equivalents. For parents to qualify for the deduction, the child would have to be placed in a recognized childcare centre, cared for by a childminder, subsidized and regulated by the ONE (now the *Office de la naissance et de l'enfance*) or its Flemish equivalent, the *Kind en Gezin* (Child and

Family), or looked after by an 'independent' childminder regulated by one of these organizations.

The plan elicited much debate and many suggestions for amendment. The Ecologists, speaking from the opposition benches, argued that any taxpayer should be able to deduct childcare expenses; the measure should not be restricted to those already in the labour force. They claimed that their amendment would encourage non-employed single mothers to use childcare while getting trained, which would help their integration into the labour market (AS, 26/10/1988: 70; AC, 30/11/1988: 394). For his part the minister of finance, a Francophone Social-Christian, opposed transforming the childcare deduction into a more general financial benefit for families; the objective of universal coverage was best met by the family allowances (AS, 27/10/1988: 122, 134). As for the Flemish Liberals, they proposed a 100 per cent deduction, to eliminate any 'penalty, even a partial one,' associated with having children (DS440/2, 21/10/1988: 84). Nonetheless, they opposed offering the deduction to any taxpayer already claiming the conjugal quotient (for a non-employed spouse). They felt that such a tax break was justifiable only in the case of single parents or two-income married couples (DC597/4, 24/11/1988, no. 56). The minister of finance did not share this perspective, contending instead that even households with a single income should be able to deduct childcare expenses if the non-employed spouse fell sick or was hospitalized (DC597/7, 24/11/1988: 127). He also wanted to keep the 80 per cent limit, to discourage childcare providers from raising their rates. He assumed they would be less likely to do so if parents still had to cover part of the costs (DS440/2, 21/10/1988: 84).

It was from the ranks of the majority and its Social-Christian wing (especially the Flemish part) that the greatest objections came. 'Being a supporter of equal treatment of all children in this country,' a Social-Christian senator felt he must argue against the deduction. He sought to eliminate any 'discrimination' among children. Any parental decision or choice about the kind of care to provide for their children, whether at home or not, should receive a tax advantage. To do otherwise would be to discriminate and to treat children differently (AS, 26/10/1988: 112; AC, 30/11/1988: 395). He also framed the issue in budgetary terms, arguing that one category of children would cost the community much more than another. As one of his colleagues had calculated, 50,000–80,000 children placed in day nurseries would share close to 1.2 billion BF (that is, the amount calculated to be lost to the treasury by the deduction); whereas the other 300,000 cared for at home would have to be content with less than half of this amount (this figure is based on an estimate of the amount of the tax deduction termed the conjugal quotient) (AS, 26/11/1988: 72). Therefore, the senator demanded that single-income households with children be compensated (DS440/2, 21/10/1988: 85).

Despite the fact that the statistical analysis appended to the draft bill demonstrated that households with one income, especially those at the lower end of the income scale, would benefit most from the tax reform, a Flemish Social-Christian proposed an amendment to increase significantly the basic income tax credit of families with a child under three and no childcare deductions. This proposal was justified in terms of choice and the need to make the income tax regime, like the other state activities in this domain, neutral on parents' decisions about whether to care for their own children or to use childcare facilities (DS440/2, 21/10/1988: 60).

In the end a compromise was reached, one that no doubt involved a concession to the Socialists, then part of the majority coalition. The government accepted a Social-Christian amendment that set a maximum 10,000 BF deduction for the conjugal quotient (this limit had risen to 12,000 BF by 1997) (DS440/2, 21/10/1988: 61). At the same time, the minister of finance also accepted an amendment that authorized the government to set a ceiling on total deductions of childcare expenses for cost containment reasons (DS440/2, 21/10/1988: 86).[15]

The amendments did not please those promoting the egalitarian model, in this case primarily Ecologists and Flemish Liberals. Although supporting policies favouring families and children, they did not want such goals to provide an excuse to return to old-fashioned values, sending women back home to raise children. The secretary of state for finance, a Flemish Social-Christian, rejected the implication that the government was reviving the traditional model. In her view the tax reform was doing exactly the opposite, because it gave 'men and women a chance for labour market participation' (AC, 30/11/1988: 393).

Most of the supporters of the amended bill were found among the promoters of the new familialist model. Thus, a Francophone Socialist senator, in terms that also exemplified how much this party had distanced itself from feminism, vaunted the reform as putting single- and two-income families on the same footing before the tax man and thereby conferring 'the freedom to choose between work and home'

(AS, 26/10/1988: 63). This was a clear stance in favour of 'neutrality' in the tax regime, providing no encouragement to use non-parental rather than parental care or vice versa. This was far from the feminist critique presented by a Flemish Ecologist deputy, for whom tax advantages to mothers who care for their infant children did nothing less than

> make then opt for returning home. This means that the woman must abandon her plans for her own life, postpone her career, and focus on mothering and child-rearing ... However, women with young children who choose to stay at home today, without being aware of it, are opting to be at home for the rest of their lives ... Staying home three, six, nine years means that she is out of the labour market. She no longer accumulates work experience. She is not keeping up with technological innovations. She is completely 'out of the loop' ... At a time when this society, this policy, provide no measures to reintegrate stay-at-home women into the labour market, I find dangerous, and even hypocritical, policies that are advantageous only to housewives. They are far from any truly free choice by women to work outside or to stay at home. (AC, 30/11/1988: 394)

The debate on tax reform shows that the egalitarian model had not triumphed over the rhetoric of free choice. The debate also provided an occasion for promoters of traditional familialism, primarily Social-Christian deputies, to become more adept at using gender-neutral language to present their ideas about – traditional – gender roles. Thus, the speech of one senator lauds 'The irreplaceable quality of care given to children in the family setting, above all during early childhood. Those *parents* who provide childcare at home render other incalculable services to society. They seek no job outside the home and save their Community the exorbitant costs ... of a space in a day nursery' (AS, 26/10/1988: 71–2; emphasis added). Or, as another intoned, 'we have too great a tendency to seek from the state certain things that the *household* is well-equipped to provide. When one relieves the household of some of these essential tasks [there is a risk] of selecting the most costly solution' (DS440/2, 21/10/1988: 85; emphasis added).

Such remarks also reveal the way that a discursive link was developing between the supposed need for spending restraint and the advantages of parentally provided care, in a political context forged by economic crisis. For example, when certain Social-Christian senators criticized the draft bill for not providing the same tax breaks to single-earner households, the minister of finance declared: 'we would do more for such households if there were no budgetary problem' (DS, 26/10/1988: 63). Here the minister was using an argument about the financial difficulties of the government to avoid having to settle the ideological conflict about using state resources to foster a particular kind of childcare. To have made a choice would have been contrary to pluralism. The minister relied on the budgetary argument, just as had been done during the parliamentary debate on the ASP, in order to moderate claims that he judged would lead to disequilibrium.

The Impact of Employment Policies on Childcare

The economic situation, at the beginning of the 1980s oriented most of federal political activity[16] towards the fight against unemployment and the improvement of business competitiveness. It is symptomatic of this new situation that the parental leave allowance, an idea floated in the 1970s, was finally created within the framework of a larger program. This is an allowance permitting a Voluntary Career Break (*Interruption volontaire de carrière*). Officially, the primary goal of this measure is to redistribute work (DC757/1, 6/11/1984: 36) via part-time employment and flexible working time.

The Voluntary Career Break as a Parental Leave

At the end of 1984 the Social-Christian-Liberal government proposed a strategy to relaunch economic growth. The 'employment and competitiveness' dimension of the project established the Voluntary Career Break. It permits workers to take a partial or full leave from their job with no risk of being laid off. It is a paid leave and may last from six months to a year. The employer must consent to the leave or it must conform to conditions set out in a collective agreement. The final condition is that workers on leave must be replaced by another worker receiving full unemployment benefits.[17] The leave is renewable, up to a total of five years. The allowance is paid at the lowest unemployment insurance rate, that is, the one available to an unemployed worker who is cohabiting (DS757/2, 3/11/1984: 132, 139). In the case of a half-time leave, the benefit is halved. Any worker taking such a leave maintains all Social Security benefits, for example, access to family allowances and health care.

Workers can request a Voluntary Career Break for any reason. Nonetheless, the government and the majority of parliamentarians imagined that the major use would be for 'child-rearing, family reasons, or other personal reasons' (DS757/1, 6/11/1984).[18] Seen as a form of parental leave, the Voluntary Career Break generated a fair amount of consensus, even if certain defenders of the egalitarian model noted that 'It will probably be mostly women who will ask for the leave. This factor then constitutes an additional labour market disadvantage for them. Employers will tend to hire a man in order to avoid such interruptions. Fathers would also do well to ask for parental leave. The current text only partially tackles this problem' (DC1075/21, 3/1/1985: 173). What dispute there was came mostly from Social-Christian deputies. They sought to link this new program to the legislated but non-functioning child-rearing allowance, the ASP (DS757/2, 3/12/1984: 135). In doing so, they revealed the extent to which they were now committed to the new familialism. They accepted the legitimacy of mothers' employment as long as it did not interfere with child-rearing. Therefore, they claimed that the Career Break Allowance and the ASP would complement each other. On the one hand, a paid leave from employment was available for those workers wanting to care for their own children but then wishing to return to their job without putting their employment rights at risk. On the other hand, the ASP should be available to parents not yet in the labour force. 'Equal treatment is necessary for reasons of equity and justice and requires that the two programs be activated at the same time and for the same duration of time' (DS757/2, 3/12/1984: 143–4).

Other issues soon entered the debate. Briefs advocated extending the Voluntary Career Break – described as a parental leave – to partners who helped their self-employed spouse, to the unemployed,[19] as well as to any spouse in a household whose income fell below a certain level. Again, limiting a paid parental leave to two-income and single-parent families was described as being unfair to two-parent but single-income families: 'This [Voluntary Career Break] discriminates according to families' choices and in favour of one family model ... It amounts to a form of political apartheid, experienced by families who live side by side' (AS, 7/12/1984: 601).

In addressing such matters, rather than invoking the primary goal of the measure – that is, work sharing – the minister insisted that the integration of women into the workforce was inevitable: 'The societal perspective to which this project subscribes is one that assumes that men and women now wish to engage in paid employment. This is the reality of today's society, and of tomorrow's' (AS, 8/12/1984: 641; see also AC, 8/1/1985: 1250). A new version of the theme of reconciling work and family life was here being sketched in. Originally, this notion had buttressed the egalitarian model, with the accent being on collective responsibility for tasks traditionally assigned to mothers (including childcare), to permit them to integrate more smoothly into the labour force.[20] By the mid 1980s, however, as we will see clearly in the discussions of part-time work and flexible working hours, the theme of reconciling work and family came to be anchored in the rhetoric of 'free choice.' As such, it fit with the new familialism, serving to re-domesticate several tasks (including childcare) by inducing 'the parent who [so] wishes' to withdraw temporarily or partially from the world of paid employment.

Promotion of Individualized Working Time

Employers are fond of the idea of part-time work or reduced working hours. Seen as a way to deal with unemployment (DS264/1, 9/1/1978), by the end of the 1970s draft legislation (often promoted by the Social-Christians) was used to produce a better fit between the Social Security regime and a reduction of working time. Such proposals were stymied by the unions' refusal to come to a general agreement with the employers over the redistribution of work, including a generalized reduction in the definition of 'full-time' work (CG ONAFTS, A127, 18/7/1978).

Agreement had still not been reached in 1989, when the Social-Christian-Socialist government introduced a draft bill that, among other things, provided new regulations for part-time employment and flexible working time. Given that such flexibility was judged to be crucial for ensuring the competitiveness of firms, the government set out to protect the conditions of employment of part-time workers (AC, 8/12/1989: 797). In legislating, the government granted new recognition to part-time work; above all, the goal was to end 'false part-time.' Such employment practices deprived the Social Security regime of income (when firms made under-the-table payments) or resulted in overpayment of benefits (to 'false part-time' workers who received an allowance because they suffered from part-time unemployment). This initiative was part of the budget-cutting efforts of 1989 (DC975/10, 4/12/1989: 44).

Having made reconciliation of work and family life one of his priorities,[21] the minister of employment and labour, a Flemish Social-Christian, declared that, while the need for budgetary equilibrium should be respected, it was also necessary 'to reconcile ... employers' need for flexibility with workers' need to balance the demands of working and family life' (DC975/10, 4/12/1989: 42). Or, as one of his fellow Social-Christians said of the new regulations with respect to flexible working time, 'they make possible a better adjustment of the effects of working life on the family' (AC, 7/12/1989: 752).

The defenders of the egalitarian model, Ecologists and Flemish Socialists (even though the latter, as members of the majority, voted in favour of the project), argued that the proposed regulations actually undermined the objective of reconciliation. For example, they would allow an employer to assign an employee to work half-time eight hours a week for two weeks and then forty hours in the third week, and the worker might be informed of this schedule only five days in advance (DC975/10, 4/12/1989: 69; AS, 18/12/1989: 1025). Claiming that these were nothing more than 'theoretical' examples, the minister insisted that it was necessary 'to give every chance to those who want to work part-time' (AC, 8/12/1989: 797–8). He went on to say: 'everyone knows that, more and more often, the two partners have a job, whether full-time or part-time. In order to permit free choice, we must design a framework compatible with the aspirations of each of them' (AS, 18/12/1989: 1025). Again, seeing the inevitability of women's labour force participation, the minister linked the rhetoric of free choice, already seen as a tenet of the new familialism in the childcare debate, with the theme of reconciliation. Subsequently, the latter was part of the new familialism whenever work-sharing was on the agenda.

Supporters of the egalitarian model deployed their classic criticisms of supposedly free choice against the notion that part-time work offered an opportunity to foster 'reconciliation of work and family life.' Pointing out that part-time work had become the norm in certain highly feminized sectors, they underlined the fact that many such jobs do not provide any real choice between full-time and part-time work (AC, 7/12/1989: 756; AC, 8/12/1989: 790). A Flemish Socialist set out the full list of feminist objections to part-time work:

First, part-timers cannot be assigned major responsibilities; therefore, they are assigned low-skilled jobs. Second, they do not have promotion opportunities; they remain marginal, thereby reinforcing secondary labour force status that women already generally have. Third, the working conditions of part-timers are poor ... with shorter working hours, their rhythm of work is faster. Very often, too, they work outside normal working hours. This is *not positive* for family and social life. Fourth, part-timers have more difficulty participating in works councils and in unions. Already there are too few women in these bodies ... Fifth, a part-time job makes it difficult to achieve economic independence ... [while] such independence is the condition of the women's development. Sixth, women continue to carry all the household tasks: they have the time! Men don't need to help them. In this way the gender division of labour is reinforced. Seventh, collective infrastructure no longer needs to be developed (day nurseries, laundromats, etc.) if, while doing their mothering, women also do laundry ... (AS, 7/12/1984: 631).

The deputy was worried that, given the traditional gender division of labour in the family, a workforce that concentrated women in jobs in which they are easily replaceable and a female psychology that was less career oriented, a real and free choice between full- and part-time work would be nothing other than 'a joke.' This Flemish Socialist concluded: 'The new work-sharing formulae favour women's return to the home ... This is of course nothing new: it is well known that whenever there is a crisis women are chased out of the employment network ... If they are not yet banished from the country, as immigrant workers are, they are nonetheless banished to the traditional gender division of labour, for the greater comfort of men' (ibid.: 629). Accused of seeking a return to the traditional model, the ministers of employment and labour vigorously denied that this was their motive. Supporters of the new familialism, they described their measures as enabling 'parents' to equilibrate family time more effectively in relation to working time, giving them the means to choose freely. In the words of the Francophone Social-Christian:

Far be it from me to want to send back women home. Today no one could even imagine doing such a thing. We are constructing a society where, little by little, as many women as men will have access to the labour force. But we must also be welcoming to children, able to rear and take care of them. We can no longer imagine a system in which certain people are permanently excluded from the labour market. By means of career breaks, we are trying to place new value on certain ways of spending time: the time spent as a couple and in family activities, the time taken for training, as well as other goals, all without negative consequences on one's career (AS, 8/12/1984: 641–2).

A few Social-Christians remained nostalgic for the traditional family model. They raised financial, educational, and even pro-natalist arguments to push for child-rearing by mothers, but they sought to marry these ideas to an acceptance of the reality, indeed legitimacy, of mothers' labour force participation. Thus, starting from the premise that many long-term unemployed women 'do not wish to find a job because they consider, quite rightly, that it is more important to devote themselves to child-rearing, and that the income from work, compared with that coming from unemployment insurance, does not justify the efforts and sacrifices they would have to make,' one Senator judged

> that a lot of these women, if they had the chance, would take a much longer career break than the one now available ... [It would also be a good idea] to give priority in employment to women who have raised a large family. The service rendered to the community is immense: more stable children, less delinquency, better training and education ... Our current demographic problems are such that we must pay more attention to these women, as well as to those who, also thanks to a career break, care for elderly persons, the sick, the handicapped, rather than imposing this burden on our old-age homes, nursing homes, or other public services. One day we are going to have to recognize the savings we make because some people care for their own children, the elderly, the sick, or the handicapped and have to offer them a fair remuneration for their contribution. We only need to think of the cost of day nurseries! (AS, 18, 12/1989: 1006).

The Senator concluded, 'Obviously everyone must have complete freedom to make a choice' (ibid.).

As the 1990s dawned, the egalitarian model of gender relations had succeeded in diffusing the view that mothers' labour force participation was both inevitable and legitimate. Being linked to Belgium's pluralism, however, it could not avoid being in competition with, and even in representational terms being surpassed by, the rhetoric of 'free choice' and 'reconciliation' in the realms of employment policies and childcare. The latter two representations of gender relations were the tenets of the new familialism and were employed even by those nostalgic for the traditional family model.

It was, then, much more fiscal pressure on state spending than any ideological commitment that precluded the state from implementing the ASP. In the debates about the child-rearing allowance, it was obvious that pluralism and the balance of forces among different views of the family and gender relations had generated a recognition of 'parents' right to choose' not to participate in the paid labour force and personally to raise their children. Furthermore, it was more the struggle against unemployment and for competitiveness, rather than any ideological commitment, that led the state to institute financial incentives for temporary or partial career breaks particularly for 'parents who choose' to look after their own children. That the non-implementation of the ASP flew in the face of the new familialism, while the Voluntary Career Break was alien to the egalitarian model, attests to the axiomatic neutrality that still characterized Belgium's citizenship regime, even as the welfare state was being redesigned. The 'mega-goal' of the Belgian state still is, as it has been for many decades, to foster the material conditions that will permit all citizens, no matter which of the 'three worlds' they belong to, to lead a life in conformity with their personal convictions.

Towards a Frontal Assault on the Egalitarian Model?

The story just recounted ends in 1990; the major decisions were by then in place. We have not, for reasons explained above, analysed the effects on Belgium's three Communities of the decentralization of family policy and care for young children that has been going on since 1980. It is possible, however, to continue the story into the 1990s by quickly surveying more recent legislative initiatives. Here, we can identify two dynamics that continue to put equality to the test and threaten its place in the citizenship regime.

On the one hand, state actions in the realm of non-parental childcare reveal a continuing trend towards the multiplication of childcare options. Employment policy fosters the creation of jobs with lower status and fewer rights than classic full-time jobs. They include, for example, programs that provide large subsidies to employers who hire an unemployed person and are used, inter alia, to remove childcare workers from the ranks of the unemployed and into paid, albeit low-paid, jobs. There are also now tax-deductible job vouchers (*chèques-service*) available to persons willing to hire an unemployed worker through a local employment agency (*Agence locale pour l'emploi*; ALE). In 1995, 91 per cent of the working hours remunerated by means of such vouchers, 75 per cent of which were worked by women, were for housekeeping, but already 2 per cent of them covered care for the sick and for children (*Le Soir*, 10 September 1996).

An assessment of such programs in terms of equality would include an examination of the differential situation of women as users and providers of childcare. The question would be asked: Can equality accommodate programs that foster integration of some women into the labour force on the basis of programs that relegate others to less advantageous forms of employment? In a document published in 1994 by the minister of employment and labour, a Flemish Social-Christian woman, who was also the minister responsible for equal opportunity policies, proposed doing just that. It was suggested in this set of guidelines for municipalities seeking concrete examples of measures that would foster gender equality that local governments should promote the provision of care for sick children by unemployed women hired through the ALE.[22]

This idea restarted a polemic that had raged in the 1980s over childcare provided by childminders working in individual homes. In contrast to the childcare workers employed in day nurseries, 'mother's helpers' (*assistantes maternelles*) require no formal training and do not have the status of salaried worker. The 1990s controversy again pitted Socialist women's organizations against Social-Christian ones. The former, as supporters of the egalitarian model, sought a 'real' professional status for childcare workers. This would involve, they argued, putting childcare workers on a salary and employing them in a real workplace, a day nursery. The Social-Christian organizations, in contrast, as proponents of the new familialism, were satisfied with much less training while extolling the quality of contact (closer, more 'maternal') between the childminder and the child when the latter was at home (Humblet, 1996: 121–4).[23]

A second trend is the reinforcement of state efforts to foster parental rather than publicly provided care. This strategy is not new, of course, but it is seen in the strengthening commitment to part-time employment as a solution to the unemployment problem and as way of making firms more competitive. After having first reduced the supplementary allowance paid to 'involuntary' part-time workers, 85 per cent of whom were women, the Social-Christian-Socialist government reinstated the allowance in 1995, albeit making it variable as a function of whether the part-time worker lives in a household with another adult or is head of a household.[24] The Social Security rights of workers who opted for part-time employment through lack of a full-time job were also improved. The government thereby also encouraged part-time employees to maintain that status if they so wished or if they were using one of the programs for reduced working time, such as a half-time Voluntary Career Break. Finally, a full-time employee who temporarily reduces working hours in order to care for a child under three has the same rights to unemployment benefits as a full-time worker.[25]

Seduced by the efficiency of the 'Dutch model,'[26] Belgian policy-makers, particularly those of the Social-Christian and liberal world, have called for a new pact between the social partners that would bring moderation in wage increases and more work sharing through an increase in part-time jobs. In the Netherlands, more than two-thirds of employed women have only part-time jobs. (Dock and Janssen, 1996).[27] Moreover, since the 'Dutch miracle' reinforces their ideological convictions, certain business and financial leaders no longer hide their preference for the traditional model. The president of the Walloon Business Association (*l'Union wallonne des entreprises*) announced that 'the labour market could not absorb all the baby-boom women, nor all the foreigners. His solutions followed. Half-time jobs for women and a refusal to welcome all the world's misery' (*Le Soir*, 23 October 1996).

Finally, and most strikingly, we hear again today, just as we did when the traditional family model predominated, a discourse about work and the care of young children that is no longer gender neutral. It is as if the goal is again to bring women into the labour force under different conditions than apply to men, so that they will continue to take responsibility for domestic labour, especially care for the youngest children. With respect to the representation of mothers' work, history seems to be repeating itself. Nonetheless, the dénouement of this story still will depend a great deal upon the political appeal of this 'new' discourse. More than that, it will depend on whether young people who, in contrast to their parents, have grown up with the egalitarian model, can resist the new familialism.

NOTES

1 Until 1974 a wife could sue for divorce 'for fault' only if her husband had brought his mistress into the conjugal home, whereas any act of adultery (in the home or elsewhere) by the wife was grounds for a husband to seek a divorce.
2 This hypothesis remains to be proved, given that the liberal parties inter-

vened very little during the legislative processes examined here, perhaps because they were more open to Catholics than were the Socialist parties from the 1960s on.

3 This Management Committee is composed of equal numbers of representatives of employers, unions, and sociocultural organizations, including the two family leagues, the Socialist women's movement (*Les Femmes prévoyantes*) and the Social-Christian women's movement (*Vie féminine*). In collaboration with the department responsible for social affairs, the Committee manages the ONAFTS and the FESC. The authors wish to thank Mr Verstraeten, the general administrator of the ONAFTS, for allowing us to consult the archives of this organization, and Mr Darge, assistant secretary general of the FESC, for his support and the information and insights he shared with us.

4 When we cite the documents of the Management Committee (CG) of the ONAFTS, we use the following abbreviations: 'P' for proposals, 'A' for advisories, and 'D' for decisions, whereas when we refer to the ONAFTS' reports of its own activities we use the abbreviation 'RA.' The quotations in the next few paragraphs are taken from ONAFTS, P17, 19/5/1970.

5 This would have been added to the 'thirteenth-month' supplement that already existed.

6 This action angered the Socialist organizations; they then decided to boycott future meetings of the Management Committee devoted to this matter (ONAFTS, RA 1971: 9–10).

7 See DS466, 2/6/1971 and 627, 8/7/1971; AS, 14–14/7/1971; DC1062, 15/7/1971; AC 1/7/1971; MB, 12/8/1971. When we cite parliamentary sources, we use the following abbreviations: 'DC,' for the parliamentary documents of the House, 'DS' for the parliamentary documents of the Senate, 'AC' for the 'Hansard' of the House, 'AS' for that of the Senate. Finally, we use the abbreviation 'MB' for *Moniteur belge*, and 'AR' for royal decree.

8 To this end, it received from the reserves of the ONAFTS an endowment of 400 million BF. The law stipulated that the FESC could receive other endowments from the ONAFTS reserves, as well as from other sources. An amendment, no doubt of Socialist origin, tried in vain to make annual the endowment from the ONAFTS reserves (DS627, 8/7/1971: 14–16).

9 Certain other senators conformed to traditional familialism. For example, one said: 'Given that, due to economic changes, certain mothers are obliged to work outside the home, it is imperative to take steps to provide for the care of their children. Nonetheless, the best child-rearing is that done by the mother herself. As the director of a day nursery in France recently stated: "day nurseries are a necessary evil"' (DS627, 8/7/1971: 3). Such rhetorical

flourishes, however, did not generate enough support to undermine the original text.

10 See DC 680, 1975–76; AC, 9–12/12/1975; DS742, 1975–76; AS, 30–1/12/1975 and 2–3/1/1976; MB, 6/1/1976.

11 Even if a feminist version exists (see, for example, the work of Luce Irigaray), differentialism has been developed primarily by the philosophers of the traditional, anti-feminist model.

12 The budget crunch also affected funding of publicly provided care. At the same time as it promulgated the royal decrees implementing the FESC, the government substantially increased the portion of childcare costs covered by parental fees (AR, 1/8/1974).

13 In a general way, one could claim that each world (in the sociological sense) is preponderant in one region: the Roman Catholic world in Flanders, the socialist world in Wallonia, and the liberal world in Brussels.

14 DS440, 1988; AS, 26–7/10/1988; DC597, 1988–9; AC, 30/11–1/12/1988; MB, 16/12/1988.

15 A royal decree fixed this ceiling at 345 BF per day (an amount still in place in 1997). The average contribution of parental fees to childcare expenses has been estimated, in 1992, at 300 BF per day in the day nurseries of the French Community, and at 362 BF in those of the Flemish Community (Dubois et al., 1994: 34).

16 Even if Belgium formally became a federal state only with the constitutional reform of 1993, in practice it has been one since the constitutional reform of 1980.

17 See DS757, 1984–5; AS, 5 and 8/12/1984; DC1075, 1984–5; AC, 7–9/1/1985; MB, 24/1/1985.

18 Typically, sectoral collective agreements concluded under this legislation linked a Voluntary Career Break to family situations such as the birth of a child or caring for young children (Maingain, 1993: 78–9). Since 1991, moreover, a small supplement to the Career Break allowances used to care for a child under three is available.

19 The Volksunie, the Flemish Democratic Nationalist party, proposed to convert into family allowances the unemployment benefits of unemployed workers who provided all the care for children or parents (DS757/2, 3/12/1984: 68–9; DC1075/2, 15/12/1984: 12). In response, the minister announced his intention to create an equivalent of the Career Break for the unemployed. He did so in 1985.

20 See, above, the arguments made by Socialist women during the FESC debate.

21 Concretely, the ministry's priority can be identified in the following actions.

Voluntary Career Break benefits were higher if child-rearing was the reason for the leave. A new right to an unpaid leave (maximum ten days) for 'compelling family reasons' was created. Specialized studies of the issue abounded. The ministry organized a round table among associations whose work involves fostering such reconciliation.

22 The document is entitled: *Une politique communale d'émancipation dans la pratique.* It is also worth noting that gender-neutral language was not considered necessary in the text. The ministry clearly had only female unemployed in mind, as indicated by its use of the feminine form in French.

23 Note that, in conformity with pluralism and the rhetoric of free choice, the ONE decided to develop the services of 'mother's helpers' as well as those of the day nurseries. As a result, with the support of ONE subsidies, between 1985 and 1992 the number of 'trained childminders' increased tenfold in the French Community.

24 Exercising its responsibility over employment policy, in 1994 the Region of Flanders instituted a subsidy to encourage full-time workers to become part time.

25 Workers did not, however, have the right to supplementary benefits when working part time.

26 At the beginning of the 1980s the Netherlands unemployment rates were as high as those of Belgium. By the mid-1990s the Dutch rate was half that of Belgium (Hemerijck and Visser, 1997).

27 Between 1983 and 1995, part-time employment in the Netherlands rose by 550,000 jobs, whereas in the same period in Belgium part-time jobs increased from 280,000 to 480,000, one-third of which were held by women.

Chapter Four

France: Reconciling Republican Equality with 'Freedom of Choice'

Jane Jenson and Mariette Sineau

A modernist societal paradigm shaped the first three decades of post-war French politics, bringing new family policy and representations of women's social roles. The shift was made in two stages. During the Fourth Republic a certain consensus prevailed, centred around a 'familialist' vision, founded on the ideal of the woman at home raising her children (Prost, 1984). Responding to the preferences of the *Mouvement républicain populaire* (MRP), in particular, family policy had three major characteristics. First, its objectives were pro-natalist. Second, programs discouraged labour force participation of women, especially mothers, despite labour shortages during post-war reconstruction. Finally, there was little investment in day nurseries (*crèches*). The last element reflected a particular ideology; for the religious right the mother at home, not the state, should be responsible for the care of young children. 'The social imagination' (Borne, 1988: 9) rallied around the model of the housewife and her special responsibility for child-rearing.

In the next two decades, however, the state moved towards a more egalitarian, or feminist, vision that accepted the legitimacy of women's labour force participation and of devolving care to institutions specializing in education and child development. The birth of the Fifth Republic in 1958 was key. Pro-natalism lost support as the MRP went into terminal decline. In addition, rapid social and economic changes modified behaviour in markets, workplaces, and homes, and the consensus over family policy was shattered. The technological breakthrough of the birth-control pill made family planning easier, even if contraception was still illegal. The baby boom ended (although the fertility rate remained above 2 until the beginning of the 1970s). The economic growth and low unemployment of the 1960s led to a surge of women into the labour force. Many were mothers of young children.

Policy-makers realized that socio-economic change – soon pushed further by the rebirth of feminism – made some adjustments in family policy necessary. By the early 1970s, because of a series of reforms, women's employment was penalized less (reform of the 'single-salary allowance' (*l'allocation de salaire unique*)); new benefits covering some of the costs of non-parental childcare, etc.). At first timidly and then more decisively, services for the youngest children were developed, even if supply always fell short of the childcare spaces needed (Laroque, 1985).

These changes brought a new discourse about women's employment, replacing that of the first post-war decade. Analysts began to describe the rising rates of female employment as an 'irreversible' fact, part of the logic of post-war modernization. A job became a condition for women's economic and social autonomy. As schools took over more responsibility, the family lost its central role and mothers were no longer necessarily seen as those best equipped to raise young children. Specialists in child development began to extol the advantages of early childhood education. A new model of gender equality took hold, based on equal rights and opportunity.

Soon the low growth rates and high unemployment of the economic crisis that started in 1973 began to threaten this vision of equality. The labour force participation rate of mothers never faltered, however, although the birth rate continued to drop. In the context of a weak economy and an expensive welfare state, rising employment rates among mothers clearly was a major policy dilemma: who would care for the children and would there be enough babies? Policy networks reacted in two ways. First, there was mounting pressure for employment policies fostering part-time and non-standard employment, such as temporary and short-term contracts.[1] Although France traditionally had had low rates of part-time employment, there was soon a significant increase. The impact on women's employment was immediate, since the vast majority of part-time employees were women (Maruani, 1995).

Second, policy networks began to shift their perspectives on childcare. Early childhood education themes declined, while the 'reconciliation of family and working life' took pride of place (Hantrais and Letablier, 1995). In the rest of this chapter we look in detail at these changes. We do so by identifying two periods: the Giscardian era, corresponding to the first years of economic crisis; and a second period that began in 1981 when the Socialists first took office and continued through the years of cohabitation and right-wing governments until the late 1990s. The new programs of these years provided representations of gender relations departing significantly from the early 1970s model, thereby weakening the equality discourse of the citizenship regime.

Upheaval and Crisis: Modernity and Ambivalence in the Giscardian Years

The leader of a coalition of right-wing parties, Valéry Giscard d'Estaing was president from 1974 until 1981. This single mandate bridged the modernist paradigm and its replacement. On the one hand, childcare programs were modernized by new programs, reinforcing the egalitarian model of gender relations. On the other hand, however, in these years also policies emerged that made the future of gender equality much more ambiguous.

Modernity and the Politics of Childcare

Policy-makers took to proclaiming that their stance towards women's employment was 'neutral.' Asserting that it would be useless 'to deny that change is taking place' or to try 'to reinvent the family of earlier times,' Simone Veil, minister of health, acknowledged in 1975 that family policy must adapt to sociological changes, among which were women's employment (Steck, 1993: 28). The state began to respond to the needs of dual-career couples. Thus, in 1977 new legislation created the Family Complement by merging several programs,[2] which included the single-salary allowance that been offered to the non-employed and programs available to the employed that helped to cover childcare costs. Modernism also underpinned the legislation (dated 17 May 1977) that recognized the employment status of child-minders (assistantes maternelles). Until the change, there was no official definition of babysitters' (nourrices) rights and obligations on the job. Some authors claim that this reform marked a 'revolution' in the history of infant care (Designaux and Thevenet, 1982: 102).[3]

Childcare spaces multiplied and variety increased. Between 1974 and 1980 infrastructure (essentially day nurseries and family day care) grew by 43,000 places, an increase of 72 per cent. Expansion was significantly faster in the first four years of Giscard's presidency, however, than in the last three, when the rate of increase declined to below

10 per cent per year. In addition, a directive setting out the fɪ entation of the local institutions responsible for family benefiɪ *d'allocations familiales*; CAF) identified for the first time the infrastruc- ture of childcare as a priority.[4] Policy commitment to variety appeared in the permission for drop-in childcare centres (*haltes-garderies*) to adapt to the 'market.' A 1979 directive loosened the regulation of such centres, allowing them to provide care to children whose parents worked part time.[5] They thereby received the green light to become – which they would do in the following years – part-time day nurseries (Leprince, 1987: 510).

A third sign of modernism was major public investments in pre- elementary education: between the 1975–76 school year and that of 1980–81, the percentage of 2-year olds in school rose from 26.6 to 35.7 per cent, that of 3-year olds climbed from 80.4 to 89.9 per cent, while that of 4-year olds reached 100 per cent.

Ambivalence

Despite these commitments to a modernist paradigm, there were still reasons for scepticism about the neutrality of Giscardian family policy with respect to women's employment and about its commitment to gender equality in citizenship. The president's rhetoric was contradic- tory. He had to deal with both a declining birth rate and crisis-induced unemployment. Speaking to demographers in 1981, Giscard d'Estaing framed in this way his worries about fertility and mothers' employ- ment: 'The problem is this: how can we raise the fertility of couples with two children ...? It is clear that cross-nationally there is no correla- tion between the amount fertility falls and the rate of female employ- ment. Nevertheless, common sense indicates that, with several young children, it becomes more and more difficult for a mother to fulfil her work and family responsibilities.'[6] Answering his own question, the president called for ingenuity: he wanted 'experiments with new for- mulae,' as much in the realm of employment policy as in that of child- care. In particular, he saw the need for greater flexibility at work: 'The uniformity and rigidity of working life corresponds less and less to current desires, particularly those of mothers. Why should everyone be at work at the same time and for the same number of hours, regardless of age, sex, family situation or financial goals? In other large industrial- ized countries, such as the United States or Great Britain, part-time jobs are much more numerous than in France.'

Second, Giscard d'Estaing called for recognition of what he termed the 'status of mother.'[7] The result for old-age insurance, for example, would be measures to treat child-rearing as the equivalent of employment. Throughout his presidency, various categories were affiliated without charge to the insurance program for mothers, beginning with recipients of the single-salary allowance.[8] In the words of one commentator, 'here the state was behaving as a quasi-employer of mothers at home, assuring them a "full career"' (Strobel, 1997: 179). Right-wing parliamentarians soon began to echo the president's call for recognition of this status in their own debates.

Third, policy biases against women's employment were never completely eliminated. Income tax continued to be calculated on the basis of family income rather than being individualized (CES, 1991: 76). Abandoned virtually every else in the European Union, this system usually results in higher tax payments for two-income couples than if each is taxed separately. Nor was the Family Complement totally neutral; the way of calculating benefits was more advantageous to single-income than to two-income couples (Laroque, 1985: 262).

Fourth, even if Giscard's presidency did mark a highpoint in the construction of the infrastructure of childcare, the president was already thinking about less expensive solutions. He called for an open mind about alternatives, particularly those being developed in local communities: 'We need good answers to the following questions. What kinds of care for young children can be developed close to home? How can we organize simple initiatives, based on a spirit of mutual help, in local communities or neighbourhoods? What is the place of community groups in this field?'[9]

A final sign of ambiguity was the decision to create two new programs, neither of which did as much as one might hope to encourage women's equal participation in the labour force. A new benefit developed for single parents, the *Allocation de parent isolé* (API) – which we can only mention here – was one of the first measures of 'national solidarity,' paying a minimum income in exchange for raising children (Messu, 1999: 122–3).[10] The second program was an unpaid parental leave (*Congé parental d'éducation*). It had been proposed by the Seventh Plan, and the president's speeches had already expressed support for what he termed a 'mother's leave.' The legislation creating this unpaid leave marked further commitment to creating variety in childcare, to the detriment of day nurseries.

The Direction of Change Is Set: The 1977 Parental Leave

The law of 12 July 1977 inserted into the Labour Code the right to unpaid parental leave. It permitted an employed mother of a child under three years to suspend her employment for up to two years in order to care for the child. This leave was available only to women who had at least one year of seniority with their firm and who worked in a company with more than 200 employees. Fathers could use the leave only if the mother formally renounced her claim to it. Because the woman kept her acquired rights within the company and could return to her job, the new leave was supposed to be attractive to parents who preferred parental to non-parental childcare.

Even if such a leave might appear to fall on the modernity side of the ledger, it had its own ambiguities. Parents who took leave lost some of their retirement benefits, and there was no realistic guarantee that the woman would return to the same or an equivalent job. Nor did the fact that the leave was unpaid make it helpful to many young families already struggling to make ends meet with two salaries.

The government's draft bill (dated 27 April 1977) had initially proposed a 'mother's leave,' to 'permit salaried women more easily to reconcile their professional and family obligations' (AN, no. 2830: 3).[11] This name for the new program was roundly criticized by parliamentarians, who sometimes ironized about why the reconciliation of work and family concerned only women. In its report, the Commission of the National Assembly that considered the draft bill alleged that the proposal was discriminatory, reflecting social and gender inequalities (AN, no. 2968: 38).[12] In addition, deputies from left parties accused the government of trying to reduce the unemployment rate by undermining women's right to work.[13]

The National Assembly, therefore, amended the project. It changed the name to 'parental leave,' and insisted that gender-neutral language be used throughout the text of the law. The more conservative Senate scorned the approach adopted by the National Assembly: 'The right to parental leave naturally belongs first to the mother. Even if both parents meet the conditions, and even if the mother earns a higher salary than the father, her natural aptitude for child-rearing must take priority over her contribution to the household's income. Financial considerations certainly should not be a priority when families decide who will take parental leave' (S, no. 406: 14). In the end, despite the new name, the leave was targeted to mothers. Moreover, regardless of loudly voiced criticisms, the leave remained unpaid. Law-makers feared weakening the competitive position of French firms.

Traditionally, childcare falls within the realm of family policy. For those initiating this program, however, the objective of the parental leave was, first and foremost, to free up jobs for the unemployed. As early as 1977, in other words, the seeds of what would rapidly become a new paradigm were planted. A link was being made between women's right to work, childcare for young children, and the unemployment unleashed by economic crisis.

The Crisis Continues: The Invention of New Services

The 1981 election of the Socialist François Mitterrand as president of France opened a new era for childcare. Demography again became an important issue, since the declining birth rate provoked concerns. Mitterrand himself frequently claimed that 'large generations are creative generations' (Jenson and Sineau, 1995: 250). While some policy-makers tried to play down any threat, pointing out that France still had one of the highest birth rates in Europe, they were definitely in the minority. Far more numerous were those, within the ranks of the Socialist party as well as on on the right, who gravely spoke of what in common parlance was termed a 'demographic crisis.' Moreover, confronted with the electoral successes of the National Front, a neo-fascist party that made much of the supposed demographic difficulties, traditional parties on the left as well as on the right felt it necessary to compete on the same terrain.

Analysis of the unemployment rate was also changing. After more than ten years of economic difficulties, policy-makers were forced to recognize that the increase in women's labour force participation – particularly that of mothers with young children – had not been halted by high rates of joblessness. Expert report after expert report documented this 'sociological revolution.' The issue for family policy was how to respond to these two social facts.

Initially, the new government seemed about to give priority to the child and to infrastructure, in the name of a philosophy of republican equality, ranging from equality among classes to that between the sexes and among children. In an early report a substantial increase in spaces in day nurseries was proposed, described as the only way to right the balance in childcare and enlarge the opportunities for parental choice. In addition, the document was very prudent about part-time work, describing it as 'only a solution for parents who can accept a fall in income. It too often confirms the traditional division of roles within the couple.'[14] Within two years, however, the conversion of the president to austerity policies as well as efforts to put the finances of the Social Security system in order brought about a radical alteration in priorities. The Socialist government shifted the spotlight from the child and early childhood education towards the need for reconciliation of work and family life.[15] In doing so, attention to gender equality and women's autonomy was significantly lessened.

The president lent a hand in bringing about this substitution. Speaking to the family movement on 21 November 1981, François Mitterrand had already lauded 'flexibility' as a boon for parents, above all for employed mothers. He claimed then that some mothers working full time might want a temporary break or reduced hours of employment. Therefore, if one gave them the financial means to do so, a number of them might opt to become (at least temporarily) full-time mothers or part-time employees.

Eventually, state support for day nurseries became the weak link in the strategy to reform the work-family relationship. By the mid-1980s the *crèches* (or day nurseries) were being supplanted by forms of childcare described as better able to meet parents' preferences for wider choices and individualized services. Alleging that day nurseries were too 'rigid' to respond to diverse parental needs, governments – whether Socialist or on the right – promoted other forms of care. In particular, there was a proliferation of programs targeted to different social groups. These supposedly more flexible measures were of two kinds. The first involved benefits that compensated for some of the financial burden of childcare, ranging from allowances available to parents who hired a childminder to care for the child in their home (if the families were well off) or who employed a childminder who cared for several children in her own home (*assistante maternelle agréée libre*) (if they were of modest means). A second set of programs was focused on adjusting working time. They incorporated incentives to work part time and to take parental leaves, both paid and unpaid.

Support for Day Nurseries: The Weak Link in the Chain

In 1983 the government implemented a major policy by which authority devolved from Paris to regional and local governments. As part of this reform, the latter gained enhanced responsibility for day nurseries. Next, a system of grants was created, intended to encourage municipalities to improve the day nursery infrastructure.[16] For the five years the program was in operation, however, the record was very modest: only one-fifth of the forecast 100,000 places were created (CES, 1991: 112). A more flexible program with farther-reaching objectives followed in 1988, providing for contracts between municipalities and the CAF to cover a wider variety of services and providers. Then, the Family Law of 25 July 1994 provided funds for a 'local development plan' for the care of children under six. All communes were eligible to take part, but participation was not required.

Despite such programs, the rate of increase in day nursery places suffered a decline over François Mitterrand's two mandates. The increase was 44 per cent between 1981 and 1988 and only 29 per cent from 1988 to 1995, compared with an average increase of 72 per cent for Giscard's seven years in office. In the 1970s the average was 10 per cent per year, but by the 1990s the growth rate had fallen below 5 per cent. In absolute numbers, 45,500 spaces were created during Mitterrand's first mandate and 43,400 during his second. While this remains a real accomplishment, it came nowhere close to his campaign promise in 1981, which was to create 300,000 spaces in day nurseries. Nor did it come near to meeting the rising demand.

Several reasons can be found to account for the slow increase in publicly provided childcare. Lack of dynamism and neglect by local authorities were certainly factors, particularly in rural areas (Commaille, 1993: 84–5). In addition, however, the national government seems to have used its decentralization policy to offload its responsibilities onto local governments. It proclaimed the need for day nurseries but neglected to give the local authorities sufficient financial resources to build them (CES, 1991: 156; Vielle, 1994: 118). This strategy for saving money by offloading responsibility reflects both an ideological commitment to less state provision and the austerity policies that marked the second half of the 1980s. The president, himself, singled out day nurseries as particularly costly; he explained: 'day nurseries are expensive to build, then to manage, and the financial resources of the state are limited.' While he admitted that the new programs marked a scaling back of commitments, he claimed they were 'not halting our program but [only] slowing it down owing to financial problems.'[17]

In brief, the consensus around austerity had a direct effect on the design of childcare and family policy. The principal political actors acknowledged that spending restrictions were incompatible with making access to day nurseries available to all children. Therefore, publicly funded childcare would no longer be primarily provided as a public service, that is, one organized by public authorities and available to all, either without charge or at a price far below its real cost. The state began to pay for – and thereby encourage the expansion of – other types of childcare. There has been a significant shift in forms of provision of spaces in day nurseries associated with the decentralization (Ullman, 1998). Municipalities provide fewer spaces, while community groups and non-profit associations have become important providers, often in partnership with the local CAF (Ancelin 1985: 444–5). Nonetheless, even such diversification was not enough; other solutions had to be found.

Individualized and Targeted Solutions

Attention was turned increasingly to aiding individual families to find their own childminders as well as to provide their own childcare. A new set of benefits and subsidies created two different policy tracks. One encouraged a form of reconciliation of work and family in which two-income families purchased services in the market, and new allowances and tax benefits compensated some of the cost of private childcare. The other track encouraged adjustments in working time. Eventually, the result was a childcare mix that was integrated with the labour market flexibility that policy-makers were simultaneously seeking to promote. Employed mothers were given a range of choices from which they could construct their own '*à la carte*' selection. They could work full time or part time, take a full-time or part-time parental leave, and use a day nursery full time or a drop-in centre part time. They could use tax breaks and other benefits to hire a childminder on a full-time or half-time basis or to provide care at home or outside the home. That childminder could be licensed and regulated, or not.

A detailed analysis of parliamentary debates both reveals the details of the programs and helps us to understand how decision-makers went about constructing a replacement for the egalitarian model of gender relations. Overall and increasingly over time, policy-makers deployed decidedly less gender-neutral representations of childcare provision, thereby creating a citizenship regime also less egalitarian.

Parental Leave: The Labour Code Becomes Family Oriented

The law of 4 January 1984 that reformed the unpaid parental leave marked the Socialist government's entry into the childcare domain. Whereas in 1977 there had been vigorous debates about whether fathers should have access to such leave, this time the matter was barely raised. The new legislation allowed both parents to take a leave, simultaneously or consecutively. In addition, it could be taken half time while combined with a part-time job. When Georgina Dufoix, secretary of state for the family, first presented her draft bill, she described it as fitting within 'the policy framework of "chosen time," which seeks to reduce working time via a combination of collective and individual initiatives' (AN, debates, 25 November 1983: 5667).

Fighting unemployment was not the government's only objective; the program was also given a definite demographic tinge. It eliminated the requirement that a parent return to work for at least a year before taking another leave. If a woman had two children within two years, she or her partner could take a longer leave without losing employment rights. This can be termed a pro-natalist provision, because demographers agree that closely spaced pregnancies encourage the creation of large families. Indeed, pro-natalist goals would henceforth exist alongside those of reducing unemployment and encouraging flexibility in working time. As part of this construction, mothers were designated a privileged pool of potential part-time workers.

The Labour Code was again modified in 1986 after the right's return to government. By making unpaid parental leave available for three years, the code was aligned with the duration of the child-rearing allowance, which will be discussed below. In 1991 the Socialist government again reformed the program, permitting unpaid leaves to be combined with a work week that was only one-fifth (but not less than sixteen hours) the usual length.[18] The law of 25 July 1994 extended the program in two ways. Any employed parent could take parental leave, regardless of the size of the firm, and parents could take an additional year to care for a seriously ill child.

The Parental Child-Rearing Allowance of 1984 and 1986:
Paying Mothers to Care

The law of 4 January 1985, termed the 'Dufoix law,' created a paid parental leave for the first time in France. The child-rearing allowance

(*Allocation parentale d'éducation*; APE) was available to parents who left work to undertake childcare full time at the time of the birth, adoption, or arrival of a child under the age of three in the household. The allowance was available, however, only if the infant raised the number of children in the family to three. In addition, the parent had to have been employed, or similarly occupied, for twenty-four of the preceding thirty months. The allowance was paid for a maximum of two years and was open to any parent in the labour force, whether employed or unemployed.

Seeking to make its own mark in the domain of family policy, the Socialist government managed to confuse the boundary – already blurred as a result of the changes to unpaid parental leaves – between family and employment policy and between family law and the Labour Code. The draft bill defined the child-rearing allowance as a measure whose principal objective was promotion of 'solidarity and demographic renewal.' In itself this was not surprising, given the extent to which French family policy has traditionally been shaped by attention to the birth rate. The bigger surprise was that the government described the allowance as 'extending' the unpaid parental leave program. By doing so, it again focused on the discourse about the reconciliation of work and family life (AN, no. 2429: 2–3). As presented by the minister, the draft bill reflected these two objectives and thereby created a link between the choice offered to families and the needs of the country: 'Family policy is a policy of free choice for families ... The state ought not define a model, but it must aid [families] in achieving their family goals, because if the drop in the birth rate continues, there will be a serious problem for social stability and social policy' (AN, no. 2470: 27).

A first series of criticisms of this perspective came from the majority benches. Certain Socialist members contested the very principle. For example, Véronique Neiertz, spokesperson of the Socialist group in the National Assembly, claimed that the allowance posed 'a fundamental political problem,' because it constituted a first step towards a 'salary for mothering.' Such a measure would be discriminatory on more than one count. She also questioned its effectiveness as a tool for raising the birth rate, and she proposed other ways of reconciling maternity and working life, such as alterations in working time and more public facilities for care of the youngest children. In an article in *Le Monde* (dated 3 January 1985), she expressed her criticisms of leading demographers, who were celebrating the allowance as a 'revolution.'[19] Other Socialist deputies, such as Jean-Michel Belorgey, also criticized it as incoherent and unfair: 'What is this child-rearing allowance? [Is it] a catalyst for parents to take leaves? [Is it] an allowance to permit the mother or the father with three or more children to withdraw from the labour force, if they have not already spontaneously done so, or have not yet had the bad luck to be banished by long-term unemployment? [Is it] essentially 'rewarding damages' to women who in the past took a low-paid job and now are making the sacrifice of giving it up in order to contribute to work-sharing ...?' (AN, debates, 4 December 1984: 6647). The right-wing Senator Jean Cauchon, who was the spokesperson for the upper chamber's Social Affairs Commission, made a similar argument: 'This allowance confuses two objectives. It has a pro-natalist, that is familial, objective, of which we approve, and the objective of fighting unem-ployment' (S, debates, 18 December 1984: 4694).

Such an allowance, combining the goals of employment and popula-tion policies, reflected more continuity than divergence between Socialist initiatives and those previously adopted by right-wing gov-ernments. It also demonstrates that concerns about gender equality were disappearing from the radar screens of ministers and ministries. Although either parent could take advantage of the child-rearing allowance, rare were those who truly believed that fathers would use their right to take a leave paid well below the level of the minimum wage. Communist and Socialist deputies continued to pressure the minister to acknowledge that the APE was really a salary for mother-ing. Georgina Dufoix tried to defend it, affirming that 'the goal was not, nor would the effect be, to encourage women's return home. Women's employment is now a given of social and economic life; it is irreversible' (AN, no. 2470: 33). This declaration, however, is some-thing less than a ringing statement of principle. It did not proclaim a firm commitment to an egalitarian concept of gender rights and roles.[20] Indeed, Georgina Dufoix adopted an offhand attitude when she spoke of the consequences the allowance might eventually have for working women: 'The child-rearing allowance is proportionally more interest-ing for low-income earners and might be more attractive to them. This effect is not something worth criticizing, to the extent that the jobs they hold are often the least rewarding' (AN, no. 2470: 33).

When the Right won the legislative elections of 1986 and formed the government, the child-rearing allowance again appeared on the agenda. The Barzach law (dated 29 December 1986) named for the minister of health and the family, essentially broke any remaining links between the allowance and labour force participation. Any parent employed for a minimum of eight trimesters (two years) in the ten years preceding the birth or adoption of a third child could receive the allowance, for up to three years.[21] Demographic concerns were even more important. The influence of the National Institute of Demography (INED) was clear. The documents clearly specified that the 'new child-rearing allowance should encourage the birth of the third child and help mothers who remain at home' (AN, no. 427: 3). With this bill, the government sought to overcome the shortcomings of the original allowance, which had had very limited success, attracting only 25,000 takers a year. Both houses of Parliament called it a 'lamentable failure.'

Critics of this program, however, continued to accuse it of being a threat to gender equality, as no more than a 'salary for mothering' that threatened women's right to work and harked back to the bad old days of the single-salary allowance.[22] Proponents did admit that it was meant to be a 'replacement salary.'[23] During her presentation before the Commission of the National Assembly, Michèle Barzach was pleased to confirm that 'thanks to the new terms [of access], giving up paid work will have, for low-income couples, no significant financial consequences.' These words are eerily close to those of Georgina Dufoix in 1984 (AN, no. 438: 57).

Employment issues were not absent from the policy project. The National Assembly proposed that during the third year mothers should be able to combine the child-rearing allowance with part-time work. The lower house justified this amendment by claiming that the change would permit both expansion of part-time employment and the introduction of flexibility in working time (AN, no. 438: 31, 66). This orientation fit very well with employment policy, where part-time work was seen as a solution to two problems, that of unemployment and that of the high costs of publicly provided childcare (Afsa, 1998).

Save Some Time, Employ Someone: Two Subsidies for Hiring a Childminder

The second direction that diversification of public support for child-care took involved programs that offset some of the costs for parents who hired their own childminders. With these subsidies, the government further diversified its representations of women's work. The first program was created (law dated 29 December 1986) by the right-wing government. The objective of the allowance for childcare at home (*Allo-*

cation de garde d'enfant à domicile; AGED) was to enrich the panoply of government programs.[24] At the same time, a two-track system was being constructed. Hiring a personal caregiver, as envisioned in this program, was feasible only for high-income parents.[25]

The new allowance was available to any employed parent of a child under 3, regardless of the family income. In two-parent families both parents had to be in the labour force; single parents could also claim the benefit. The allowance covered (up to a fixed maximum) the employee and employer's contributions made on behalf of the babysitter to the social security system (Steck, 1993: 71). Parents could also claim a tax credit on the base salary.

Michèle Barzach justified her bill as one that 'encouraged the development of a more flexible type of childcare, so as to reduce the pressure on day nurseries and to permit parents better to organize their working and family life' (AN, no. 427: 3).[26] It was supposed to expand 'real choice.' Moreover, because other types of care, whether provided by parents or in day nurseries, were subsidized, it was 'unfair' that babysitters working in the child's home did not benefit from similar public support (AN, no. 427: 3).

Deputies and senators vied to argue the merits of the program, describing it as a form of childcare that 'weighed much less heavily on the community.'[27] The report of the Senate Commission started by stating: 'by lightening the demand for publicly provided childcare, this measure will help the financial situation of local governments' (S, no. 90: 5, 33).[28] Another objective was job creation.[29] The program would encourage babysitters to stop working 'under the table'; as such, it was part of a broader set of initiatives to end black-market work, especially in the area of personal services (AN, no. 438: 49; S no. 90: 5). Third, this type of childcare would be flexible and available to parents, regardless of their working schedules, especially to those employed part time.[30] Finally, making the hiring of a babysitter 'accessible to middle-income earners, particularly those working part time' (S, no. 90: 35), would help to create part-time jobs in service work.

The program was again modified by the Family Law of 25 July 1994, a major change in family policy initiated by the right-wing government. It was extended to families with children aged 3–6, and the amount of the allowance was significantly increased, as was the tax credit that accompanied it (Fagnani and Rassat, 1997: 79–86). When the left-wing government of Lionel Jospin came to power in 1996, significant cuts to the program were made; nonetheless, the allowance remained an option among the array of possible ways for parents to organize childcare.

The second program created an allowance subsidizing the employment of a licensed mother's assistant (*Aide à la famille pour l'emploi d'une assistante maternelle agréée*; AFEAMA, law dated 6 July 1990). It is one of the Rocard government's principal contributions to diversification as well as individualization of childcare services (S, no. 219). The benefit is available to any parents, regardless of income, who hire a self-employed licensed childminder to care for a child under six. The subsidy targets the middle-income families who have provided the major clientele of day nurseries. The allowance makes it often less expensive to have children cared for by a self-employed childminder.[31] Its supporters described the allowance as also enabling 'a real freedom of choice' for parents (S, no. 219: 4).

The program responded to more than the needs of working parents; it also addressed a category of workers, the licensed mother's assistants (*assistantes maternelles agréées*). Their number had been declining, falling from 238,000 in 1977 (when they gained formal recognition) to 129,600 in 1989–90. The deputies attributed this drop-off to the growth of 'under-the-table' employment (AN, no. 1402: 12). As senators indicated during their consideration of the draft bill, both the subsidy for employing a babysitter and that for engaging a licensed childminder actually were quite similar measures. Each sought 'to relieve families from paying [the employer's portion of social security] contributions so as to encourage the mother's assistants or domestic help to declare their earnings' (S, no. 282: 31). The bills improved access to health and retirement benefits, a change also expected to increase the attractiveness of such jobs. Therefore, in presenting its bill in 1990, the government emphasized that 'childcare is a field with significant employment potential,' while it also helps parents to combine work and family life (S, no. 219: 2).

It is clear, then, that the two allowances were tied to employment policy, with little, if any, attention to quality of childcare. They were an element of what might be called the 'strategy of exoneration.' Governments had been excusing certain employers from making contributions to the social security system for most of the 1980s. This familiar solution had already been applied to programs for youth employment and for the long-term unemployed. They fit well with the ambient neo-liberalism of the time and therefore would be applied to the childcare sector.

Part-Time Work

Working-time adjustments, either via reduced hours or flexible schedules, was another approach that policymakers used in seeking to provide parents with 'choice' about childcare. They could reconcile work
and family life 'by alternating' between the two. After 1981 the first
Socialist governments quickly began to regularize this type of atypical
employment, viewing it as both a cure for unemployment and an
incentive for work-sharing. Although the candidate, François Mitterrand, denigrated part-time employment as a ghetto for women, once
elected president, he began to see it as part of the fight against unemployment.[32] Little by little, a new model was taking form and gaining
support from a majority of politicians, on the left as well as on the
right. Their representation of the situation hypothesized a close association between work-sharing, new childcare services, and women's
'interests.' For example, in 1988 then Prime Minister Jacques Chirac
described part-time work as a form of employment for which mothers
should have priority: 'Women now work outside the home ... We well
know the problems [that result]. Even if they are still incomplete, some
solutions are being tried out, such as more options for childcare, more
spacious housing for families, part-time work for women who wish it.
All the programs adopted over the last twenty years are going in this
direction, such as the child-rearing allowance [APE], the allowance for
childcare at home [AGED], and the law on adjustment of working
time' (*Les femmes An 2000*, 1988: 210).
   A number of official reports also promoted part-time employment.
Experts well knew that more part-time employment would almost
automatically help to reduce the demand for non-parental care; mothers working part time are much more likely to provide their own childcare than those employed full time (Leprince, 1987: 513). Thus, the
report of the *Haut Conseil de la Population et de la Famille*, entitled *Working and Family Life: Creating New Balances* (*Vie professionnelle et vie familiale. Des nouveaux équilibres à construire*), is a veritable hymn to part-
time work. It recommends making part-time employment of all kinds
a more normal part of working life, ranging from half time to three-
quarter time as well as Wednesdays off. It would involve making the
working conditions of a reduced-hours job as similar as possible to
other forms of employment (1987: 36).[33] In a 1991 brief on family policy
the Economic and Social Council also promoted part-time work and
new arrangements for working time.

In a major initiative in employment policy in 1993 the Balladur government reiterated its commitment to atypical forms of work. Among the many measures found in the government's five-year plan for employment (*Loi quinquennale pour l'Emploi*) was provision of job vouchers (*chèque-emploi-service*). They could be used partially to offset the costs of hiring personal service providers, such as cleaning women, providers of home care for the elderly, and babysitters. This measure reduced even more the distinction between family policy and employment policy.

The 1994 Reform

The law of 25 July 1994 marked another step towards the development of atypical work among young women. The reform was overseen by Simone Veil, minister of state for social affairs, health and urban affairs, and was put into place less than a year after the right-wing parties had won legislative elections. The legislation significantly increased the reach of the child-rearing allowance (APE). For the first time, parents could claim it at the birth or adoption of a *second* child. They could also hold it in combination with a part-time job, and the amount paid was significantly increased. Accessibility to the subsidies for hiring a child-minder (AGED and AFEAMA) were extended, and the unpaid parental leave (CPE) was available on a part-time basis. Finally, public-sector employees were provided with new opportunities for part-time employment. All the reforms were described as contributing to choice and flexibility. Presenting her bill to the Commission of the National Assembly, Simone Veil said: 'In career terms, having a choice between working part time or using the subsidy for hiring a babysitter will permit women with positions of some responsibility more freely to manage their professional lives' (AN, no. 1239: 40).

At the same time the changes confirmed the government's strategy of encouraging women to take up atypical jobs. Targeted were both mothers' part-time employment and part-time jobs in the personal service sector. The allowance for childcare at home (AGED) is a good example. The goal was to encourage more parents to use it. Subsidies became available to hire a babysitter part time and to combine this option with a part-time child-rearing allowance. As Simone Veil assured the National Assembly: 'Both parts of the proposed childcare policy will contribute in a significant way to employment. We estimate this bill will foster the creation of 100,000 jobs. About 50,000 will come from freed-up [by parents on leave] places. The extension of the child-rearing allowance [to the second child] will induce some parents to reduce or suspend their labour force participation ... Another 50,000 will be jobs created either in individual homes or in public institutions, notably in day nurseries' (AN, no. 1239, Annexe: 2483).

A new model had been born, one that can be described as 'double dualism.' Some women would work part time and care for their own children part time. Other women would be employed to care for the children of women who were working full or part time. This new model elicited very few objections. Although they wrote voluminous reports, the commissions of the National Assembly and the Senate formulated only a few criticisms of the draft bill, and, on the whole, the two chambers were in agreement.

The 1994 child-rearing allowance, to a much greater extent than earlier subsidies, was directly linked to employment policy: in order to use the allowance parents must have worked for at least two of the five years preceding the birth or the adoption. Second, the allowance could be combined with a part-time job at any time, not only in the last year. This modification permitted parents to supply more of their own childcare while still remaining in the labour force, albeit in an atypical manner.[34] Yet, hoping simply to encourage women to leave the labour force or to have an atypical relationship to it, policy-makers paid little attention to the longer-term needs of women who opted for the child-rearing allowance. Few asked what would happen once they tried to get back into the labour force or to take up more typical, full-time employment.

Freedom of Choice versus Republican Equality?

In the last fifteen years there have been major changes in the range of childcare choices offered to parents. The direction of change has been towards more individualized services and practices as well as towards those for which the market, especially the labour market, are central. This policy shift results from France's adhesion, in the context of economic crisis as well as neo-liberal ideology, to a new societal paradigm, including a less egalitarian model of gender relations. Analysis of the discourse of the principal actors situated at the centre of the institutional system (the presidents, governments, and parliaments) allows us to retrace the slide towards consensus.

The Presidents of the Republic

All three presidents, those maestros of French politics and the embodiment of the Republic, made important pronouncements on the family and contributed to policy redesign. Tracking the ideas of Valéry Giscard d'Estaing, François Mitterrand, and Jacques Chirac provides an opportunity to observe changes in representations of gender and class equality. It also uncovers areas of agreement and disagreement about care for young children among heads of states who have different political sensibilities.

Valéry Giscard d'Estaing's declarations on matters related to the family and mother's employment reveal two main ideas. The first is clearly a discourse of 'reconciliation.' A 1976 speech given on the occasion of the thirtieth anniversary of the major organization of the family movement, the UNAF, listed the four objectives of family policy.[35] The third objective was 'to permit both parents better to reconcile working and family life.' The president refrained, however, from identifying state support for the development of day nurseries as crucial to achieving this goal. Rather, he focused on means of temporal adjustment, among which he saw 'the development of part-time work and flexible schedules, a chance for mothers to stop working for two years after the birth of a child, all the while having a guarantee of returning to their job and even to continuing their career. [These are] the directions in which [we must] make progress, in order to lighten the tensions that paid employment too often imposes on family life.' At this time the president clearly considered that responsibility for such reconciliation fell primarily upon the mother.

The second central term in Giscard d'Estaing's discourse was that of the 'choice.' In a press conference on 9 March 1977 he said: 'The position adopted leaves the choice to mothers. This choice must be as free as possible. Women [must be able to] to choose to devote themselves entirely to raising their children or to employment. [They must also be able to choose] whether during their lifetime they will alternate between times of child-rearing and times when, by contrast, they focus on their jobs. The two measures adopted this morning [the reference is to the draft bill on the 'mother's leave' and the family complement] affect this freedom for women, for mothers, to combine child-rearing and labour force participation as they wish.' In this statement, the president did not mention publicly provided childcare or day nurseries. He preferred to evoke less expensive services. When neo-liberal ideology was taking shape, the presidential discourse was not spared its effects. Individualized and private family-based solutions were being called on to supplement state services already falling prey to budgetary restrictions.

When François Mitterrand was elected, many hoped that the principle of republican equality, threatened by the right-wing approach of Giscard d'Estaing, would again be the touchstone of childcare policies. Once he was in office, his discourse and action required a nuanced assessment. Without a doubt, Mitterrand's rhetoric differed in many respects from that of Giscard. For example, he willingly accepted that gender roles had changed, volunteering that 'the image of the woman that is out of date is that of the woman at home, the housewife' (de Singly, 1993: 60). Nor did he ever openly call, as had Giscard d'Estaing, for recognition of the 'status of mother.' He also demonstrated full awareness that, with the high labour force participation rates of women, publicly provided services were needed if women were not to refrain from child-bearing altogether. Thus, he said in 1984, 'I have always thought it necessary that a woman wishing to have children be able to raise them without having to sacrifice her working life. This makes an ambitious family policy necessary.'[36]

Mitterrand's rhetoric, however, soon came to resemble that of Giscard. The Socialist was no less attentive than his predecessor to family policy in general and, in particular, to demographic matters (Jenson and Sineau, 1995: 239–67). Second, from the first year of his initial mandate, he identified reduced working time and temporary withdrawals from the labour force as steps towards the diversification of childcare. The theme of 'variety' – a *leitmotiv* of his family discourse – was already present in a 21 November 1981 speech to a UNAF Congress: 'It is by a variety of different means, chosen in collaboration with families, that care for children can be achieved ... Reduced working time is one major element, following from the modification of parental roles our society is experiencing.' Here, François Mitterrand echoes a speech given five years earlier and to the same audience by Giscard d'Estaing. We see Mitterrand making the same 'semantic slip' as Giscard d'Estaing made. Despite careful language ('respect for the rights of each – father, mother, child'), and always speaking of 'parents,' he seems implicitly to envision maternal care. He, like Giscard, in general terms evoked forms of reconciliation that would concern the two parents equally. But when both presidents got down to brass tacks, mothers were really the targets of programs. Moreover, he proposed the same actions as his predecessor. Diversification of childcare would occur by means of individualization and, in particular, by means of greater parental care through leaves and part-time involvement in the labour force.

More than once the president remarked that a 'cumulative' model (that is, both full-time employment and raising children) did not suit all women. Some women might prefer, if not a return to the post-war 'alternating' model (that is, employment or children), to be able to have a form of alternation. They might wish to withdraw from the labour force and have a three-year child-rearing allowance, in order to care for young children, then return to work when children entered school. Thus, in a 1994 interview Mitterrand said: 'In my view what is most important is women's right to choose what they want. It is necessary to do everything so they can do so. This is a major political battle. A mother may very well wish to care for her child (or children) at home when they are very young. She needs the time to do this, while keeping her job.'

On this occasion, François Mitterrand explicitly rejected the notion that family policy should be used to salvage employment policy. He said that using the child-rearing allowance 'as an anti-unemployment remedy would be an absolutely reactionary measure, in the true sense of the term.' Nonetheless, he accepted without any apology that family policy would support population policy and demographic goals. Thus, in October 1985, speaking to the *Haut Conseil de la Population et de la Famille*, over which the president presided, he underlined the negative consequences for fertility if parents encountered difficulties in reconciling work and family life: 'That women work is a significant step forward, [indeed] desirable progress, but its consequences have not always been examined directly ... It is true that the arrival of a third child, if necessary for society, seems very often to compel the mother to drop out of the labour force. There are a variety of ways of addressing this question. [Unfortunately] conflict between career and children is too often resolved on monetary grounds. We see such a solution as unjust.'

Thus, one can conclude that, for a variety of reasons, François Mitterrand, like his predecessor, came to accept that dualism is inevitable. Some mothers would pursue their working lives without interruption, whereas others would swell the ranks of contingent and part-time workers. Mitterrand's justification for this breach in women's right to full labour force participation is no different from that of Giscard. Free choice for mothers was the fundamental principle. The result was, for Mitterrand as for Giscard, that defence of individual liberty overshadowed any threats to republican equality that the new childcare programs might imply.

The presidency of Jacques Chirac continued much that was already evident in Mitterrand's discourse on the reconciliation of work and family life. The terms employed by our third president show that he, too, invoked 'free choice.' The proposals of President Chirac largely reflected the promises of Candidate Chirac. In 1993 he pledged to create an 'Allowance for Free Choice.'[37] Speaking to the *Haut Conseil de la Population et de la Famille* on 12 April 1996, the head of state devoted a long passage to the family and family policy, unveiling his understanding of the needs of young children and working mothers. Describing the high rates of women's labour force participation, he emphasized the difficulties of two-career couples: 'It is already difficult to reconcile work and family responsibilities with one or two young children. It becomes almost impossible with the birth of a third child. Yet the growth of women's employment reflects a profound longing of our times, and it must be encouraged and supported. Today 80 per cent of women age twenty-five to thirty are employed, and these 12 million women must be better able, just as men are, to reconcile family and professional life without penalizing their careers.'

How might a good family policy marry these opposites? 'Rethinking our relationship to time'[38] was the answer, an ambitious notion as it was formulated by Jacques Chirac. He had adopted several ambient ideas, such as altering the school year and school week or setting up a 'time savings account, ' an as yet poorly defined concept: 'We must learn how to master time better so as to use family and working time intelligently. This must be done in a variety of ways, each appropriate to different points in the life cycle, and so as to respond to family goals.' The president spoke of part-time work, flexi-time, changes to school hours, 'time-saving accounts,' parental leaves. He described them as major issues in negotiation among the social partners. He called on the French to take inspiration from experiments abroad, notably in Sweden. According to Chirac, that country provided an example worth imitating of how to respond to demographic decline. His discourse reveals the real stakes involved in childcare, whether defined in a national or local framework. As he went on to say: 'I find it symbolic that the first agreement concluded by the social partners of the [European] Community was one on parental leave. Defining a new relationship to time will permit us simultaneously to encourage natalism, create jobs, and promote the employment equality between men and women.' It is hardly surprising that Jacques Chirac advertized the pro-natalist goals of family policy, but his two other objectives might seem more surprising. In effect, he unabashedly accepted that family policy must support employment policy, whereas François Mitterrand had sought to disguise such a link.

Beyond the rhetorical differences due to the different personal styles of the three men, the similarity in presidential prescriptions for childcare for young children is striking: they are founded on the same principles – reducing the role of the state and enlarging the role for the labour market, especially for childminders; and they encourage mothers to provide childcare at home. These prescriptions are justified as providing freedom of choice, the key value of the citizenship regime.

Governments and Parliaments

The new model was also fashioned in these two institutions. If the French state still spends significant amounts of money on a wide variety of forms of childcare, it is because of the way these institutions have combined representations of work, women, and families. As documented in this chapter, elected officials as well as governments had many irons in the fire when they designed the unpaid parental leave, the child-rearing allowance, and the subsidies for hiring childminders. They never hesitated to deploy the pro-natalist discourse long traditional in France. Thanks to consensus on the right and the left about the need to encourage a higher birth rate, the state still makes generous public expenditures. The legitimacy of this financing is rarely, if ever, in dispute. A neo-liberalism implying that the French state ought to get out of the business of paying for childcare never had much purchase. The influence of neo-liberal ideology was sufficiently strong, however, that the new measures depended on market relations rather than being delivered as public services as well as requiring less public investment. Incentive programs for parents to hire babysitters or licensed mother's assistants were widely preferred over spending on the more costly and publicly provided services such as day nurseries.

The government also deployed a pro-natalist discourse as justification for weakening its commitment to the model of gender equality in employment. Representing mothers as having a vocation for child-rearing did not shock pro-natalists, who remained convinced of the advantages of 'mothering' and were faithful to the traditional view of the sexual division of labour.

Pro-natalist discourse did place some limits on the government, however, as it set out to make family policy subservient to employment policies. Legislators expressed suspicion that some programs were simply props for employment policy rather than a response to the goals of family and population policy. Nonetheless, as demonstrated by the reform of the unpaid parental leave of 1984 birth-rate strategies and employment policy could be combined to target mothers as part-time workers and to reduce obstacles to closely spaced pregnancies. Indeed, acceptance that childcare was actually a branch of employment policy gradually spread.

The idea of 'choice' was then the crucial linking concept, as the combinations of full-time and part-time employment and child-rearing options expanded. On the one hand, several ministers and deputies extolled the appeal of parental care in comparison with low-paid and tedious jobs for low-income women. Mothers gradually became a sort of 'reserve army' of part-time labour. All parental leaves and allowances for childcare now can be combined with part-time employment. The combination of a pro-natalist discourse and the 'targeted' discourse of employment policies permitted the projection of an image of the mother at home who works only when she has time free from childcare. Family life takes precedence over employment. Women, however, were less enthusiastic about the programs, especially the child-rearing allowances.[39] They were also aware of the problems of being reintegrated into the labour market after an absence.[40]

On the other hand, policymakers projected another representation of working mothers. Some women were devoted to their careers or high salaries who could not envisage leaving their job. Rather than alternating between work and family, these women cumulated roles. Their way of reconciling family and working lives was to purchase – highly subsidized – childcare services. Here again, the concept of choice was crucial. They were represented as exercizing 'consumer sovereignty, ' often needing to avoid the rigid schedules of day nurseries or demanding licensing provisions. The discourse of choice left it up to families to determine how much money they wanted to invest in childcare and the quality of care they preferred to purchase from among the several options on offer.

In this vision, other working women were also present. They were the childminders who had to be induced to quit the black market and declare their – generally part-time – incomes. Regularizing the labour force status of childminders was part of the struggle against unemployment, one of the 'job mines' evoked by Martine Aubry when she was labour minister. These programs could be positive, but nonetheless, they still had the drawback of accentuating the gender division of labour and the dualism of the labour market.[41] These are classic personal service jobs, lacking recognized skills, poorly paid, often part time, and with few career prospects.[42] In this context the objective of gender and class equality tends – in the name of the freedom of choice for families – to be sacrificed on the altar of the struggle against unemployment and the development of civil society (Ullman, 1998).

A logic of inequality underpins a hierarchy in childcare services and the groups of women to which they are addressed. At the upper end of the social scale there are programs that transform working mothers into employers, in the words of André Gorz, a kind of 'new domestic labour' (*néo-domesticité*) (1988: 212; see also Fraisse, 2000). At the other end of the social scale are low-income mothers for whom a small child-rearing allowance is sufficient inducement for them to leave a paid job and provide their own childcare. The societal paradigm of neo-liberalism, in other words, sustains socio-economic as well as gender inequalities.[43] Childcare programs that actively promote parental 'liberty of choice' may be undermining another republican principle, that of equality. Ultimately, then, it can provide no more than limited freedom, constrained by class barriers and by power relations between the sexes.

NOTES

1 This shift was never simply a response to rising rates of women's labour force participation. It also reflected employers' desire for more flexibility in hiring and firing and in organizing the labour process.

2 The Seventh Plan (1976–80) announced the need for this reform. Giscard d'Estaing also subscribed to the change. See, for example, his speech to the 30th Anniversary Congress of the family movement (UNAF), 12 June 1976, and the press conference held at the conclusion of the Council of Ministers, Elysée Palace, 9 March 1977. The law creating the *Complément familial* is dated 12 July 1977.

3 Another goal of this law was to reduce under-the-table working by unli-

censed babysitters. In 1977 approximately one-quarter of them were not licensed (*Cahiers Femmes d'Europe*, 1990: 27).

4 This Directive (2 March 1981) established 'les orientations générales 1981–85 de l'Action Sociale et Familiale des Caisses d'Allocations Familiales.'

5 Fifteen years earlier, regulations limited *haltes-garderies* to caring 'for a short time and occasionally' for children under six years of age whose mothers did not have a job. In 1979, 93 per cent of drop-in centres closed at the lunch hour, and children whose mother worked part time were rarely accepted.

6 Address to the *Colloque national sur la démographie française*.

7 The president used this term during his 12 June 1976 speech, then again at a press conference on 9 March 1977. During the latter he said: 'What does this status mean? It means that a mother, simply by virtue of raising her children, would gain some protections or rights.'

8 This was the AVMF (*Assurance-vieillesse des mères de famille*).

9 Speech of 25 June 1980.

10 The rate at which the benefit was paid was high enough to make it competitive with a minimum-wage job.

11 References to the *Journal Officiel* are made as follows. Documents of the National Assembly are labelled AN, followed by the number of the document for the year being discussed. Similarly, Senate documents are indicated by S.

12 For example, accusation of discrimination against poor families and women was the central theme of Gisèle Moreau (Communist) when she spoke in the debate (AN, debates, 16 June 1977: 3860).

13 Maurice Andrieu (Socialist/MRG) accused the minister, Christian Beullac, of acting 'as if man's fundamental role is to work in a factory or office, but part of woman's life could take place elsewhere' (AN, debates, 19 June 1977: 3859).

14 This report was submitted to the secretary of state for the family in 1982 and entitled *L'enfant dans la vie. Une politique de la petite enfance*. The quote is from p. 76.

15 On the conceptual fluidity of this notion see Junter-Loiseau and Tobler (1995).

16 Funds were distributed via *contrats-crèches*, organized by the CNAF and available between 1983 and 1989.

17 Interview with Kathleen Evin, *Hommes et Libertés*, 3, 1984.

18 This measure applied to firms with more than 100 employees. In smaller firms, the employer could reject the request for reduced hours, based on the needs of the firm. The law is dated 3 January 1991.

19 See the article by Gérard Calot, director of the National Institute of Demography (INED), *Le Monde*, 19 December 1984.

20 Georgina Dufoix always claimed that the child-rearing allowance was gender neutral. She fell into a trap, however, when speaking hypothetically about a parent deciding to take a leave: '"For two years, I will devote myself to my young child rather than to my work, and then I will go back to my job." Because, basically, what do women think? What am I saying – women? Here, I am catching myself in your snare!' (AN, debates, 4 December 1984: 6651–2).

21 The Senate never wanted access to the child-rearing allowance to be conditional on having participated in the labour force. Again, describing the legislation as discriminatory, the Senate Commission proposed to widen the definition of 'employment' to include volunteer work (S, no. 90: 51). Invited to testify, the UNAF claimed, for its part, that raising children should be sufficient in itself to give parents access to the allowance (S, no. 90: 70).

22 Socialist deputies, now in the opposition, fell upon this criticism. Ghislaine Toutain (Socialist) also accused the government of threatening women's right to work (AN, no. 438: 62). Throughout these debates, Michèle Barzach was forced to repeat several times that the allowance was not a 'salary for mothering' (see, for example, AN no. 438: 33–4 or 50).

23 The National Assembly used a CNAF text to ground its argument about a 'replacement salary' (AN, no. 438: 12).

24 During the debate few allusions were made to the tax credits that actually constitute one of the most important forms of public financial support. Over time the state tax expenditures via credits for expenses for care for children under seven rose dramatically. These credits increased from 6 million FF in 1981 to 720 million FF in 1989 (CES, 1991: 82).

25 Childcare at home, despite tax credits and relief from making employer's contributions to social security, is an expensive type of care (AN, no. 438: 38). It is used, therefore, by high-income parents.

26 Despite careful use of gender-neutral language, it was obvious that the minister and her colleagues understood that the new measure addressed the needs of mothers more than those of fathers (see, for example, S, no. 90: 68).

27 The quote is from the Senate Commission (S, no. 90: 33, 35), but the National Assembly also strongly favoured reduced public spending (AN, no. 438: 38, 48, 59, 69).

28 Each commission paid obeisance to Prime Minister Jacques Chirac's notion that family policy could be improved only when state spending was under control.

29 At the time, the government anticipated creating 100,000 jobs, which was a

very generous estimate. According to the *Cour des comptes*, the number of jobs created or declared was only about 20,000 in 1994, of which a mere 10,000 were full time (Fagnani and Rassi, 1997: 86).

30 Owing to the limited number of places in day nurseries, priority is generally accorded to parents who work full time.

31 The law of 31 December 1991 supplemented the benefit (Steck, 1993: 48–9), while the 1994 Family Law increased the amount paid.

32 Speech of 8 March 1982 during the first celebration of International Women's Day.

33 Wednesday-off is relevant in France because, although school days are long, thereby alleviating problems of after-school care, there is no school on Wednesday. In an earlier report, entitled *Demographie et politique familiale en Europe*, the *Haut Conseil* had already addressed the need for improvement: 'extension of a variety of leaves (parental leaves, remunerated leaves for caring for a sick child), part-time and temporary employment, individualized working hours, and improvement in the school day, week, and year move in this direction' (1989: 63).

34 Low-income mothers may not have access to the child-rearing allowance because they had not worked enough before the birth of the second child (Fagnani, 1996a: 115).

35 The first objective was to 'adapt family benefits better to the real needs of families, ' the second 'to create the "status of mother,"' and the fourth to 'adapt housing policy better to family needs.'

36 Interview in *Hommes et Libertés*, 3, 1984.

37 See *Le Monde*, 2 December 1993. When Jacques Chirac became president, this allowance was announced (24 May 1995) as part of the prime minister's general policy declaration. Nonetheless, for budgetary reasons it was never implemented.

38 The president again used this expression in a speech on 3 June 1996, while presenting the Medal of the French Family at the Elysée Palace: 'In the last quarter century, family situations profoundly changed. More and more mothers are employed, or hope to be. This is legitimate, and we must help them to do so. In order to do so, we need to reconcile employment and family responsibilities better. Therefore, we need to rethink our relationships to time.'

39 Until the early1990s a very limited number of parents used the child-rearing allowance. It was in fourth place among all family benefits, absorbing 5 per cent of spending (CES, 1991: 50). Once available at the birth or adoption of a second child, after 1994 the number of beneficiaries climbed (Afsa, 1996: 1–8).

40 One of the difficulties faced by recipients of the child-rearing allowance is finding a job at the end of the leave (Fagnani, 1996b).

41 Mother's assistant is a highly feminized job, being a kind of 'professionalized mothering' (Kniebiehler, 1997: 311. See also Bosse-Platière, 1999).

42 In 1992 there were 342, 000 childminders (*assistantes maternelles*), all of them women and 47 per cent working part time (*INSEE-Première*, December 1992). Of the 120,000 jobs for childminders created between 1982 and 1992, more than 60 per cent were part time.

43 These varied motives and differing effects help to account for the high level of controversy the programs have evoked. See, for example, Fagnani (1998), Math and Renaudat (1997), and *Conseil d'analyse économique* (1999).

Chapter Five

Italy: Policy without Participation

Franca Bimbi and Vincent Della Sala

Italy's post-war citizenship regimes contained a number of paradoxes with respect to the care of children and the representation of women in work. The role and nature of the family were a source of tension in the drafting of the constitution, yet the political elite avoided confrontation on family policy throughout the post-war period. Italy has developed an extensive welfare state and forms of social assistance; yet many of the groups that are central to family policy – such as the elderly and youth – remain largely outside the sphere of state intervention. Although Italy has a centralized unitary state, there are great regional disparities in the delivery of key programs such as childcare. Beginning in the late 1960s, Italy set out a series of seemingly progressive policies that directly affected women in work and the care of children, without demands for either of these policy areas to occupy a prominent place on the political agenda. Moreover, when the bases of those policies began to be transformed as a result of fiscal pressures in the 1990s, there was little space available for the representation of resistance to decentralization, cuts in funding, and individualization of childcare policies.

In this chapter we argue that Italy's consensual politics left little room for an open political debate about social citizenship as it relates to the family, the representation of women in work, and the care of children. The dominant model was a familial one, which represented the care of children as a matter for the family and the care of the family as the responsibility of women. It went largely unchallenged in the political discourse of the major political parties until the 1990s. Nonetheless, there were undercurrents of social and economic change in the 1960s and 1970s that did produce policy changes such as the introduction of publicly funded day nurseries and maternity leave. However, these policies neither reflected nor led to equality rights in the representation of women's work or responsibility for the care of children. They were marginal adjustments that slowly eroded the familial model but never supplanted its dominant position in shaping policy.

Italy seems like an odd case when compared with the other countries examined in this volume. It has few children under the age of three in the public childcare system, while over 90 per cent of children between the ages of three and six attend public pre-primary schools. Progressive maternity leave policies were implemented as early as the 1950s, but unlike the situations in the other countries, at the time there was no widespread debate about the care of children and the representation of women's work.

The puzzle presented by Italy is why policy changes took place without any major challenges to the familial model. The answer is that introducing new representations of women and the care of children would threaten to unravel a series of political and institutional compromises that were seen as essential for the consolidation of liberal democratic structures. In order to understand the Italian case, we also have to look at a number of policy areas, such as the pre-school and family allowances, that might not seem directly relevant to the broader questions of the representation of working women and children in the citizenship regime. They are essential, however, to an understanding of a policy process that allowed only gradual and marginal changes that could not be seen as a threat to the dominant model and the political and institutional impasse upon which it rested.

The chapter is divided into four major sections. In the first section we provide a brief historical background, emphasizing the constitutional foundations of the post-war citizenship regime. In the second section we examine the gradual process through which a number of policies were introduced in the 1960s but in which there was little change in the basic principles and nature of representation. The primary focus will be on pre-schools in order to illustrate that they provided an important step in establishing the principle that the care of children was not a monopoly of families. In the third section we examine the opportunities for change in the 1970s and some of the policy changes thus introduced. In the final section we look at the changes in the 1990s, which reveal that the debate about the family and the care of children that was avoided for fifty years has finally begun. This debate, however, is taking place within a context where primacy is given to monetary considerations and controlling public finances. We concentrate on two major policy areas, maternity and parental leaves and preschools, and also briefly discuss family allowances.

The Long Arm of the Post-War Constitutional Compromise

Representation of the role of women and the family, while not occupying a prominent role, was central to the debates in the Constituent Assembly (CA) in 1946–7 that helped to fashion the post-war citizenship regime. The Assembly that drafted the constitution left little room, however, for the articulation of notions that did not arise from the ideological and partisan claims of either the Roman Catholic or the Communist political forces.

At the political-institutional level, the ideological conflict centred on differing concepts of women and the family. On the one hand, Catholic ideology considered the state-family relationship in the light of the principle of subsidiarity and defined the family as a social unit based on natural law; on the other hand, it found in Catholic doctrine the foundation for the legal, moral, and social regulation of the family. Within this vision the representation of women in labour markets is subservient to women as mothers, as spouses, and as persons responsible for domestic chores. The Italian Communist party (PCI) position was no less ambivalent. On the one hand, the PCI supported equality rights for women, especially economic rights such as equal pay and job security. The representation of women as workers centred primarily on women in industry. On the other hand, Communists rarely challenged the basic premises of the familial model. They did not try to place on the political agenda a different representation of women and the care of children for fear of upsetting the broader political objectives of consolidating Italian democracy and gaining legitimacy as a party, committed to the Republic's basic principles.

The drafting of the constitutional text to be considered by the Constituent Assembly was assigned to the Committee of 75, which, in turn, was divided into subcommittees to consider constitutional principles and the institutional architecture to govern them. It was in the subcommittees that the chasm between the parties became most apparent, but also where accommodation was sought and found. In the case of constitutional principles on the family, the first subcommittee met on 30 October 1946 to consider draft articles prepared by the Christian Democrat Giovanni Corsanego and the Communist Nilde Iotti. They presented to the subcommittee a relatively innocuous proposal that would have inscribed in the constitution the statement that 'The Republic ensures the necessary economic conditions for the defence and development of the family' (Assemblea Costituente, 30 October 1946: 330). Corsanego quickly revealed that there was a tension between Christian Democratic (DC) positions and those of the PCI, represented by Iotti. He said that he regretted that they could not present a clause that would also designate a head of family; Iotti did not agree that this should naturally be the father. For his part, Corsanego did not want to include Iotti's demand to grant full rights to illegitimate children. Therefore, the innocuous statement was a compromise.

The largest gulf, however, was over the definition of the nature of the family. Iotti described the Communist position, and that of most of the secular forces, with the following article: 'The State protects and defends the family, which is fundamental for the material and moral prosperity of citizens and the Nation' (Assemblea Costituente, 30 October 1946: 332). The DC members wanted to go further and enshrine in the constitution the idea that the family was a 'natural' unit with 'natural' rights. Giuseppe Dossetti argued that the constitution's description of the family should also state that it was based on the indissolubility of marriage, thus raising within the constitution the question of divorce. Dossetti, one of the leading figures of the DC, told the subcommittee that the rights of the family as they were perceived by Christian Democrats, were just as important as individual rights were for the secular members of the CA (Assemblea Costituente, 30 October 1946: 334–6). Therefore, there was little room for the DC to compromise on its position on the family, and he expected concessions from the opposition, just as Christian Democrats were ready to concede and accept principles based on citizens' individual rights and duties in other parts of the constitution. The DC, it seemed, was ready to jeopardize agreement on a constitutional settlement if its views on the family were not accommodated.

The subcommittee, upon reaching an impasse on defining the family and its links to the indissolubility of marriage, decided to adjourn and asked that Aldo Moro (DC) and the leader of the PCI, Palmiro Togliatti, join Iotti and Corsanego in finding a new wording for the draft text. The fact that the top leaders were asked to deal with the issue was an indication that there was a genuine fear that progress on the entire constitutional project would be hindered by failure to find some accommodation. When the committee reconvened, it became immediately clear that, although Moro and Togliatti seemed to be in agreement, some members of the DC were not ready to accept the new text (Assemblea Costituente, 6 November 1946: 343–53). The revised articles included provisions that would charge the state with the 'moral and material well-being in motherhood, infancy and youth,' as well as entrenching equality of spouses within marriage. On the question of divorce, however, the DC remained intransigent. The left and secular parties were satisfied with keeping divorce, which was prohibited, untouched in the Civil Code and did not want to risk mobilizing popular resistance to the entire package if divorce were made a constitutional matter. The DC, on the other hand, seemed willing to use divorce as a bargaining tool to gain concessions on the definition of the family as a 'natural' unit.

In the end, as it was in so many other parts of the constitutional debate, accommodation was reached. It reflected a consensus on a set of broad principles but avoided the deeply divisive issues. The secular parties accepted article 29 of the constitution, which stated that the family was a 'natural' unit, based on marriage. The DC accepted the principle of granting equal rights to children born outside marriage.

The constitutional settlement and, perhaps more important, the process of accommodation by which it was reached helped to establish the basis for consensual democracy in Italy (Fabbrini, 1994). The onset of the Cold War on both domestic and international fronts ensured that the mutual suspicion of the major parties would make it difficult for the liberal democratic institutions and procedures to function smoothly. Fragmentation of representation was guaranteed, as the many cleavages in Italian society found political expression in Parliament, in large part owing to an extremely generous system of proportional representation. The parties of the centre and the right quickly established that the Communist party and its Socialist allies were not to be trusted as coalition allies, and they banished the PCI to seemingly permanent opposition.

This accommodation process had long-term consequences. It did not mean that all policy demands had to be filtered through the DC or one of its governing allies; nor did it mean that the policy agenda was dictated and imposed by the governing parties. Rather, most policy decisions were the result of an interaction among all social and political forces with no party or faction imposing its will on another.

This decision-making process had consequences for family law. For instance, the deliberation and approval in the Chamber of Deputies on a series of measures on maternity leave that became law in 1950–51 (Law no. 860, no. 986–7: 1950; Law no. 394, no. 1904: 1951) reveals the ideological polarization that existed between the major parties, yet it also demonstrates that this was not an obstacle to widespread agreement on legislation that would allow working mothers as well as those that worked at home to benefit from state assistance. The legislation, proposed by left-wing women in textile unions in 1948, produced one of the most generous maternity leave policies in Europe. It instituted a mandatory five-month leave (three months before and two months after birth) to be paid at 80 per cent of salary. The remaining 20 per cent could be paid by employers, according to provisions of collective agreements.

The Christian Democrats who spoke to the legislation emphasized the role of women as 'mothers' and how the legislation would have a negative effect on this supposedly natural role. Antonio Repossi called on the Chamber to imagine a day when the head of the household would earn enough that the mother would not be 'forced' to leave the household to work and thus abandon her familial 'duties' (Camera dei Deputati, I Legislatura, 1950: 20082). Such a policy, he claimed, would ensure the large families that were necessary for the 'moral health' of the country.

Within the Catholic world, however, there was support for maternity leave, which stemmed from representations made by its trade unionists and women, along with the ACLI (*Associazioni Cristiane dei Lavoratori Italiani* – Christian Workers Societies). They worked to develop support for notions of social justice that tried to strike a balance among help for the disadvantaged, maintaining the basic principles of familialism, and protecting the rights of workers. The provisions of the maternity leave legislation allowed them to rally support from different parts of the DC, whose basic anti-Communist base was suspicious of any intrusions into the private sphere of the family, for all three parts of this delicate balance (Miccoli, 1976; Pace, 1982).

The Communist position centred primarily on protecting the rights of working women rather than on addressing the role of women in the care of children and within the family. For instance, Noce Longo, speaking on behalf of the PCI, emphasized the extent to which the bill would help women working in industry – it would provide three months' leave prior to childbirth for women working in industry, six to eight weeks for the rest – and raised concerns that the bill might not provide enough for women working in other sectors (Camera dei Deputati, I Legislatura, 1950: 20085). This opinion reflected the tendency among Communist women to concentrate on achieving equality rights in the workplace and the trade union support for policies guaranteeing income parity and reducing night shift work for women (Caravaggi et al., 1976). Thus, marginal gains could be made in these areas without risking an open conflict with the DC on the nature of the family. For some Communist (and some DC) women, these marginal adjustments represented the thin edge of the wedge that would eventually lead to broader social rights of citizenship.

However, the Communists did not focus exclusively on the protection of working women. For instance, the women's association closely linked to the PCI, the UDI (*Unione Donne Italiane* – Association of Italian Women) represented a 'maternal' wing of the party. While maternity leave provisions were being introduced in the early 1950s to help working women, the UDI was calling for pensions for women who stayed at home and an increase in social services for children. Its concern with helping with the care of children was limited to a view of women's employment as emerging from need, not choice, and was concentrated primarily on industry (Rodano, 1976).

The short debate on maternity leave – it was discussed in the Chamber during two brief afternoon sessions – exhibited many of the features that shaped decision-making in Italy's consensual democracy. First, even in the early 1950s the DC was not a monolithic bloc; thus, the way for bargaining between left-wing Catholics and opposition parties was open. There were those who opposed any state intervention in areas regarded as a purely 'private' sphere, but there were equally strong voices in the DC who hoped for a broad program that would put in place extensive social programs and a welfare state. Second, even those in favour of state intervention within the DC were divided on their motives. The interventionists included left-wing factions whose ideological roots were in Christian socialism and were inherently suspicious of market forces (see Titomanlio in Camera dei Deputati, I Legislatura, 1950: 20078–9). However, within the DC there has always been a group that looked to using state resources as a means of mobilizing support from middle-class voters. The motives here were less ideological or programmatic than they were electoral; the party's lack of organizational base to match its main political rivals was compensated for by its control of state resources, which could be used to attract support from key groups.

Those within the DC opposed to the maternity leave legislation also reflected such divisions in the party. There was one group who, like those who hoped for more social programs, saw maternity leave as the thin edge of the wedge. Others emphasized market principles and were suspicious of any attempts to extend state protection for workers. It is interesting to note that they saw this bill as extending protection to 'workers,' which they claimed would have a negative impact on women in the labour force because employers would see them as carrying added costs (see Sabatini's comments in Camera dei Deputati, I Legislatura, 1950: 20086–7). The other group within DC that was opposed to the bill saw state intervention as an intrusion into the private sphere that was best left to associations – almost entirely Catholic organizations. They were suspicious that the extension of the state sphere would be at the expense of Catholic influence.

An additional feature of the debate on maternity leave was the emphasis that the PCI placed on mothers as 'workers' and its defence of industrial working-class interests. The party, apparently relegated to permanent opposition, used what little influence it had at its disposal to provide some returns for its political and social base. To accumulate such resources the PCI always was careful not to antagonize Catholic sentiments or threaten Catholic interests. Maternity leave was not presented by the Communists as something to challenge the traditional role of the family and of women within it; nor was it seen as part of a broader program in which the state would play a larger role within the 'private' sphere. Rather, the PCI sought common ground with the other parties in Parliament for a bill for which it could claim credit, at least partly.

On the surface, it seemed that the extreme ideological polarization of the Cold War left little room for dialogue between the ostracized PCI and the governing majority. As the case of maternity leave indicates, however, the fragmented nature of the DC meant that those forces looking to extend state intervention in areas of social and family policies could find willing allies in the left wing of the party. The PCI did not seek a confrontation on the nature of the family or on the role of the state in securing social and economic conditions to support families. Consequently, it was possible for policy changes to be approved, but they could not be introduced as responding to new forms of representation of women in work, the care of children, or the very nature of the family. Changes in the balance of power between and within the major parties allowed a small space for new policies. The result was only marginal, incremental policy changes based on compromises that satisfied a wide variety of goals. These changes did not challenge the familializm that placed the care of children and the representation of women in work within the private realm of the family.

Signs of Movement in the 1960s

Despite attempts to interpret article 29 of the constitution as preventing the state from intervening in the 'private' and Catholic sphere of the supposedly natural family unit, changes began to occur by the 1960s and accelerated in the 1970s. There was a subtle change as the representations shifted within the citizenship regime. Three different ways of representing women emerged: as workers; as members of a collective movement, such as the women's movement, bearing rights; or as individuals. As we will see shortly, however, space for the articulation of these representations remained limited and marginal to the central decision-making sites in Parliament and between the major parties.

Debate of the law (no. 444, 1968) creating pre-primary public schools (for children from three to six years old), was an important turning point in establishing the principle that the state had a role to play in the lives of children. The proposal was to make the pre-primary schools part of the public education system, under the control of the central Ministry of Education. The central government would fund the teachers and provide subsidies for the schools, which would be run primarily by local authorities, or in some cases by private organizations. Regional and local authorities would also contribute to the funding of state-run pre-schools.

This proposal marked an attempt to limit the Catholic influence over schools and the care of children in early childhood. It challenged some of the basic principles of the citizenship regime, particularly the monopoly of familialism. Although it brought only marginal adjustments that did not alter the foundations of the regime, it did open the way for other, later changes.

The debate in 1968 was only marginally concerned with the presence of women in labour markets; it centred more on the relative balance between the public and private spheres (in this case, it meant the balance between the Catholic Church and the state; see Pedrazzi, 1966). The traditional secular centrist parties, the Liberals and Republicans, as well as the Socialists, saw the law as part of the long struggle to separate Church and State. Progressive elements to the left of the DC, governing with the PSI at the time, saw the pre-school as part of a broader strategy of social and economic modernization. The PCI was the least interested and least involved in the debate, concentrating primarily on establishing the principle of women's right to work outside the home.

Two issues emerged in the parliamentary debate: the role of the state in the training of schoolteachers; and whether pre-primary schools were to be obligatory. Both issues had a direct bearing on women's employment. For instance, religious orders controlled the *Magistrali*, the institutes that trained the predominantly female teachers for the pre-schools. The 1968 law referred specifically to teachers (*insegnante*) and directors (*direttrice*) of the pre-primary schools in the feminine form, a clear indication of the feminization of the teaching staff and administration of the pre-schools. The fact that the schools would not be obligatory reflected, perhaps, a compromise. On the one hand, there were those who believed that the function of the pre-schools was to complement the family, not substitute for it. On the other hand, there were those who looked to them as an opportunity marginally to lighten the focus on family responsibilities (mostly women on the left, but also some DC women). They hoped that making no charge for the pre-schools would help to establish a social service and begin to shift the care of children into the public realm.

The number of children who were in some form of pre-primary schools at the time of the debate on Law no. 444 in 1968 was not insignificant. According to the Education Commission of the Chamber of Deputies, 48.5 per cent of children between the ages of 3 and 5 already attended such schools in 1962–63; the figure had reached 50.8 per cent by 1968–69 (Pinnelli, 1983). However, the overwhelming majority were in private schools: only 4.8 per cent of children in this age category were in an institution funded and controlled by the central government. Fully 70 per cent were in private schools, while the rest attended schools run by local authorities or some other public body (Pedrazzi, 1966: 191). It also was clear that the 'private' schools were largely under the control or influence of religious orders; thus, any overt attempt to set up a rival 'public' system could face serious challenges from Catholic forces.

Passage of a law designed to make the pre-schools part of the public education system took place in the absence of two factors: any debate over declining birth rates and any significant rise in the percentage of women in the work force. Between 1946–50 and 1966–70 the birth rate dropped from 21.5 to 17.4. The magnitude of the change may have been masked by the slight rise in the fertility rate. In addition to the baby boom, large internal migration and significant differences in demographics across regions helped to give the impression that Italian families remained prolific (Livi Bacci, 1980). Thus, there was hardly any mention of a 'crisis' of the family based on its size; there was, instead, some concern of the effects of individualism and consumerism on conventional family structures. There was simply no vision of the pre-schools as an integral part of a childcare system that would make raising larger families more appealing.

Throughout the 1960s women's labour market activity rates declined. In 1959 women constituted 31.2 per cent of the labour force; the figure had dropped to 27.1 per cent by 1966 (OECD, 1968). Perhaps this decrease was due to the displacement of women workers from agriculture without a corresponding increase in their employment in industry. In addition, women who were employed in industry tended to be found in weaker sectors such as textiles, while the range of benefits available to predominantly male workers in strong industrial sectors allowed them to be the 'breadwinners' and keep their wives at home.

Therefore, publicly provided pre-schools were instituted in the absence of any increase in demand due to employed mothers. The introduction of the pre-schools for children between 3 and 6 as part of the public education system did not materialize as part of a broader debate about how to deal with changes to families resulting from women's entering the workplace, or as a means of encouraging larger families. There was no challenge to the Catholic representation of the role of women within the family. There was little change in the Catholic view of the family as a natural unit with rights beyond the limits of state intervention. There was little recognition that the social economic and social changes in Italy in the post-war period were beginning to have an impact even on those women who were not entering the labour markets, as the general drop in birth rates indicated.

Those same economic and social changes, however, began to break down the autonomous nature of the family and generated a diffuse range of demands from young people and women. There were social transformations under way that began a process of the gradual secularization of the family that would have a direct bearing on the representation of women in work. For instance, the position of many on the left, for whom the rights of women were emerging from the rights of workers and social citizenship as rooted in economic citizenship, also began to face challenges from new collective demands from student and women's movements (Calabro, Grasso, 1985). As a result, the strategy of achieving political gains for women, primarily through the defence of single women in the workforce, was beginning to reveal its limitations. Despite these undercurrents in favour of change, they were not strong enough to bring about a broad public debate on the fundamental questions arising from the economic and social citizenship rights of women and from the balance between public and private in the care of children.

The establishment of public pre-schools, then, was presented primarily as an educational reform designed to train future generations and help to modernize the system of public education. The reform, however, was also a social policy. Children living in poverty were guaranteed meals and health care in the pre-primary schools. The educational and social policy objectives of the reforms help to explain why policies aimed at providing care for children took place despite the lack of demand generated by an increase in the number of working women. They could be presented as responding to social policy needs, not to those of women who chose employment.

The Missed Revolution? The 1970s

During the 1970s the representations of the demands of women as workers, as individuals, and as a collective movement flowered. The period, as we will see below, produced grand declarations and objectives but only marginal policy achievements.

A number of constraints upon women's entry into the work force were removed. For instance, the improved access to university education introduced in 1969 helped to break down the traditional and limited educational careers for women (Franchi, Mapelli, and Lipando, 1987). There continued to be resistance, however, from a wide range of forces, which included parts of the trade union movement and some Communist women, to the introduction of conventional policies that facilitated the reconciliation of work and family life for women. This was particularly the case with respect to a legislative vacuum in the area of part-time work.

There were two important legislative developments in 1971: the law (no. 1044) that established a childcare system financed by the central government and the reform of maternity leave provisions (no. 1204). Neither, however, was the result of broad programmatic or policy responses to the changing needs of women. The first proposed a five-year plan to increase the number of day nurseries from less than 1,000 to 3,800, and to shift them from being almost entirely in the private sector to being state run and financed. The law committed the central government to provide 0.1 per cent of employer contributions to the Institute for Social Security fund to regional governments for the day nurseries (Network on Childcare, 1995: 23). This central government grant constituted only a small percentage of spending by a day nursery. The bulk of funding would be provided by regional and local authorities, whose primary source of revenue was central government grants.

The law that introduced changes to maternity leave (no. 1204) proposed to extend job security to maternity leave by prohibiting the dismissal of working women during the period from the beginning of pregnancy to the first birthday of the child. It also allowed women to choose a further optional six months of paid leave at 30 per cent of salary.

The genesis of both projects could be traced back to 1963, when proposals similar to the ones that became law eight years later were approved by the Senate but died on the order paper in the Chamber of Deputies. Arguments were made that public funding of day nurseries was necessary in order to establish them as a social service and to begin to erode the monopoly of the private sphere in the care of children. At the same time, the unions – both the Socialist-Communist and the largely Catholic confederations – presented proposals to reform maternity leave provisions. They sought job security, an additional six-month optional leave, and to have women in public sector jobs receive the employer's portion, that is, the remaining 20 per cent of salary. The proposals were to languish for the rest of the 1960s, as the political climate changed after the 1963 elections. The new centre-left coalitions were not ready to risk a delicate political balance between the left wing of the DC and the Socialists.

The social and political unrest of the late 1960s helped to generate support for reconsideration of the proposals in 1971. Their approval after the eight-year break reflected three important political factors: the connection between the creation of the day nurseries and the extension of maternity leave; the conflict between those parts of the DC that sought to protect traditional conceptions of motherhood and the growing claims for the representation of work as an expression of women's identity (by the left, trade unions, and parts of the women's movement in the DC); and the debate over the devolution of powers to regional and local governments. The last point proved to be an important political and institutional factor that would shape policy responses. For instance, the Episcopal Conference was particularly critical of the transfer of social and health services to the regional level. The Church, although recognizing that regional planning could guarantee that families would retain their 'pre-eminent role' in the education of children, feared that the Catholic associations and organizations that provided social assistance would lose their central position at the national level (Inchiesta, 1972: 60).

The DC's support for the two laws in 1971 was not motivated primarily by a concern with the demands of women entering the labour force; rather, there were political factors at play that shaped the DC response. Approval of the proposal to extend maternity leave to as much as a year was designed to temper criticism from the Catholic public that the conventional representation of the maternal role was undermined by the extension of day nurseries. In addition, the Christian Democrats were reluctant to support a decentralization of social services to the regional level, since this might strengthen the hand of the left in those areas largely controlled by the Socialist and Communist parties. As we will see below, the legislation on day nurseries provided little coordination, no common standards, and poor financial coverage. Thus, the DC in the early 1970s was able to be seen as trying to help establish a modern system of social services without offending its Catholic base and without providing 'red' left-wing administrations at the regional and local levels with sufficient policy-making powers. Policies that produced marginal adjustments were accepted so long as they did not challenge the foundations of the citizenship regime. Even policies that might have represented a major shift – such as that on funding day nurseries and extending maternity leave – were limited and constrained so that they would not undermine the existing regime.

The left provided a much broader range of reasons for supporting the establishment of the day nurseries. It was recognized that real needs existed, generated by the increase of work by women in activities outside the home. In addition, the left argued that the day nurseries could serve to more effectively protect the health needs of early childhood, and they could serve as a defence of the family against 'fragmenting pressures.' In these issues women were not placed at the centre of the project; the health care needs of children and families were. The left, while trying to exploit the space afforded by the gradual secularization of the family, was reluctant to represent the creation of an extensive childcare system as part of a process of responding to the growing needs of women in the workforce.

Surprisingly, the representation of the needs of women in the labour force were articulated forcefully by some Christian Democrats. For instance, Tina Anselmi, the *rapporteur* for the law on maternity leave, introduced to the Senate in 1971 the notion that women seek employment as a means to self-realization and self-expression as well as a way of achieving greater freedom (Senato, 1971: 493). She reflected the position of a part of the DC that held that paid work is one of women's basic civil rights. However, even this stance was balanced by the innovation in the law introduced by the Catholic association, ACLI, that allowed a combination of an optional – paying 30 per cent of salary for six months without loss of job security – and supplementary maternity leave for the first year after birth. This provision would help to make it easier for women to stay home so as to 'guarantee the protection of the child who needs the presence of its mother in the first twelve months of existence' (Senato, 1971: 493), in contrast to changes to the regular compulsory leave, with compensation at 80 per cent of salary for two months prior to birth (instead of three) and three months following in the successive period (instead of two). This position reflected a more social, rather than biological, construction of pregnancy and motherhood and was favoured by the left-wing unions, which did not want women to be off work for long periods of time.

It is interesting that despite what seemed to be conflicting visions of motherhood, pregnancy, and the representation of the demands of women in work, there was little open contestation of the dominant model of familialism that placed children at the centre of policy decisions. The political and institutional dynamics that shaped Italy's consensual democracy ensured that an open debate would not take place but afforded enough space for policy changes to be introduced.

An indication of how the consensual nature of Italian policy-making prevented the emergence of more egalitarian forms and responses to women in work may be found in the short debate in 1971 on legislation (Law no. 1044), establishing a national childcare plan to be administered by regional governments. As mentioned above, the law that would create 3,800 childcare centres over a five-year period merged three almost identical private-member bills presented by Communist, Socialist, and Christian Democratic deputies. The bill was sent to a joint session of the Health and Internal Affairs committees meeting in legislative session, which meant that there was no debate in the Assembly (Camera dei Deputati, vi Legislatura, Commissioni Riunite: 18 November 1971). This unique feature of the Italian legislature allows parliamentary committees to approve bills without having to return to the floor of the Assembly. The aim was to have legislation deliberated upon in the less visible committee, where it was easier for parties to seek an agreement behind closed doors. The three original bills were brought forward after extensive pressure from, and collaboration with, the three major trade union confederations (each with close ties with one of the parties that sponsored the private member bills). The government's original position was to resist the plans to create a new childcare system, since the Health and Internal Affairs departments were locked in a jurisdictional dispute as to which of the two would regulate the implementation of the program. The merged bill was brought forward to the committee, where it was discussed briefly, found little dissent, and was approved in the second sitting. The only criticism of the bill was that it was not part of a broader social policy agenda.

The childcare example is useful as an illustration of the institutional features of representational politics in family policy. First, the fragmented nature of decision-making structures created many avenues to seek accommodation among a range of political interests. It also meant that the access points for approving legislation were multiplied within the legislature and they were far from the public eye, which made it easier to bargain among competing claims made by political and institutional demands. Second, the fragmented nature of the policy-making process meant that programs such as childcare might find consensus, but broader policy agendas were difficult to implement. Third, the bill would charge the central government with financing a program implemented by regional governments and delivered at the local level. This gave the regions power to decide on broader principles, such as the private-public mix in the delivery of services. However, there were no measures put in place that ensured national standards, or, perhaps more important, to monitor whether funds destined for child care would, in fact, be used for that purpose (Visco Comandini, 1992).

It is clear that the day-nursery legislation was generated by misunderstanding of, or lack of willingness to address, difficult political choices. Instead, as in the situation of pluralist Belgium, the reform sent many different messages that accommodated a broad representation of interests. For instance, the duties and responsibilities of the public sphere in organizing services for children are explicit in the case of the day nurseries, but not for the pre-schools. In addition, the former were specifically referred to as being a public service within family policy and described as part of broader social policy framework facilitating women's labour force participation. The link to women's economic and social citizenship was explicit. Nonetheless, the text of the law covers all bases. It speaks of 'temporary child care in order to assure aid to families as well as to facilitate women's access to employment.' The rights arising from the recognition of broader citizenship claims were clearly conditional in the law.

Another problem emerged almost immediately in the case of the day nurseries: the law seemed to implement a universal system of childcare for children under the age of three, while in practice, delivery was rather selective. Regional and local rules and regulations restricted the service to employed women, in particular, single mothers, poor families, and children with a disability. In many instances, parents were charged fees on the basis of their incomes.

Such limited access to services may be traced to a number of factors: the historical legacy; the representation by social actors, many of whom wanted to protect women working outside the home; and the lack of financing and coordination provided by the central government. Italy's complex network of centre-regional/local relations was highlighted by two phenomena in the case of childcare: the discretion allowed to local and regional governments in the delivery of services, and their ever-increasing costs. The differences and discretionary powers at the local level reflected the different needs to mobilize support, the variation in administrative capacity, and the significant differences in regional economic development. Almost immediately in the 1970s the regions began to increase the personnel-to-children ratio, while the local authorities quickly abandoned the notion that day nurseries were a free social service. Families had to pay fees set according to income (Censis, 1978: 344).

The two major policy measures at the beginning of the 1970s did not present a significant breakthrough in the social, political, or cultural representation of women in work and the care of children. In practice, they were not part of a welfare state model based on universal principles, nor did they promote a clear commitment to unconditional rights for women's social and economic citizenship. A number of significant elements were introduced, however, which began to challenge the dominant, conventional representation of women and families. As was the case in France at the time, the day nurseries were intended, in part, to focus on child development. This intention undermined two traditional images of services for children: (1) the 'natural' supremacy of maternal care and (2) that institutional care of children was limited to the poor.

Yet the discussion of the day nurseries illustrates that there was still little room in the debate for new social actors to put their imprint on policy choices. The key determining factor remained the delicate balance of political and social relations between the Catholic and Communist worlds as it was articulated by the DC and the Communist party. This might help to explain the paradox of how important services and policies – which the maternity leave and day nurseries certainly were – could be introduced without any public political debate about principles or the details of policy. The search for consensus was overwhelming in the mid-1970s, when, although support for the Communist party was at its strongest, tension caused by left- and right-wing terrorism led the PCI to support the minority DC governments rather than seek an open challenge.

The result of bridging such contradictions was that national laws that defined social policy and were meant to underpin women's economic and social rights of citizenship often lacked the structures, financing, and commitment necessary for implementation. As we will see below, concerning the care of children, local authorities were allowed space to interpret national initiatives in ways that often either enforced the most traditional policies or introduced innovative and exciting programs.

One other measure passed in the 1970s deserves mention, that is, legislation on the equal treatment of men and women at work (Law no. 903, 1977). In addition to guaranteeing equal treatment for female workers, the law introduced parental leave and extended maternity leave for mothers of adopted or foster children. Fathers, according to the law were entitled to take leave for the care of children at 30 per cent of salary. In addition, they also could take leave at 30 per cent of salary to care for sick children. Fathers could make use of this right, however, only after mothers had explicitly chosen not to avail themselves of it or when fathers had sole responsibility for the child. There is no evidence to indicate how extensively parental leave has been used by fathers, and the law has sent mixed messages with respect to leave for the care of sick children. From the father's perspective, the care of children is a responsibility shared by the couple. From the point of view of the rights of women, children remain fundamentally a responsibility of mothers.

The law was the product of the convergence of trade union mobilization and feminism – to create a 'feminist syndicalism' – in the late 1970s. The mobilization began around the '150 hours' courses (Balbo, Capecchi, and Facchini, 1974).[1] This term refers to a provision of the Workers Statute of 1970 that allowed 150 paid hours of non-professional training for workers. In many universities, trade unionists and feminist academics used the time to discuss not only issues related to women's work but also questions about motherhood, women's identity and social services. At about the same time there was much discussion about the 'double presence' of women (Balbo, 1978). A model of citizenship was articulated, mainly by feminist sociologists who sought to deal with employment, domestic responsibilities, and emancipation within the family. In this context, the law on equality for male and female employment was seen as legitimizing not only the increasing presence of women in labour markets and their increasing economic rights, but also the representation of women's rights by trade unions. The latter would ensure, in part, that the interests of women workers would not be secondary to their male counterparts, especially in those sectors with a strong trade union presence.

Before we trace the development of day nurseries in the decades following the 1971 law, it is useful to examine some of the constraints on the implementation of social policy. While the principles and objectives of many areas of social policy seemed progressive and almost too ambitious, financial and administrative structures remained ill defined and poorly developed (Fedele, 1988). A number of problems became apparent as the decade progressed. First, it became quite clear that the absence of clear national standards in setting social policy, with universal standards defining the rights and responsibilities of citizens placed severe limits on the Italian welfare state. Second, the central state maintained considerable control over the budgetary powers of the regions. The latter had minimal capacity to generate their own revenues and were subject to the uncertainty of national budgetary decision-making. This allowed regions and local governments to engage in deficit spending, since there was little control over their expenditures, and possibly to divert funds from the original destinations set out in legislation (Desideri, 1995).

The case of the day nurseries reflects many of the tensions and contradictions of the Italian welfare state. By 1976, 1,080 day nurseries had been established; ten years later, there were 1,964 day nurseries, despite a five-year plan (1972–76) of the 1971 law, with central government special funds for the regions to be distributed to local governments to create and administer 3,800 day nurseries (Saraceno, 1990). The doubling of the number of day nurseries may seem impressive, but it was not unprecedented. There were 562 day nurseries administered by the ONMI (*Opera Nazionale maternita ed infanzia*) in 1963 (Faustini, 1963) and over 1,000 ten years later. The fact remains that the original objective of 3,800 day nurseries has never even come close to being achieved, since the number stabilized at about 2,100 in the 1990s (ISTAT, 1995: 92).

It is not surprising to find that the number of children attending day nurseries has never reached a significant level. In 1963, 2.2 per cent of children at or below the age of 3 attended one of the day nurseries administered by the ONMI; the figure dropped slightly to 2.1 per cent in 1976 and rose to 5.2 per cent in 1986. A number of factors may be seen as contributing to the limited presence of the centre-based care, including the reluctance of many regions actually to build the day nurseries, the high cost to local governments to deliver the service, and the high quality standards for personnel, which drive up the costs. The basic problem was, and has remained throughout the period since 1971, a lack of adequate funding by the central government to achieve the initial objectives set out in the legislation. More important, the central government was incapable, and perhaps unwilling, to ensure that objectives set out in the law would be implemented by regional and local governments.

Growing concern with the state of Italy's public finances meant that financial considerations created pressures to redefine the very nature of childcare services for the very young. For instance, in the mid-1980s the national government stated that the day nurseries were demand-driven services, and it indicated that it would likely weaken or abandon the commitment to universal provision of childcare services. The central government was not precise on what this statement meant in practice, but visible signs of a change included an increase in the percentage of costs that local governments must pass on to parents from 25 per cent in 1983 to 32 per cent in 1987 (Moss, 1990). This increase contrasted with the fact that the only charges to parents of children in the pre-schools were small amounts for meals. The day nurseries, which had begun, to some extent, as a selective policy for the poor and had been transformed into a quasi-universal service for working mothers, thereby became a selective service increasingly dependent on financing by local governments and parents. Never adequately financed, they did not fully develop into a universal and extensive social service.

The fragmented nature of Italian policy-making and the welfare state, however, resulted in different outcomes in the provision of child-care for children and different responses to changes in objectives and funding in the regions. Authors of a recent study of regional models of day nurseries, who examined standards set in regional laws and regulations, found that Emilia-Romagna maintained the highest-quality standards, while the general quality was high in the central regions, such as Tuscany and Umbria, mixed in the northwest regions, relatively low in the northeast, and low in the south (Becchi, Bondoli, 1992).[2] As a result, accessibility to childcare services for young children showed great variability across regions. This is quite different from the pre-school situation. In Emilia-Romagna, 18.9 per cent of eligible children frequented a day nursery, while in the northeastern Veneto region, though it shared many similar economic characteristics, only 4.8 per cent of children attended. The contrast with the south was even greater. In Sicily the statistic was 1.8 per cent, and in Calabria 0.8 per cent (Ghedini, 1995).

Political and Financial Crises in the 1990s

By the beginning of the 1990s a number of processes that had been developing throughout the previous decade began to undermine the consensual nature of Italian democracy (Sylos Labini, 1995). First, a party system that had seemingly 'frozen' representation suddenly starting generating unpredictable electoral outcomes. The subcultural bases of the two major parties no longer had the same effect on voter behaviour, especially in the case of the DC. A new electoral system, introduced in 1993 and based on a plurality system for three-quarters of the seats in Parliament, has contributed to party competition and introduces the possibility that elections may produce a governing majority. A corruption scandal that began in a Milan nursing home in 1992 grew to national proportions and led to the replacement of almost the entire leadership of the parties in the governing coalition between 1992 and 1994. Finally, the anomaly of post-war Italian democracy that led to the search for a consensual democracy – that is, the permanent exclusion of the PCI from government coalitions – disappeared. As a result, not one of the major parties in the 1994 general election ran in the 1987 election; the PCI became the *Partito Democratico della Sinistra* (PDS) in 1991, and the DC dissolved into various parties of the centre-left and centre-right before the 1994 election.

Second, popular initiatives led to a series of referendums throughout the 1990s that rejected many of the compromises of the political elite and brought about changes in the electoral system and the dismantling of government ministries such as the ministry for public holdings (Corbetta and Parisi, 1994). Fabbrini has argued that the popular nature of the referendum movement – 500,000 signatures are required to put a motion on a ballot – reflects the widespread rejection of the 'oligarchic' nature of the consensual politics (Fabbrini, 1996: 10–11). Along with the emergence of parties such as the Northern League, which made much of the fact that they did not want to be part of consociational politics, the referendums reveal the extent to which parts of civil society no longer look to party elites to bargain policy outcomes for them.

Third, it is difficult to underestimate the impact of European integration and, more generally, the global pressures for greater economic interdependence. The introduction of the single market and the convergence criteria of the European Union became tools to reduce the space for consensual politics. The political and business elite argued that Italy could meet the convergence criteria for economic and monetary union only with policy-making instruments that no longer placed a premium on representational functions. Concerns about Italy's public deficit and debt began to shape discourse in almost every policy area, at the expense of accommodation and consensus among major political parties.[3] The central points in policy-making, for one of the few times in post-war Italy, have shifted away from the search for consensus towards clearly defined final objectives, creating the possibility that one of the rival policy preferences may be imposed on the others.

The emergence of new political forces and the end of consensual politics has created a space for new representational structures. The First Republic has yet to be completed, however, and it is not clear what decision-making structures will replace fragmented, diffused consensual politics. Indeed, such changes are going in several directions that may hinder this openness. On the one hand, economic interdependence has contributed to a displacement of national state capacity to other levels of government and to markets. In Italy, this 'hollowing out' of the national state may be seen in major changes to central pillars of the welfare state. Modifications have been made to pensions and the health service, privatization has begun, market principles have been introduced in the public sector, and there are plans to transfer powers to regional governments. All these changes have occurred in addition to acceptance of European constraints (Macchiato, 1996; Ferrara, 1995; Cazzola, 1996). On the other hand, there is an emphasis on enhancing the capacity of state structures to determine policy outcomes. The goal is to make them less permeable and accessible to political forces. One might say that, rather than 'hollowing out,' the state is 'hardening its shell,' demarcating clearer boundaries between itself and civil society. These two changes are not unrelated. Displacing national state authority towards markets or other levels of government can be facilitated by limiting the sites for representational and consensual politics. Within this context in the period since the late 1980s the convergence of a political-institutional crisis and severe economic pressures has placed on the agenda a number of difficult decisions that have affected policy areas related to the care of children and women's work.

Family allowances provide a useful introduction to the evolution of policy in the period. They were seen as one of the few universal social benefits that parents could use towards the care of children. Moreover, they had been one the least controversial ways in which the state could intervene in family life. At the beginning of the 1980s, the existing regime provided for the universal provision of non-indexed family allowances based on the number of dependent children and financed by employer contributions. The funds gathered from these contributions have always resulted in a surplus, but it has never been suggested that it be used to broaden the allowances. Rather, the money has been redirected to cover deficits in other areas of social policy.

The universal nature of the child allowance was undermined on a number of occasions in the 1980s and 1990s. In 1983 the allowance became dependent on the number of children and on family income. A further change in 1988 (Law no. 153) strengthened the principle that allowances would grow proportionately with the number of children but decrease proportionately and significantly with family income. The result of the move away from a universal to a selective provision was evident. Whereas in 1983 close to 15.7 million family allowances were distributed, by 1989 the number fell to about 3 million (Gorrieri, Saraceno et al., 1986; Presidenza del Consiglio dei Ministri, 1994). The selective nature of the family allowances and the tax concessions for dependent children have led some to conclude that Italy's financial help to families, especially concerning the care of children, provides scant support for low-income families (Dumon, 1992; Golini, 1994). In addition, family allowances were cut sharply and means tests were introduced in the 1996 budget (Camera dei Deputati, Servizi Studi. Commissione speciale competente in materia di infanzia, 1995).

By the 1990s almost the sole criterion for judging a policy was its effect on public finances. The result was divergent paths for the representation of women in work and the care of children. The former produced an emphasis on 'choice' for women, including proposals for salaries for women who choose to stay at home. This idea has long been promoted by several Wages for Housework groups. For instance, the 1996 budget extended retirement benefits to housewives and extended allowances to families with only a single income. In the case of the care of children, two issues emerged: a concern with demographic decline (Golini et al., 1991) and the increasing costs for local governments for the care of children. In 1988 the central government moved away from conditional grants and towards a block grant that gave the regions the responsibility for making difficult decisions about how to distribute a smaller amount of funds. Thus, day nurseries now must compete for regional government funds that must be divided within a range of social services, all of which are under financial pressure. The preliminary evidence seems to indicate that those regions that had a weak commitment to childcare in the past, such as Calabria and Sicily in the south, now dedicate even fewer resources to the care of children (ISTAT, 1995: 143–8).

The change in central government funding also had consequences for local authorities, since they had to deliver services with even fewer resources flowing from the regions. The result has been that local governments have had to use different forms of delivering the service, including an increasing reliance on non-governmental organizations and attempts to combine day nurseries and pre-schools. As already noted, they now also generate a greater percentage of their revenues from parental fees. For instance, between 1990 and 1992 the percentage of revenues for day nurseries across Italy that came from fees increased from 11.8 to 15 per cent. Although the – minimal – central state funding remained the same, the percentage of regional funds decreased from 14.6 to 12.7 per cent of costs, and the local government contribution also dropped from 71.4 to 69.8 per cent (ISTAT, 1995: 143).

One clear consequence of such changes is that decentralization of discretionary decision-making has further fragmented a citizenship regime that lacked coordination and coherence. In this rather confused context, it has been easier for authorities to make changes to the nature of childcare and indirectly to the rights of women as workers without any visible political debate. We see now that policies that had been implemented without any noticeable debate or policy commitment in the 1960s and 1970s are being eroded by decisions based on financial constraints. Thus, in the 1990s an open and visible debate has taken place about the nature of the family and the representation of women's concerns with respect to the care of children and work.

The lack of a coordinated, coherent family policy was lamented throughout the 1970s and 1980s, but it is only in the 1990s that a minister for family affairs – renamed the minister for social solidarity – was created. The minister was without portfolio, however, had no department, and was a very junior member of the government without the institutional resources to design and promote a family policy.

Almost all the political forces that spoke in the only debate on the issue of family policy in the post-war legislatures raised this issue. The discussion, on 7 February 1995, addressed a series of motions presented by almost all the parties in Parliament that called upon the government to establish and implement a family policy. In many ways, the debate was no different from that over the definition of the family in the Constituent Assembly in the 1940s. Rosa Jervolino Russo, from the ex-DC Popular party, reminded the Chamber of what Giuseppe Dossetti had told the Committee of 75 close to fifty years earlier about the importance of the family for Roman Catholics (Camera dei Deputati, xii Legislatura, 1995: 7799). The parties of the left did not challenge the constitutional provisions, nor did they try to reopen the debate. Livia Turco, speaking on behalf of the PDS, presented its position, one that was little different from that of the other parties: she lamented the fact that there was no comprehensive family policy addressing the broad social and economic needs of the family (Camera dei Deputati, xii Legislatura, 1995: 7793). As they had done in the debate on maternity leave, the deputies from the PDS and Communist *Refoundation* (a faction that created its own party in opposition to the change in name and direction of the PCI when it became the PDS) stressed the needs of women as workers. The parties of the centre and right concentrated on women's 'natural' role as mothers. However, these differences did not lead to an open conflict or real debate. The approved resolution simply called on the government to establish a 'family policy' that would provide for the social and economic needs of families.

That consensual politics actually were eroding can be observed more clearly in the Social Affairs Committee hearings in June 1996. Livia Turco was the new minister for social solidarity in the centre-left government of Romano Prodi. She described her plans for her mandate, promising to increase family allowances and develop a comprehensive family policy as called for in the February 1995 resolution approved by the Chamber. She did admit, however, that her capacity to carry out her plans was limited by the fact that her institutional position provided only a coordinating role, and a limited one at that. The minister was then challenged, from both the left and the right, in terms that left little room for accommodation (Camera dei Deputati, XIII Legislatura. Commissione Affari Sociali, 1996: 3–5).

On the right, the deputies of *Forza Italia* (FI) criticized Turco for not being realistic about public finances, whose 'disastrous state' left no room for any increases in programs to help families. The FI indicated that, while it supported the principles of family policy, it doubted the capacity of the national government actually to provide for one (See Giuseppe Barone of FI in Camera dei Deputati, XIII Legislatura. Commissione Affari Sociali, 1996: 15). On the left, Tiziana Valpiana of the Communist *Refoundation* stated that the nature of the family had to be addressed before any 'family policy' could be established. She objected to the constitutional definition of the family as a 'natural' unit and stressed that families were particular social constructs with changing needs and rights (Camera dei Deputati, XIII Legislatura. Commissione Affari Sociali, 1996: 16). RC deputies also expressed concern about public finances, but unlike those from *Forza Italia*, they feared that European convergence targets would be used to justify cuts to programs that helped families.

The centre-left governments, elected in 1996 and led first by the centrist Romano Prodi and after October 1998 by Massimo D'Alema (PDS), initiated two important measures with respect to family policy. In March 1999 the government introduced a bill that would reform the childcare system (Camera dei Deputati, Proposta di legge, N.5838, 23 March 1999). It does little to ensure that the wide regional differences in the delivery of services will be addressed, nor does it promise a large number of new spaces. It is stated quite clearly, however, that childcare is an important part of the education and socialization of children, and that it facilitates access to labour markets for women. This marks a shift in the view of childcare as a residual service for mothers and families unable to find their own services. In an attempt to introduce elements of flexibility into the system, in the bill the government proposes to support care provided in homes, complemented by standards that would regulate the qualifications of caregivers and directors of services; it also calls for the setting of professional and educational requirements. Finally, the bill sets a limit of 30 per cent of operating costs as the maximum amount that parents are to pay for spaces in public day-care centres.

The second initiative was a government bill that brought together a number of private member bills on parental leave. The bill extends parental leave to eleven months over the first eight years of a child's life. An incentive of an extra month of paternal leave is provided for fathers who choose to stay at home with a new child. A 'sabbatical' year of unpaid leave for up to eleven months is proposed, that could be shared between parents. Parents can take this leave not only to care for children but also to further their education or to take some form of training. Mothers in 'atypical' work are also given consideration in the new regime, since they will have the right to 3 million lire as a 'maternity benefit.'

The two initiatives do signal an attempt to break new ground in trying to design policies for the care of young children. It is no coincidence that they have been initiated by a government of the centre-left that has tried to present itself as a catalyst of modernization. Part of this discourse has been to move away from the concept of the welfare state as based on male industrial workers and to recognize changing patterns of work and the growing importance of women in labour markets. However, the government coalition contains many centrist elements with deep roots in the old Christian Democratic party. The two bills represent a start, but many of the obstacles mentioned earlier remain, and the care of children still is very much a family matter.

It seems that by the middle of the 1990s, nearly fifty years after the Constituent Assembly, the dissolution of the post-war citizenship regime, especially its institutions of representation, has finally sparked a debate about the nature of the family and family policy. In the previous regime, the dominance of the principle of consensus meant that debates about the definition of a family, the balance between public and private sectors in delivering programs, and the role of the state were muted. Any policy that did affect families was a collection of disparate decisions that reflected a series of compromises, primarily, but not exclusively, between the PCI as the guarantor of industrial working-class interests and the DC, whose Catholic base contained a number of different ideological strands.

If in the 1990s Italy finally has begun to address such matters, it is in a context of financial constraint in which there seems less room available to use public resources in the name of equality or even public support for families. Thus, its childcare programs for the under 3s remain poorly financed and diversified both across space and across classes. If Italy still leaves responsibility for children to families, now it is more for reasons of 'free choice' than because of a commitment to Catholic ideas of subsidiarity. For parents, especially working mothers, however, the difference is hard to discern.

NOTES

1 The importance of the '150 hours' was that their roots were beyond the confines of the conventional party and trade union structures.
2 Quality was measured by three indicators: the pedagogical and psychological model for the day nursery, the training of its personnel, and the legitimacy accorded to the demands of families.
3 An interesting example was an editorial that appeared in the newspaper *La Repubblica*. The author, trying to recall attention to the perennial problem of a lack of running water, gas, and electricity in many parts of Sicily and southern Italy, called for the delivery of these basic services as a criterion for entry into the single currency. The assumption is that only policy objectives that are seen as gateways to the single currency will gain attention from policy-makers. Antonio Ramenghi, 'Acqua, luce e gas per Maastricht,' *La Repubblica*, 17 July 1996.p

Chapter Six

Sweden: Models in Crisis

Anne-Marie Daune-Richard and Rianne Mahon

Sweden has often been considered a model social democracy where much has been done to take the sting out of class inequalities, but it has also come to stand for equality of the sexes. This reputation is due in no small part to policies that have eased the tensions between domestic and paid labour, faced especially by working mothers. Of particular note are generous parental leave insurance and a publicly funded, and largely publicly run, childcare system, which has gone a long way to meeting potential demand.[1] The egalitarian Swedish model of family policy and the citizenship regime within which it is embedded grew out of the challenge posed in the 1960s to the initial vision of Swedish women's place in 'the People's Home.'[2] In that vision the child-rearing housewife was ensconced in a modern home by a supportive social democratic state.

In this chapter we analyse the development of and renovations to the egalitarian Swedish citizenship regime. The story is focused on a series of struggles and compromises in which the Social Democrats (SAP) and their union partners, the blue-collar unions of the LO (*Landsorganisation i Sverige*), with their class-centred discourse, often played an important role. Nonetheless, the story also shows that new representations of women's citizenship were brought into Swedish discourse – and kept there – by Swedish feminists.[3] In the first two sections of the chapter we provide the historical backdrop, tracing the shift from the modern mother-housewife celebrated in the political discourse of the 1930s and early post-war years, to the feminist humanism of the 'sex roles' debate, sustained and radicalized by the emergence of the New Left in the 1970s. In the last section we cover the recent period, marked by a growing sense of crisis. In the 1980s the model came into question in partisan debate and on the discursive terrain in civil society, while the economic crisis of the 1990s undermined its material foundations.

The Modern Mother-Housewife in the 'Small World' of the People's Home

In Sweden, as elsewhere, the economic disruption wrought by the Great Depression was matched by turbulence in the world of representations. Here, the 'big' struggles focused on (re)setting the parameters of class relations.[4] After more than a decade of labour market strife, the Saltsjöbaden Accord of 1938 between the LO (the union central) and the SAF (the employers' federation) established the principles that were to govern collective bargaining until the 1970s: the unions recognized management's right to manage, and management conceded the unions' right to represent workers' collective interests as wage earners, while both sets of peak associations agreed to work for socially responsible agreements. Political turmoil gave way to relatively stable government by a cross-class partisan alliance of workers and farmers, cemented in the 'Cow Deal' of 1932. The latter, in turn, paved the way for Keynesian economic policies and for developing a comprehensive set of social policies. The foundation stones of the People's Home – full employment and a universalistic welfare state – thus were laid.

The family was not untouched by these changes, as was evident in the tumbling fertility rate – from 4 children per woman in 1900, to 3 in 1920, and to 1.7 by 1930 (Pauti, 1992) These figures were brought to political life with the publication in 1934 of *The Crisis in the Population Question*, written by two leading social democratic thinkers, Alva and Gunnar Myrdal. The debate that ensued helped to bring into focus contending views of the family and the key figure therein, the 'modern woman.' Here appeared an early version of the feminist-humanist vision that was to take hold in the 1960s and 1970s: the modern woman as an economically independent individual, willing and able to combine child-bearing and full participation in civil and political society. In the discourse of social engineers like the Myrdals the representation of woman was of a rational individual, able to achieve the same full citizenship as her male counterpart, with the assistance of the social democratic welfare state (Hirdman, 1994: 73). There were also other, less radical, versions of the modern (social democratic) woman. Thus, some advanced the figure of class-conscious housewives exercizing the enhanced purchasing power promised by Keynesian-welfare reforms to create a better match between exchange and use-values.[5] The vision that triumphed, however, was more modest still: the modern mother-housewife.

The two Commissions on Population that grew out of the debate sparked by the Myrdals provided the Social Democrats an opportunity to forge a tactical cross-class alliance that supported the expansion of the welfare state in the name of this figure. Conservative pro-natalists and Social Democrats came to agree on housing loans to encourage earlier marriage and eventually, on the building of new apartment blocks for large families; special aid to 'mothers in need of assistance,' albeit without the stigma of poor relief (Ohlander, 1988); and in the 1940s universal child allowances (Pauti, 1992). Behind these policies shone the figure of the modern housewife, ready to listen to the scientific advice of the newly created network of experts on nutrition, child-rearing, and modern household management in general.

In the early years of the post-war boom, it was this figure who predominated in popular representations of modern family life, such as those to be found in Astrid Lindgren's well-known children's stories. Thus, the mother in the Mårten family is depicted as busily at work in the 'small world' of home and neighbourhood with her three mischievous children, while her husband goes off to work in the 'big world.'[6]

Although women had also won the formal right to remain in the labour force after marriage in 1938, employed mothers were not to receive the kind of generous state support accorded their housewife sisters, either in the 1930s or in the early post-war years. A universal maternity allowance (at a flat rate) was instituted in the mid-1950s, as part of a move, inspired by class politics, to introduce universal sickness insurance. Yet the working mother still was considered a product of dire necessity (e.g. single parenthood) and thus was a rarity.[7] Although the tightening of labour markets in the early 1950s gave rise to some discussion on how to draw Swedish women into the labour force,[8] little was done to facilitate this idea; for instance, no new child-care spaces were created in the 1950s.[9] Tax policy constituted a disincentive to married women's labour force participation,[10] and the new labour market policies were focused on the male breadwinner (Sainsbury, 1994). Women remained barely visible at the margins of the labour market,[11] and it was primarily to foreign labour reserves that employers looked to meet labour shortages (Kyle, 1979; Knocke, 1986).

Thus, 'full employment,' one of the core principles of the Swedish model, did not apply to Swedish women. Yet unlike many welfare states, which took the male breadwinner as their paradigmatic citizen, the Swedish welfare state directly incorporated women, first as citizen-beneficiaries of universal social programs and second as mothers. Maternity and other related benefits applied to all mothers, irrespective of their marital status or their connection to the labour market (Sainsbury, 1994). In this way, the Swedish welfare state recognized the principle of care, albeit in a manner consistent with a traditional division of labour between the sexes. As we shall see, in the 1960s the recognition of a public responsibility for the care work performed by women would provide an avenue for those who sought full equality of the sexes to challenge the supremacy of the mother-housewife.

The 'Right to Be Human': Towards the Egalitarian Model, 1960–1980

Both men and women have one main role, that of human beings. Taking care of one's offspring is part of one's role as a human being, as a necessity and as a moral duty, but also as a rich resource, a sweet experience and much else ... it is towards this utopia, a society of free, independent individuals, that we are striving.

Moberg, 1961; reprinted in Baude et al., 1992: 197

In many respects, this period marks the golden age of the Swedish model in general and of egalitarian family policy in particular. Until the mid-1970s the Swedish economy enjoyed boom conditions which, along with major policy innovations, mitigated the impact of the accompanying structural shifts as people moved from the sparsely populated regions to the thriving metropolitan areas of Stockholm, Malmö, and Göteborg and from primary to tertiary sector occupations. Sweden also managed to weather economic crisis without sacrificing full employment through active labour market measures and the continued expansion of public services. These two decades were also a time of renewed political turbulence. The end of the old alliance between the Social Democrats and the Farmers' party[12] in the late 1950s contributed a new fluidity to party politics at a time when the SAP, the Liberals, and the Centre party were discovering the new middle class.[13]

Although the existing party system generally proved capable of absorbing these new social forces, the parties had to open up to new representations of class, national, and gender relations. These representations, in turn, sustained the wave of important policy innovations that have come to characterize the Swedish model of social democracy.

The great innovations in the citizenship regime put in place in this period included the Rehn-Meidner adaptation of Keynesian economic policy, a new tier of social insurance benefits based on the income replacement principle, and the provision of high-quality public services. Seeking a progressive solution to the trade-offs between full employment and price stability, equity, and efficiency, the designers of the Rehn-Meidner policy aimed to provide conditions for all to benefit from the high-growth, export-oriented economic policy. In addition to its macroeconomic and labour market policy aspects, the Rehn-Meidner strategy provided justification for the LO unions' policy (increasingly shared by the white-collar union central, the TCO) of solidaristic wages bargaining.[14] The renovations to the welfare component of the People's Home were also designed to make it attractive not only to its earlier inhabitants of blue-collar workers and farmers but also to the burgeoning category of white-collar workers. Thus, the People's Home would achieve such quality that even the better paid white-collar workers would call it their own.

Women's citizenship was not left untouched by these developments. In fact, alongside the primary discourse centred on an emergent collectivity of genderless 'wage earners,' a renewed debate about appropriate gender roles appeared. As it did in the 1930s, this debate took place against the backdrop of renewed concern about population policy. Fertility rates, which had risen in the 1950s, once again fell (Näsman, 1990: 5). This time, however, it was the mother-housewife who would ultimately be confined to the margins, yielding central place to her 'working-mother' sister. This outcome certainly was partially a product of the tight labour markets, where the fastest growth was occurring in the service sector. Employers turned to Swedish women, rather than immigrants, to meet these needs (Kyle, 1979). Yet falling birth rates and tight labour markets are not the whole of the story. The politics of representation also mattered; for it was in the name of a recharged feminist-humanist vision that these reforms were launched. The aim was not only to liberate women from the small world of home and family to allow for their full participation in the big world of markets and politics through paid work. It was also to free men to be fathers. In other words, men and women alike were simultaneously to play two roles, as parents and as workers, assisted by the social democratic state.

Progressive elements in both the Liberal and the Social Democratic parties pushed this vision. The publication in 1961 of an important essay, *Women's Conditional Liberation*, by a young Liberal, Eva Moberg, is usually credited with bringing back the feminist-humanist vision into Swedish political debates. For Moberg, women's struggles for equality had thus far led to only a conditional liberation: 'Woman has been given her freedom only under the implicit condition that she constantly sees her main task as being to care for and raise children and to create the right environment for their growth. Only if she recognizes that this is her natural task, in some way built into her qualities as a sexual being, will society recognize her as a fully free individual' (Moberg, 1992: 197).

Similar voices were being raised in social democratic circles. In 1960 in an article in the Social Democratic journal *Tiden* it was argued that women's liberation required going beyond limited forms of civil and political citizenship to embrace full equality. The latter, in turn, was seen to require recognition that men as well as women had two roles.[15] Another Social Democrat argued even more pointedly that a woman's main role was not as a mother but rather as a worker and that through labour market policy reforms society should be prepared to support her in this role (Hinnfors, 1995: 109). The publication in 1962 of Dahlström et al.'s *Women's Life and Work*, with its scientific mode of argumentation, did much to widen the terms of the discourse. It moved from the 'woman question,' marginal to the main business of politics, to the 'sex role debate' of concern to all and requiring action on many policy fronts (Baude, 1992: 10).

Although the main proponents of the feminist-humanist vision were divided by party allegiance, an important network of activists was created to bring together Liberal and Social Democratic[16] activists. Subsequently known as 'Group 222,' the band included influential trade union and party intellectuals as well as those with strong media connections.[17] Its program claimed: 'We oppose all forms of sexual discrimination. Full equality should obtain between the sexes. One's opportunity for education, home and paid work and personal development in general must be independent of one's sex. To achieve this aim, traditional sex roles must be changed so that home and family become to an equally great extent men's and women's concern and so that material support and social responsibility become to the same degree men's and women's task. We believe that the national government, municipalities, educational authorities, industry, organizations, and the mass media should work for this goal' (appendix to Hederberg, 1992: 22). As we shall see, the group's demands for tax reform, educational and labour market policy reforms, supportive social services (including childcare), and a new form of child support combining a generous child allowance and reimbursement for parental childcare during the child's first year set out the policy agenda for the rest of the decade and beyond. Of particular interest was the demand for childcare services and the precursor to the parental leave policy adopted in 1974.

These groups acting within and across the Liberal party and the SAP were assisted in making headway against more traditional views by the uncertain terrain the two parties found themselves on following the breakdown of the farmer-labour alliance. After experiencing substantial losses in the 1960 election, the Liberal party became more open to the arguments made by Moberg and the Liberal youth wing, where her views had found support (Hinnfors, 1995: 129). The Liberals' move to embrace the emergent female wage earner, in turn, changed the terms of partisan competition, especially for the Social Democrats. When election results showed that the SAP was losing support among young employed women, the leadership became more open to a voice like that of Sten Andersson, who argued that women 'are the most discontented in society ... This is a movement that we cannot bring in, if we do not set to work with these questions and show the greatest possible openness to the ideas that are, to these women, obvious. If we are not radical, we will lose the groups we are dependent on' (Karlsson, 1990: 101).

By 1966 the egalitarian humanist view seemed to have won over the Social Democratic Women's League (SSKF) as well as the Social Democratic Youth. Together they produced the document, *On Equal Terms* (*På lika villkor*), which was circulated on the eve of the election in order to undercut the appeal to women of the Liberal and Centre parties. As the title suggests, *On Equal Terms* advanced the renewed feminist-humanist representation of citizenship, and it did so in ways that linked women for the first time to the full employment core of the Swedish model. Thus 'the social democratic term, *full employment*, must apply even to women. *Work is everyone's right and obligation.* Special treatment for the woman is not motivated by anything other than in connection to pregnancy and childbirth. The care of children is the responsibility of both parents' (Karlsson, 1990: 116; emphasis in the original).

This argument fit well with the position held by the LO, the blue-collar union federation that not only constituted the party's core support but was also the intellectual force behind some of the SAP's key policy innovations. By the early 1960s the LO had reached an agreement with the SAF (the employers' association) to abolish separate women's wages. From the mid-1960s, the LO became a leading advocate for the expansion of publicly supported childcare. LO staffers connected with Group 222 certainly helped to shape the LO's position on these questions, but the Group had had to learn to cast its arguments in ways that accorded with the union's class identity (Baude, 1992; Hirdman, 1998).

This attitude came through in the 1969 report of the LO's family policy committee, which complained that the sex role debate had hitherto been shaped by the concerns of highly educated, professional women rather than the large group of LO members (1969: 13). This is not to say that the LO refused to recognize gender inequality. The latter, however, was clearly seen as secondary to the larger question of class inequality (LO, 1969:11, 16). In fact, in the latter half of the 1960s the question of class inequality had begun to assume a new significance.[18] Thus, the feminist-humanist discourse did not so much fall on deaf ears in LO headquarters as it demanded a struggle to find its place in the unions' reformulated agenda.

Not all parties, however, were as keen as the SAP-LO and the Liberals to draw women into the labour market. The mother-housewife continued to have her defenders. The Centre and Conservative parties – and the socially conservative Christian Democratic Party (KDS), which split from the Conservatives in the 1960s – tried to reassert the traditional concept of the family. The classic liberals among them argued that the state should leave to parents the right to choose how to raise their children, and one of the least intrusive ways to do so was to place a lower tax burden on the individual. Nor was opposition confined to the right. There were strong advocates for the traditional sexual division of labour in the Social Democratic and Liberal parties, as well as in the unions. The main difference between the latter and their conservative counterparts was that they looked to the defence of the housewife and children in a manner more consistent with the earlier version of the People's Home, notably by raising child allowances and other measures that required an active state.

The notion of 'choice' initially adopted by feminists helped to pave the way for the formation of new compromises, just as the population question had done in the earlier period. The concept of choice played an especially important role in bringing radicals and traditionalists together within the governing Social Democratic party (Karlsson, 1990: 124). It also held an appeal in the wider political debates. Here, the convenient ambiguities surrounding the concept went beyond the right of women (and eventually even 'parents') to choose housework and paid work. It also touched on competing visions of the conditions under which that choice was to be exercized. These differences emerged in the debate over the introduction of a care allowance.

Although the notion of a care allowance has come to be associated with contemporary efforts to make it feasible for 'parents' to choose the traditional model, the idea actually originated with the feminist-humanists. In *Woman's Conditional Liberation*, Moberg proposed a child bonus system, financed through a payroll tax, which would make it economically viable for women (or parents) to choose to stay at home with children under 3 or to work full time.

At this juncture, the notion of the care allowance offered a means of implementing a compromise. It enjoyed the support of advocates of change while not alienating more traditional elements in either party. It also made it easier for the Liberals to work out a common family policy with their new allies in the Centre party who leaned towards the traditional model.[19] Ironically, given later developments, only the Conservative party opposed the care allowance in the 1960s. For the social conservative elements, the proposal was seen as going too far towards meeting the conditions for women to 'choose' paid work in the labour market. For the economic-liberal wing, it gave the state too great a role: tax cuts were the best way to encourage childbearing, because they left to families the choice of how best to care for their children (Hinnfors, 1995, passim).

Meanwhile, however, advocates of the 'working mother' were moving beyond the ambivalent notion of choice actively to promote women's employment. Under pressure from the LO and from the growth in support for the feminist humanist option within its own ranks, the Social Democrats and the Liberals began to push for the expansion of childcare services (Hinnfors, 1995: 101). Nor was the demand for childcare the dream of a political elite. Many ordinary Swedish women recorded their votes for day care in the voluminous government studies commissioned in the 1960s (Bergqvist et al., 1999:140).

While the Social Democrats and the Liberals may have agreed that the national government should offer the municipalities financial inducements to increase the supply, there was disagreement on the choice between centres run by the municipalities and publicly licensed (and subsidized) family day care. All the bourgeois parties preferred subsidized family day care, whereas both wings of the labour movement preferred municipal centres (Kyle, 1979: 185). For the former, family day care was not only cheaper. It also preserved parental 'choice' (now between kinds of services), and, most important, it did so in ways that allowed parents to choose milieux that were as 'natural' (i.e., homelike) as possible under the circumstances. LO, however, was quite critical of the fact that family day care was expanding more rapidly than places in municipal centres were increasing.[20] For the LO, the TCO, and many Social Democrats, public institutions were the best way to offer working parents the security that their children were being well looked after. The pedagogical advantages of public institutions also were important to these class-based actors.[21] Just as schools were being expanded to provide all children with at least secondary education, public childcare and specialists in early childhood education could help to erase the disadvantages associated with class origins.

In fact, both forms of childcare expanded rapidly from 1965: in that year there were 11,900 places in municipal centres and 6,000 in family day care; fifteen years later there were 136,400 municipal places and 88,500 in family day care (Hinnfors, 1995, table 11: 50). That municipal centres accounted for a modestly declining share of a rapidly growing total (from 66 per cent of places in 1965 to 60 per cent in 1980) can be explained less as a result of ideology than as a result of pragmatism. In other words, because family day care did not require the same infrastructural investment, it was quicker (and cheaper) to respond in that way to rapidly rising demand.[22] What is interesting to note, however, is that by the end of the 1970s there was a clear class difference in utilization rates. Over 50 per cent of children from SACO families and nearly 50 per cent of children from TCO families had spaces in the municipal day-care system, compared with one-third of LO families. The difference is even more marked in terms of utilization of spaces in municipal centres (the LO's preferred option). Approximately one-quarter of SACO and TCO children had places, compared with only 13 per cent of children from LO families (Hinnfors, 1995, table 12: 51). As we shall see, this issue of class distinctions in childcare use would cause some difficulties for Social Democrats when 'choice' again became an issue in the 1980s.

The debate over 'choice' via a care allowance played an even more important role in opening the door to one of the reforms that perhaps best embodies the feminist-humanist ideal: parental leave. By the mid-

1960s the Social Democrats and the Liberals had begun to take their distance from the notion of a care allowance but had not entirely abandoned it. The Centre party kept the option alive in Parliament, and this put pressure on the SAP to find an appropriate alternative (Hinnfors, 1995: 101). Traditionalists in the Centre party sought a kind of 'care wage,' to be given out to those who chose to stay at home to look after their young children. The Liberals, however, continued officially to support something closer to Moberg's ideal: a non-taxable care allowance available to all parents to help to defray the costs of raising children, whether in the form of fees or as income forgone by a stay-at-home parent.[23] The LO and the SAP began to work out a third option: parental leave. It broke with the notion of 'choice' between wage work and housewife status to clearly favour the two-earner family.

Thus, the LO's 1969 report, *The Union Movement and Family Policy*, suggested the following:

> There are good reasons to ease the family's situation in connection with the costs of child raising, and at the same time to underline the man's shared responsibility, by allowing sickness insurance to be paid during the first fourteen days to the woman's male partner or another close to her. Under the currently legislated six-month leave, after the first three months it should be possible for leave to be taken by the woman or the man. Even sick pay should be linked to this possibility. Through a change of the law forbidding firing on the basis of marriage or pregnancy, the possibility should also be created for a further six months' leave. Even this should be available to the man or the woman ... The fact of shared responsibility for child-rearing should be marked by talking of parenthood in cases where the term 'motherhood' is now used. (LO, 1969: 50)

The first report of the party's Equality Commission took a similar stance (Ohlander, 1988: 232), as did TCO's long-awaited 1971 family policy report (1971: 189–91). Thus, by the time that the SAP family policy committee finally submitted its report in 1972, the Social Democratic majority was clearly ready to reject the care allowance in favour of parental leave. At its congress that year, the SAP officially adopted the parental leave insurance option (Hinnfors, 1995: 113–14). In 1974, with Liberal support, the law changed: 'parental' leave replaced 'maternity' leave. The former, originally available for six months, was based on the income replacement principle (90 per cent of salary). Parental leave continued the principle of public support for child-rearing but did so in a way that assumed that care was to be provided by fathers as well as mothers.[24]

The introduction of parental leave marked the high point in the struggle to realize the feminist-humanist vision of the egalitarian family. It occurred near the crest of the wave of radicalization of the workers' movement: struggles for industrial and economic democracy had resulted in a series of important industrial relations reforms focused on collective rights in the workplace. There was also a parallel radicalization of the women's movement, in which the small but influential socialist-feminist force, 'Group Eight,' galvanized the younger generation of Social Democratic women.[25] Under these political conditions it seemed possible that the dream would become even more concrete through the introduction of a special 'father's month' of parental leave and the adoption of the six-hour day as a new norm that would allow time to be 'fully human.'

It is interesting that two members of the Centre party raised the issue of not allowing one partner to take the entire allotted leave.[26] The demand for the six-hour day was articulated in the 1972 SSKF policy document produced by six young Social Democratic women, *The Family in the Future – A Socialist Family Policy*. The SSKF kept the work time issue on the agenda by publishing a report on the question. Indeed, in 1974, the topic seemed to have wind in its sails: an investigation into the work time issue was established and the SAP's new party program included the six-hour day (Karlsson, 1990: 161). Yet at the 1974 SSKF conference on work time, the unions' ambivalence became apparent. A representative of the important Metal Workers Union made it clear that LO members had more pressing needs, such as a fifth paid week of vacation and reduced hours for shift workers. His position was supported by the secretary for the LO's family policy council, Aina Westin. She argued that rather than trying to adapt the societal (male) norm to women, the unions should focus on securing the rights of part-time workers in collective agreements (Karlsson, 1990: 162–3).[27]

The outlines of a resolution on the work time issue appeared, along with the first real hint of a 'father's quota' in the 1975 report of the Commission on Family Support. In it was a proposed modification of the parental leave legislation to allow parents of very young children to reduce their work time for up to twenty months while receiving partial compensation for the wages forgone. The SSKF continued to push for the reduction in the working day for everybody, but the SAP managed to defer a decision on the work time question, passing it on to an internal family policy committee. A small group of Social Democratic women MPs, however, managed to secure the party's official commitment to the introduction of the 'father's quota' in the run-up to the 1976 election (Karlsson, 1990: 169–70).

By this time, however, the radical wave had crested, and the economic crisis that had earlier hit other OECD economies had reached Sweden. The Social Democrats lost the 1976 election and would not return to office until 1982. The coalition governments that followed brought together the Liberal party, whose conception of the modern family was not far from that of the Social Democrats, and the Centre and Moderate parties, who continued to favour the notion of a care allowance.[28] The compromises they arrived at fell short of the egalitarian two-earner vision, institutionalizing instead a 'one and three-quarters' wage-earning family, wherein men continued to work eight hours (and overtime), while many mothers adopted the six-hour day, but as part-time workers.[29]

Thus, in 1978, when parental leave was extended to nine months, the last three months were paid at a flat rate, making the extension unattractive to the (usually) more highly paid fathers. The additional three months, of course, could be used to reduce the working day for one of the parents – but with no requirement that the reduction in working time be shared. In that same year, legislation was introduced that made it illegal to deny parental leave (with and without pay) until the child reached the age of 18 months. It was also illegal to refuse the reduction of a 'parent's' working day to six hours until the youngest child reached the age of 8. The language remained the gender-neutral language that the feminist-humanists had introduced into the Swedish citizenship regime, but the institutional supports for full equality were not provided. The norm that emerged from two decades of debates about women's and men's social citizenship was that of full-time employment for father and part-time jobs for mother, at least until the children were well into school.

This is not to suggest that significant changes had not been made. By the end of the 1970s the feminist-humanist vision had largely displaced that of the mother-housewife in Swedish policy discourse and practice. The rights of employed women were now firmly embedded in the Swedish welfare state and the public commitment to full employment had been redefined to include both men and women. Nor was this mere rhetoric. As Esping-Andersen (1990) rightly argued, the continued expansion of quality public services (one of the hallmarks of the

Swedish model) created 'good' jobs, many of which were filled by women. In other words, the Swedish welfare state supported women's employment both by providing crucial services such as childcare and by creating the jobs that employed many of them.

The Swedish Model(s) in Crisis?

Although in the 1980s there was little progress towards the radical ideas of the 1970s,[30] Sweden seemed to have escaped the crisis and retrenchment of the Keynesian-welfare state that had afflicted most OECD countries. Thus, mass unemployment was avoided, and from 1983 to 1990 the Swedish economy enjoyed boom conditions, started by the export sector, which benefited from the devaluation of the krona early in the decade, then fuelled by the financial and real-estate boom of the latter half of the decade. The Social Democrats returned to office in 1982 and governed for the rest of the decade. Governments were induced to 'follow market principles,' and there were efforts to trim public sector expenditure. Nevertheless, for the most part, the Social Democratic government used a 'cheese-paring' approach, which left much of the basic structure intact (Olsson, 1990: chapters 3 and 4).

Sweden's relatively egalitarian family policy also exhibited strong signs of continuity, even incremental improvement, during the 1980s. Thus, in 1985 the government made a commitment to have a childcare space for all children from the age of 18 months by 1991, and indeed, public funds continued to be channelled into the expansion of the system throughout the decade. Although increased funding proved inadequate to fulfil the promise, this failure in no small part reflected the rise in fertility rates.[31] Throughout the 1980s parental leave was successively extended, with the aim of securing the equivalent to 18 months' leave per child, based on the income replacement principle. While women continued to bear the main part of the care burden by using the leave and continuing their pattern of part-time work, an increasing share of the leave was being taken by fathers.[32]

Neither the relatively egalitarian Swedish model of family policy nor the larger Keynesian-welfare model on which it rested fared very well in the 1990s. Unemployment leapt from 2.1 per cent in 1990 to 12.5 per cent in 1993 (Huber and Stephens, 1998: 379) and did not drop below double-digit figures even when the export sector rebounded in 1994.[33] Although a Conservative-led government was in office when unemployment began to soar, the previous Social Democratic government had already abandoned full employment as the primary economic policy goal. Unlike the bourgeois governments of 1976–82, however, the Conservative government, led by Prime Minister Carl Bildt, was explicitly committed to bringing about a system shift. It sought to destroy the old model and lay the institutional basis for its neo-liberal successor (Mahon and Meidner, 1994).

Although the crisis of the Swedish model became visible only in the 1990s, a closer examination reveals its earlier roots. In the 1980s the Social Democrats may have restored full employment, but their chosen economic policy instrument – the so-called Third Road[34] – broke with the tenets of the Rehn-Meidner strategy by looking to high profits to restore growth (Ryner, 1994; Erixon, 1995). This policy, in turn, allowed the leading export companies to offer substantially more at the local level than the union leadership, schooled by the Rehn-Meidner model to 'hate inflation,' could deliver at the national bargaining table. As a result, the Third Road supported the employers' drive to destroy coordinated bargaining and with it the unions' policy of solidaristic wages, which had done so much to close the wage gap between women and men.

Instability and crisis were also increasingly apparent in the realm of politics. The 1980s has sometimes been labelled the time of the Swedish 'wars of the roses' – a reference to the signs of a growing rift between the leadership of the two wings of the labour movement.[35] By the end of the decade it had become clear that the crisis of representation extended to the party's base (Mahon, 1999). The Social Democrats not only lost the 1991 election; they watched some of their supporters (mainly young working-class men) turn to the new right-wing populist party, New Democracy. In the aftermath of the 1991 election, there was also speculation that a new 'women's party' would be formed. Coming on top of the earlier breakthrough of the Swedish Greens (*Miljöpartiet*), these movements suggested that the traditional party system was losing its hegemony over social movements, old and new.

These developments occurred against the backdrop of a measurable shift in societal values and the citizenship regime away from the more communal spirit of the People's Home towards a new individualism, a change especially marked among blue-collar workers. Pettersson and Geyer (1992) suggest that this cultural shift can be attributed to the very success of the Swedish model. In other words, material security, mass education, secularization, and even a growing cosmopolitanism have helped to undermine allegiance to the more communal concept of justice on which the model was founded. Yet the shift in values has also been created, to some extent, by the aggressive propaganda war waged in the trenches of civil society by the SAF, the Swedish employers' association (Hansson and Lodenius, 1988). In this discourse, the new individual is identified as the harbinger of a new societal model, one that breaks with the belief – held by Liberals, feminist-humanists, and Social Democrats alike – that a strong public sector constitutes a vital support for individual development.

The crisis of the broader economic and social policy model has not left the Swedish model of family policy unscathed. For its success, the egalitarian family policy depended on the state's willingness and ability to maintain full employment 'for all' and on the existence of various mechanisms, from solidaristic wage bargaining to the social democratic welfare state, designed to spread the benefits of productivity gains across the economy. Yet, while family policy has been affected by the crisis of the social democratic model in which it is embedded, the challenges have been posed in terms specific to the family policy field of policy discourse.

Thus, shortly after the Social Democrats' return to office in 1982, the twin concepts of 'choice' and the 'care allowance' returned to centre stage from the margins to which they had been relegated. In this way, the 1980s debate came to evoke the debates of the early 1960s. This time, however, new inflections were added. Choice was now defended by all three bourgeois parties (and elements within the SAP), in the name of respect for 'difference' and 'variety' (with the market seen as being best able to provide it) in contrast to the standardized solutions of the paternalistic welfare state. Under the sign of 'choice,' private for-profit as well as church-run day care were put on the agenda and with them the reinstatement of the notion of a care allowance.

The challenge to public day care can be seen as part of the SAF's broader campaign to undermine support for the public sector's 'monopoly' on social services. Thus, along with private health clinics and private health insurance, the SAF and the Swedish Federation of Industries financed the establishment of a private day-care company, Pysslingen – named after a character in an Astrid Lindgren story. The Social Democrats responded by proposing legislation – *Lex Pysslingen* – that would ban private for-profit day care and regulate the growth of other non-public forms (Olsson, 1990: chapter 5). In the parliamentary debate that ensued, advocates for Pysslingen and other alternatives to municipal day-care institutions invoked the ideas of 'choice' and the

'sovereign family.' For Conservatives and Moderates, family sovereignty was seen to include not only the family's right to choose the
kind of childcare it preferred but also the right to stay home while the
children were small (Jonsson, debates, 1983/84: 41). Both parties,
moreover, continued to push the care allowance as the most appropriate form of state financial support for such choice. While the Liberals
continued to differ from the other bourgeois parties on details, they
had never fully abandoned the notion of a care allowance. By the mid-
1980s, moreover, they were prepared to join the other bourgeois parties
in demanding some form of state support for choice among alternative
forms of childcare. Thus 'choice' – in the form of day care (now to be
widened to include for-profit and other private alternatives) and in the
broader sense (to work or to stay at home) – was back on the agenda.

For the Social Democrats, family sovereignty continued to depend
on the kind of security that a high-quality, public day-care system
could provide to the working parent/mother. In attacking for-profit
day care, the Social Democrats also emphasized social (class) justice:

> To find the right seductive and pleasing name for certain forms of so-
> called individualized childcare activities, one has turned to Astrid
> Lindgren's story world. Names like Pysslingen and Bullerby have been
> used as fig leaves, to hide the real intent of a market-directed childcare,
> which will skim off the cream, leaving the municipalities to take care of
> the problems, for example, children with special needs. Those who know
> their Astrid Lindgren know what is hidden behind the fig leaves. Pysslin-
> gen did not have it especially warm and cosy; he lived more precisely in a
> rat hole. In the so-called parental cooperative in my home municipality it
> is definitely not a question of 'all us children' in the Bullerby ... I can
> assure you. (Silfverstrand, debates, 1983/84: 162)

In other words, the unregulated growth of private alternatives would
turn municipal institutions into ghettos for the children of the low paid
or with special needs. Public resources should thus continue to be
devoted to providing high-quality public services that would appeal to
all wage earners, both white and blue collar.[36]

Although with the support of the Left Communists, *Lex Pysslingen*
was eventually passed, the Social Democrats were somewhat vulnera-
ble to criticism precisely on the question of the 'class' distribution of
the state's largesse. That is, the more egalitarian model had been
unevenly institutionalized across class lines: it applied particularly to

white-collar families, while blue-collar women were more likely to rely on something closer to the traditional model (SOU, 1990: 103). Both Centre and Conservative members of Parliament were quick to point out this distinction in both the debates on day care (a 'subsidy' to the middle class) and various opposition motions in favour of some form of care allowance. In the words of one Centre party member, 'What is wrong with parents' choosing to stay home and take care of children when they are young? Is it also a right-wing policy for the rich? Read the statistics! Which families decide to stay home and look after their children?' (debates, 1983/84: 104)

The LO had earlier raised concerns that its members were not as successful in gaining access to public day-care places as were their TCO and SACO counterparts. Subsequent studies have shown that LO families indeed were, and remain, underrepresented in public day-care institutions, although the difference fell throughout the 1980s as the number of places in public day care rose (LO, 1995a: 6). In LO families, mothers of young children are more likely to work on nights and weekends in order to manage a combination of paid work and family responsibilities (LO, 1988, 1995a; Jacoby and Näsman, 1989; Andersson et al., 1993). In addition, while part-time work is high among both LO and TCO mothers of pre-school children (58 and 54 per cent, respectively), LO mothers are more likely to continue part-time work until their children finish school. Class is also visible in patterns of parental leave-taking: fathers in white-collar families are more likely to take some parental leave (Ohlander, 1994).

The bourgeois parties thus could (and did) argue that the Social Democrats' policies favoured the better off, while some form of a care allowance would result in greater fairness for working-class families.[37] This view nicely captured in the following motion presented by two women from the Centre party: 'The working parent loses income if he or she wants to reduce work time. For the single parent this solution is often completely unthinkable. In reality, it is possible to make use of the legislated right to reduce work hours for the children's sake only for the well heeled, as long as the right is not connected with financial compensation. Thus, one of the most pressing reforms for the children's sake is the introduction of a care allowance that will make it possible for the parents to genuinely choose more time for the children' (Söder and Granstedt, debates 1988/89, So 636).

As a later survey showed, while the vast majority of women gave low priority to the notion of a care allowance, support was strongest among women and men with unskilled jobs and women with lower than average part-time hours (Björnberg, 1994). Fortunately for the Social Democrats, in the mid-1980s the bourgeois parties were still divided on exactly what form a care allowance might take. Thus, in the 1985 election, while the Centre and Christian Democratic parties favoured the 'care wage' form (a taxable allowance), the Liberals and the Conservatives argued for the more general form – an untaxed allowance – closer in philosophy to parental leave. Only on the eve of the 1988 election did the three main bourgeois parties manage to unite around a common version.

The Social Democrats were placed in an awkward position. If they went into the election promising the continued expansion of public day care, they would have nothing to offer those who continued to choose a more traditional pattern, yet the latter included a significant number of LO families, its core supporters. The LO's 1987 family policy statement suggested one solution that seemed to speak to these needs in a manner consistent with the egalitarian family model: the extension of parental leave to twenty-four months (Hinnfors, 1995: 219). At the same time, the work time issue had resurfaced: the LO called for the introduction of a sixth week of annual vacation, which put it in direct conflict with the Social Democratic Women's League, which had renewed its demand for the six-hour day.[38]

The compromise chosen was consistent with the way in which the egalitarian model had come to be institutionalized. As they did in the 1970s, the Social Democrats chose to promise the LO the sixth week of vacation, while deferring a decision on the reduction of the working day. Instead, the LO (and other) women were offered the extension of parental leave to eighteen months plus a renewal of the 1985 commitment to provide day-care places for all children of working parents from age 18 months.[39] The question of the six-hour day was handed over to a commission of investigation that would ultimately conclude that such 'standardized' solutions were passé. Flexible work time was now considered to be of greater interest to working parents as well as to employers (SOU, 1989: 53). Progress in all of these areas, however, came to an abrupt halt as the Swedish economy slid into crisis. Proposals for both the sixth week of vacation and the extension of parental leave were withdrawn as the Social Democrats struggled to manage a ballooning public deficit. These policy changes, in turn, fed the growing alienation of the party's traditional supporters shown in the 1991 election, which the Social Democrats lost.

The 1991 election also revealed a marked swing to the right. The Conservatives were now clearly the dominant party in the bourgeois bloc, while the bloc itself had grown to include the Christian Democrats, who had never before cleared the 4 per cent requirement to gain seats in parliament. The recently formed right-wing populist party, 'New Democracy,' also made it into Parliament. The turn to the right was clearly a gender-linked phenomenon. While the Liberals and the Social Democrats continued to enjoy the support of a majority of women voters (white and blue collar), the parties to the right appealed more strongly to men (especially younger ones) across class lines.

The governing coalition parties may have been able to agree on a common neo-liberal economic policy, but there were important differences among them on social policy questions in general and on family policy in particular. All parties in the coalition government certainly favoured extension of public subsidies to private, including for-profit, day care.[40] The old division persisted, however, between the Liberals, who were the most committed to the egalitarian model of two income earners, and the Centre party, for whom 'choice' also meant public support for 'parents' who preferred to stay at home while the children were young.[41] While a resurgent women's movement[42] gave strength to the former, the latter benefited from the inclusion of the Christian Democrats in the governing coalition. The tensions showed in the Bildt government's policy choices.

Thus, when in 1992 national subsidies for day care were rolled into a general grant to municipalities (a move that might have made it easier for municipalities to renege on their commitment to the continued expansion of day care), the egalitarian line was strong enough to insist on putting into legislation the state's commitment to provide day-care places for all children of working parents – only nine years after the Social Democrats had made the original commitment. The Liberals also managed to secure the introduction of a 'father's month,' which could not be traded to the mother, a position favoured by the leading feminists, the TCO, and a newly formed 'daddys' group.'[43] They were unable to resist, however, the introduction of a care allowance on which both the Centre and Christian Democratic parties, especially the latter, insisted. [44] At the same time, a version of the care allowance was introduced that more closely matched the Centre party's classic position in favour of a 'care wage.' Thus, the modest (2,000 kronor per month) taxable allowance would be paid to 'parents' who chose to stay at home until the youngest child turned three. Those who chose to reduce working hours during this period would have their income topped up, but those who chose to work longer hours would benefit instead from subsidized day care.

The Egalitarian Model at the End of the Twentieth Century: Only a Parenthesis?

It would be a mistake to exaggerate the extent of the crisis or to assume that the outcome will mean that the egalitarian model was, indeed, 'only a parenthesis.' The Swedish model of family policy has not, as yet, been destroyed. Swedish women continue to enjoy the right to work, and the old family policy mechanisms are still present, albeit at a declining level. The care allowance was rescinded by the Social Democrats when they returned to office in 1994, while the 'father's month' was left intact. At the same time, deregulation of financial markets and the convergence requirements, imposed by Sweden's decision to enter the European Union, continue to exert pressures that threaten to undermine the material basis of the egalitarian policy. Thus far, under social democratic governance, these pressures have resulted only in short-term changes.

In response to pressure on the Swedish krona, the Social Democrats (temporarily[45]) reduced the compensation rate for parental leave insurance to 75 per cent (85 per cent for each parent's quota month). The government also imposed more stringent fiscal requirements on the municipalities, making it more difficult for the latter to meet their obligations to expand (let along maintain) a high-quality day-care system. Nonetheless, once the fiscal situation had improved, the Social Democrats announced substantial increases in transfers to municipalities and counties to raise the quality of education and restore the standard of child and elder care.[46] The Social Democrats also went into the 1998 election with the promise to introduce a ceiling on day-care fees.[47] With the support of the Left and Green parties, the ceilings will be introduced in 2001.[48] Finally, a second 'father's month' that will extend parental leave to thirteen months, was promised in the spring 2000 budget.[49]

More broadly, the fate of the egalitarian family policy model, and the broader social democratic welfare state in which it is embedded, are intimately linked to the debate on the future of employment. Most agree that the trend towards 'post-industrial,' that is, service sector employment, will continue. The question is – what kind of service jobs and in which branches? In earlier work Esping-Andersen suggested that there are alternative post-industrial trajectories. The United States, with its large business and personal service branches – and the skill-income polarization associated with them – constituted one, while Sweden, with a strong public sector and substantial business services but a small 'fun, food, and wine' sector, comprised another (Esping-Andersen, 1990: 207). The latter displayed a relatively high ratio of good to bad jobs, and even the 'bad' public sector jobs offered substantially more than their private sector counterparts (Crouch, 1997: 382). The crisis of the 'full employment' Swedish economy has made it harder, however, to contest the neo-liberal claim that 'there is no alternative' to the U.S. model.[50]

In Sweden during the 1990s a new cross-party consensus began to emerge that future job growth must come from the *private* service sector and that such jobs can be generated by subsidizing personal services (via reductions to/elimination of payroll tax or personal tax deductions). The proposal was first placed on the agenda and given a (neo-)liberal feminist spin by economist Anne Marie Pålsson, who argued that housework is work whose value should be recognized; thus, government should allow tax deductions to cover the costs of domestic help. The Bildt government was quick to pick up on this plan, establishing the Vinell Commission to examine ways to promote the growth of the private service sector. Vinell recommended that payroll taxes on certain household services be reduced for households with a child under thirteen or another dependant present and where both parents work at least half time (*Välfärdsfakta* #2, 1994). Initially, Vinell's recommendation was roundly criticized for supporting the return of a 'servant class.' Yet since unemployment has remained high despite the Social Democrats' commitment to reduce it substantially, the idea seems to be gaining credence in social democratic circles. In an important debate article, three prominent Social Democratic women argued that tax deductions on domestic services could be seen as the equivalent, for women, of the construction jobs created by classic public works programs. The then-head of the large confederation of white-collar unions, (TCO),[51] went on record in support of the argument that future job growth lies in the private service sector, including domestic services (*TCO Tidningen*, 15.11.97). Several unions affiliated with the social democratic blue-collar confederation, LO, have also supported the idea.[52] Even the Social Democratic government seemed prepared to flirt with the idea, appointing the Andersson Commission to investigate.[53]

The slide towards the American model would certainly affect family policy, pushing it in the direction of the 'dark scenario' presented by an earlier government commission, in which poorer women would be paid to perform the personal services that make it easier for professional women to get on with their careers (SOU, 1990: 113). In other words, the class dimension would disappear from the egalitarian model, to the detriment of gender equality, at least in working-class families. Currently, however, the old model seems to have gained a new lease on life, as part of the Social Democrats' renewed commitment to the Swedish post-industrial alternative. This is evident not only in the decision to increase transfers to the levels of government charged with delivering child and other care services. In May 1998 Prime Minister Persson announced that the ministers of social policy and of labour were working with the county and municipal governments to come up with proposals to radically improve working conditions in this sector, with particular attention to work time (*Dagens Nyheter*, 14.5.98).[54] In a subsequent debate article, the minister of the interior was even clearer that public social services were to form a critical part of the future employment structure. Over the next decade, many new jobs will appear in this sector as the current labour force retires. To attract the new workers needed, the different levels of government have to collaborate on the issues such as work time, training, and improved work organization (*Svenska Dagbladet*, 1.7.98).

Although the egalitarian model is once again in the forefront, the left and feminists will have to work to sustain support for it and for the 'social democratic' post-industrial alternative of which it forms a part. Although the Liberals continue to back high-quality social services, it is the neo-liberal Conservative party that has become the hegemonic force on the right. This position is reflected in their common policy, which stresses tax cuts in general and a particular tax cut to encourage the growth of domestic services.[55] A change of government could indeed open the way to a transformation of the Swedish welfare state and its citizenship regime.

NOTES

1 The reform most often cited as supportive of women's labour force participation is the change in the basis for filing income tax policy, from joint (husband and wife) to individual taxation. Other policies instituted in the

name of gender equality include the gender equity law (*jämställdhetslagen*), first promulgated in 1979 and subsequently revised several times to increase its efficacy. The law supporting the right of 'parents of young children' to reduce their work time by one-quarter until the youngest child reaches school age might also be included. In the area of family policy, a substantial and non-taxable child allowance, a special allowance for multi-child families (*flerbarnstillägg*), and housing subsidies are worthy of note.

2 The 'People's Home' is a powerful metaphor for the social democratic project. In a famous 1928 speech then Social Democratic leader, Per Albin Hansson, drew a parallel between the Social Democrats' vision of the appropriate social order and the 'good home' where relations are character-ized by equality, mutual consideration, and cooperation.

3 As others have rightly argued, Swedish political parties – most notably the SAP, the small but often influential Communist party (VPK; now V), the Liberals (FP), the Centre party (formerly Agrarian), and the Conservatives (Moderates) – have remained the principal shapers of political discourse, along with their respective economic partners. (See Pontusson, 1987; Eduards, 1988; Therborn, 1992; and Jahn, 1993 on the capacity of Swedish parties, especially the SAP, to maintain their 'gate-keeping' function even after the emergence of new social movements.) In addition to the important LO-SAP link, the SAP enjoyed close ties to the coops, the Workers' Educa-tional Association, tenants associations, and seniors. Although the Centre party retained close links to the farmers' federation (LRF) in the 1960s, it developed an environmentalist perspective capable of attracting urban voters. The Centre party forms part of the bourgeois bloc, along with the Liberals and the Conservatives. The latter's fragmentation, however, has meant that the powerful employers' association, SAF, had had a quasi-partisan function. The peak associations representing the burgeoning category of white-collar workers (the TCO and the SACO, especially the former) were (and are) non-partisan, hence courted by all parties. With the exception of the VPK, all parties have affiliated women's federations. Historically, the main independent feminist organization, the *Fredrika Brenner Förbundet*, has been closer to both the FP and the Conservatives.

4 For more in English on the debates about class and the appropriate form of class relations see Therborn (1983), Martin (1984), Swenson (1989), Fulcher (1991), and Pontusson (1992a).

5 See Åkerman et al. (1983) for more details.

6 Lindgren is best known for her Pippi Longstocking character – a non-traditional girl, indeed, but one whose freedom to be different is not unre-lated to the absence of both parents (dead mother, travelling father) – and

her capacity to fend off the agents of the welfare state (teachers and social workers). The Mårten family series also features a mischievous girl, Lotta, but her shenanigans are constrained by the presence of a firm but loving housewife-mother.

7 Ulla Lindström, then minister of social policy, initiated an inquiry in the mid-1950s. She focused on the problems faced by single mothers, who 'constitute the proletariat, which at present lies at the bottom of Swedish society ... The courts demand a much too small maintenance from the father; the wage market treats women as "coolies"' (cited in Ohlander, 1988:227).

8 The LO-SAF had set up a women's labour committee (*kvinno-arbetsnämnd*) at the start of the decade, but little was done to encourage women's labour market participation. See Kyle (1979) and Waldemarsson (1998)for more details.

9 As in many other western countries at that time, in Sweden the limited childcare offered outside the home took two forms: childminding services run by voluntary agencies for poor women who had to work to support their families and pedagogically motivated half-day kindergartens for the children of the well to do (Hwang and Broberg, 1992).

10 Sainsbury argues that the barriers were fewer in Sweden than in many other countries, despite joint taxation. Thus, from 1952 working wives with children were entitled to a larger tax allowance than other working wives. By 1971 the amount had risen such that a married and employed mother's deduction was nearly twice the amount allowed her husband. This would have reduced the disincentive to dual-earner families provided by joint taxation, at least at lower income levels.

11 The famous study of women and work (Dahlström et al.) published in 1962 revealed that, although only 20 per cent of women worked full time, once part-time work was included, women's labour force participation rates rose to nearly 40 per cent.

12 The alliance split over the first of the new, post-Beveridge social insurance reforms (a pension plan based on the income replacement principle). With the 1958 pension scheme, the SAP moved to embrace the new principle, a move that gave blue-collar workers the same income-related benefits that employers had given white-collar workers and simultaneously gave white-collar workers a real stake in the public system. The Centre party continued to defend universal flat-rate benefits and this point, as we shall see, was as visible in its family policy program as in its social programs in general. As Hinnfors (1995) argues, a party's stance on social policy generally was viewed as a good predictor of its family policy orientation.

13 This is arguably true for the VPK as well. The latter was one of the first (1964) western European parties to embrace what would later come to be known as the 'Euro-Communist line.' Although the party was some distance from Moscow, it also was designed to express the radical potential of a left/socialist alliance of white- and blue-collar workers.

14 Labour market policy involved measures to promote geographic and occupational mobility, a well-developed system for short-term job creation, and a comprehensive labour exchange. Solidaristic wages policy, which originally emphasized equal pay for similar jobs irrespective of the employer's ability to pay, became focused on special increments for the lower paid.

15 Part of the context for the Swedish debate about sex roles was provided by Alva Myrdal and Viola Klein's *Women's Two Roles* (1957), in which they argued that women could be both mothers and workers – but not simultaneously. In other words, once the children were old enough, mothers could return to the labour market.

16 Although the majority was linked to either the SAP or the Liberals, the occasional Communist also was admitted (Hederberg, 1992: 18).

17 The address of their meeting place at the home of Annika Baude in the Stockholm suburb, Bromma. At that time, Baude was working for a major publishing house; she subsequently became the main researcher and author of the TCO's 1971 family policy document.

18 'Class' has always been central to LO's identity, from the moment of its formation as the union wing of the social democratic workers' movement, but its meaning has changed over time. In the 1960s a series of developments – not the least of which was the release of the findings of the Low-Income Commission, which showed that years of Social Democratic governments had failed to attenuate income inequality – contributed to a re-radicalization of class. The wildcat strike of the Kiruna iron miners in the winter of 1969 can be seen as the spark that ignited the already smoldering anger over class inequality in the workplace and in society as a whole.

19 The period from 1965 to 1973 was one of close cooperation between the Liberals and the Centre party, which left the Conservatives isolated to the right of the political spectrum (Hinnfors, 1995: chapter 3).

20 Between 1960 and 1970 the number of places in subsidized family home care expanded from 4,000 to 35,000, while the number of places in municipal day-care institutions grew from only 8,250 to 37,000 (LO, 1969:31). The expansion still left out many children. In 1960, 1.4 per cent of Swedish children from birth to six were in day-care centres and 0.5 per cent in family day care. By 1970 that percentage had grown to only 4.2 per cent and 4 per cent, respectively (Broberg and Hwang, 1991).

21 It was also professional: the TCO's support for day-care centres can be attributed, in part, to the stance taken by the teacher's unions (interview with A. Baude, May 1997).
22 The supply of day-care places grew at an especially rapid rate between 1965 and 1975: from 17,900 to 126,000 (then to 224,900 in 1980), when the Social Democrats were in office and the economy was booming. The share of family care had been as high in 1975 as it was in 1980, after four years of bourgeois government. That the number of spots continued to grow (albeit at a somewhat reduced pace) under that government, despite the unfavourable economic circumstances, is indicative of the degree of consensus that had come to prevail. It might be noted, however, that municipal day care grew more rapidly in the 1980s, such that by 1989 it accounted for 64 per cent (of a total of 337,400 places).
23 See Hinnfors (1995: 20–1) for a discussion of these three versions of the care allowance.
24 Clearly, the income replacement principle is important in this regard, given the tendency for fathers to earn more than mothers.
25 It is interesting that the unions were prepared to change their opposition to state involvement in shaping the rules governing collective bargaining to support the industrial democracy reforms but were not prepared to support the equity legislation of 1978.
26 As early as 1973 these two women MPs argued that no parent should be allowed to take more than eight months of an extended (to twelve months) leave. SSKF took up the fight within the SAP for a 'father quota.' The Family Support Commission, established to evaluate the new legislation, recommended that the benefit be extended but only on condition that no one parent could use the whole allotment. (Bergqvist et al., 1999: 142–3).
27 In its 1976 family policy report, the LO argued that the shorter day was important – in the long run – but that there was a danger that the abbreviated working day might become a substitute for the industrial and economic democracy reforms that then constituted the unions' main demand. At the same time the report did not come down in favour of a special reduction for parents of young children, arguing that that kind of solution appealed more to the 'already privileged' (i.e., white-collar workers, who already enjoyed greater freedom from control over their work time).
28 See Hinnfors (1995: chapters 6 and 7) for a discussion of the differences between the Liberals and their allies to the right, the Centre party and the Conservatives, on family policy questions.
29 To be sure, the gender wage gap between full-time men and women workers declined significantly in the 1970s (Anxo and Johansson, 1995),

but 45 per cent of women worked part time. Women's recourse to part-time work can be viewed as a kind of transition, allowing them to establish a place in the labour market (Anxo and Daune-Richard, 1991; Daune-Richard, 1993).

30 In addition to the struggle to achieve the conditions (in the form of the six-hour day, and the father's quota) for equality of the sexes, there was the important struggle for economic and industrial democracy. The co-determination accord signed by the LO and the white-collar unions in the PTK and SAF in the early 1980s was much more 'pragmatic' than the 1970s industrial democracy campaigners envisaged, and the wage earner fund that was to have advanced economic democracy fell well short of the original idea.

31 The percentage of children from 3 to 6 with day-care spaces in the public system rose from 30 per cent in 1980 to 48 per cent in 1990. The share in private care fell from 20 per cent in 1980 to 7 per cent in 1990 (*Inquiry into the Needs of Children*). In the same period the fertility rate rose from 1.6 to 2.1 per woman in the childbearing years with no attendant drop in women's labour force participation rates.

32 In 1980, 29.6 per cent of the fathers of children under two took parental leave of an average of forty-five days. By 1992 both the percentage taking leave (48.3) and the average duration (sixty-three days) had risen (Arves-Parès, 1996). Various authors have examined the obstacles that fathers face in exercising their right to leave (Näsman, 1992; Haas and Hwang, 1993).

33 Official figures have usually been below this number because around 6 per cent of the unemployed labour force were involved in some kind of labour market program and therefore are not counted as unemployed. Öberg and Danielsson provide a finer-grained analysis, which breaks the decade into four periods. Between 1990 and 1993, 600,000 jobs disappeared, mainly from the private sector and largely in the male-dominated goods-producing sector. In 1994–95 the latter experienced some recovery, since 130,000 (net) jobs were created, all in the private sector. Between 1995 and 1997, however, 110,000 jobs were lost, most of which were in the municipal and county public sector. At the end of the 1990s there was modest job growth in both sectors (*Svenska Dagbladet*, 30.8.98).

34 Reference to the third road was to indicate that the Swedes were trying to steer a course between Thatcher's monetarism and the early Mitterrand government's misguided return to Keynesianism. The main policy instrument was an aggressive devaluation, which, in addition to more modest devaluations of the previous government, meant a fall in the value of the Swedish krona by some 20 per cent. On this and other significant changes

to the Social Democrats' economic policy see Pontusson (1994) and Huber and Stephens (1998).

35 See especially Pontusson (1992 and 1994) for a good discussion of the crisis at the heart of the labour movement.

36 Hinnfors argues, however, that there was internal debate on this question and that in 1984 the party was close to giving up its insistence on public provision (1995: 218).

37 The counter-argument included references to the absence of childcare at night, to high fees in some municipalities, and to the greater ability of well-educated people to jump the queue. See, for example Aina Westin's reply in the *Pysslingen* debate (debates, 1983/84, #41: 115). Westin went on to argue that a care allowance would contribute to labour market polarization: those with higher education would remain in the labour market with places in municipal day care, while LO parents (*note*: no reference to mothers – quite typical of the Swedish discourse) would be directed to go home and collect the 'pin money' offered by a care allowance.

38 Although the LO's official position at this time clearly reflected the continued predominance of the male norm, the tide was beginning to turn as feminists started to mobilize within the LO. See Mahon (1996) for an account of their progress in changing the LO's line.

39 Children of students were included. In addition, they renewed the promise to provide children at home or in family home care access to pre-school from the age of four.

40 When the coalition took office, it abolished *Lex Pysslingen*. The Social Democrats did not restore it when they returned to office in 1994, though they did ensure that private day-care centres had to follow the same rules as the public centres if they were to receive municipal subsidies. Although still small, private day care grew in the 1990s. Thus, while in 1991 those employed in private day care constituted only 2.5 per cent of the total day-care workforce, by 1997 that figure had grown to 9.2 per cent. (*Dagens Nyheter*, 12.11.99)

41 This division was openly reflected in the media debate occasioned by the publication of an article by Bengt Westerberg, leader of the Liberals, in a prominent daily. Westerberg mused about the relative strengths and weaknesses of parental leave versus the version of the care allowance that had formed part of the electoral platform of the three main parties. Representatives of both Conservative and Centre parties were quick to chastize him publicly for breaking ranks. It should also be noted that the Liberals floated the idea of rolling all support into the form of a childcare allowance that could be used to finance any option.

42 That the 1991 election led to a decline in women's representation in Parliament (reflecting the masculine profile of the parties of the right) served only to strengthen the women's movement that had been gaining strength, especially within the LO but also in general discourse. There was even talk of the formation of a new women's party, but the Liberals, the Social Democrats, and the smaller Left and Green parties were able to retain their role as the primary political representatives of the feminist line. A feminist network – the 'Support Stockings' – was created, whose leading representatives include journalist Maria Pia Boethius and economist Agneta Stark. When the Social Democrats returned to office, the network disappeared, and many of its key spokespersons were absorbed into the government. Ulmanen (1998) is quite critical of the Stockings for not developing an institutional base. They have had an effect on the policies of the Social Democrats, however, inter alia, on the question of social versus personal service jobs (Mahon, 1999b).

43 The 'daddys' group' called for a minimum of three father's months, so that children could learn that 'men care.' See Bergqvist et al., (1999: 145).

44 Although the Centre party has been consistent in its advocacy, it did feel it necessary to differentiate between its position and that of the KDS. Thus, in its 1994 policy statement it pointed out that the Christian Democrats laid particular stress on the right of 'one parent' to choose to stay at home. The Centre party presents itself as the party that would leave to parents the right to choose either option. It is also the case that the leader of the KDS made introduction of a care allowance the price of his party's participation in the Bildt government.

45 When the government's fiscal position improved, it promised to return the rate to 80 per cent as of January 1998.

46 In the spring budget of 1997 the government promised an extra 4 billion kronor transfer for 1997–98 with an additional 8 billion kronor in each of the subsequent three years. The 1999 spring budget brought in by the new, minority Social Democratic government, dependent on support from the Left and Green parties, was even more generous.

47 Municipal governments can determine local fee structures. Some substantially raised the fees paid by higher-income families. At a certain point, such fees become an incentive to leave the public sector and opt for cheaper in-home care. As the LO argued, moreover, they constitute a disincentive for women to increase their labour force participation.

48 The version to which the three parties agreed included a sliding scale with a higher upper limit than either the Social Democrats or the Left party wanted. The Green party agreed, however, that the money thus saved

would be put towards improving the quality of daycare (*Svenska Dagbladet*, 03.30.00).

49 There are signs, however, that mothers of young children are finding the labour market more difficult: their unemployment rate has remained significantly above average (*Dagens Nyheter*, 3.8.00). Another study, commissioned by four key blue-collar industrial unions, suggested that both mothers and fathers were finding it more difficult to utilize parental leave. Lean production means that they face pressure from fellow workers, as well as from employers (*Dagens Nyheter*, 16.3.00).

50 In the 1980s the left could counter the OECD's 'Euro-sclerosis' arguments (that mass unemployment was due to the European welfare state) by pointing to countries such as Sweden. When Sweden joined the mass unemployment club, it became much harder to maintain the sense that there was an alternative to an American-style 'job machine.' This pessimism is clear in Esping-Andersen's recent work (1999). While recognizing that the Swedish model offers better pay and greater security than the American one, he is now more concerned about the growing tax burden apparently required to sustain the model. He fails, however, to consider the possibility of post-Fordist restructuring in this sector, which could simultaneously increase efficiency and improve the quality of public sector jobs. See Mahon (1999b) for a critique.

51 Inger Ohlsson, former president of the nurses' union.

52 They include the unions representing office cleaners and hotel and restaurant workers.

53 Andersson stopped short of supporting subsidized domestic services, but he did back the idea of reducing payroll taxes for businesses in the service sector, such as restaurants, hairdressers, car repair, and laundries, that lighten the burden for two-earner families.

54 The aim is to reduce involuntary part-time employment and the large number of replacement jobs.

55 The Conservatives, Liberals, and Christian Democrats have united around the proposal that households would pay half the cost of domestic help and the government would pay the remainder, up to a maximum of 25,000 kronor. This plan, they argue, would eliminate the black market and create between 50,000 and 100,000 jobs.

Chapter Seven

Europe: An Actor without a Role

George Ross

The Community has no powers in the domain of family policy. The word 'family' does not occur in the Treaty on European Union. The Member States alone are competent in this domain and free to organize family policy as they deem fit. Moreover, even in the Member States family policy has many different facets. While most Member States of the European Union recognize the importance of the family and the State's obligations in its regard, few countries have a family policy as such that is explicitly distinct from other sectors of social protection.

Teirlinck, 1994: 9

These sobering facts establish the context within which any discussion of family and childcare policy in the European Union (EU) must be discussed. The EU is a unique organization, whose Member States 'pool' parts of their sovereignty, through negotiated treaties, to confront common problems. What is not pooled remains reserved to national sovereignty. The overwhelming bulk of the matters thus combined have been trade and market related, while social policy is one important area reserved to Member States. 'Family policy,' as part of social policy, is not even recognized by all Member States as a legitimate area for public policy, even though some things under the rubric are public matters almost everywhere.

At first sight, then, discussing EU family and childcare policy is fruitless, since there is likely to be none. However, it turns out not to be true. Although it has had very little treaty power in the area, the EU (and the European Community (EC) before it) has made a number of forays into family policy. The particularities of the European political system provide part of an explanation. Both the European Commission and the European Court of Justice (ECJ) were designed to be advocates of more 'Europeanization.' For example, they were to work towards further integration by proposing new activity where treaties are vague (which they are in a number of places) and through the accretion of jurisprudence. Thus, despite the constraints of Europe's treaties and the interests of Member States in zealously protecting their sovereignty, what Europe is politically, what it can do, and how it does what it does have never been definitively fixed. At certain moments – the early 1960s, the 1970s, between 1985 and 1992 – it has been possible for European-level political entrepreneurs to argue plausibly that new policy areas, even those quite peripheral to market matters, should be incorporated into Europe's evolving mandate. Europe's constitutional elasticity, the entrepreneurial skills of European leaders, and the flexibility of European institutions have allowed the Community to try to move on family policy and childcare, with certain small, subtle successes.

The distinction is often made between 'hard' and 'soft' politics in European matters. Regulations, Council Decisions, and Directives are 'hard.' They are legislation binding Member States in areas for which the treaty base is evident. 'Soft' politics, which is primarily done by the Commission (and, to a lesser extent, the European Parliament) mainly consists of non-binding inciting and agitation on matters of common concern that treaties do not clearly cover. European institutions, the Commission in particular, have tried to 'incite,' 'inform,' and 'animate' policy debate in the social policy realm, particularly in the decade of the Delors Commissions (1985–95). Europe has thus done a significant amount of soft politics in the family policy and childcare area, via networking, informing, solemnly declaring, and officially recommending. In some instances the eventual result has been Community legislation and other mandatory measures.

Since it is important to situate social policy – and family and childcare matters within social policy – in the history of the EU, in the first section of this chapter the emergence of social policy concerns in the context of the first quarter century of the Community is reviewed, with particular attention paid to those affecting women at work. Action in this area was derived directly from the Treaty of Rome's article 119, which mandated equal pay. Out of that treaty base, the EC constructed an increasingly expansive policy and judicial discourse on equal opportunities for women in the labour market. These, were then extended in the 1980s and 1990s to incorporate caring work. Thus, representations of women's work have been at the core of EC activities in the area of childcare. In the second section these extensions are considered, with emphasis on their interconnection and their discursive contents. Europe was not only making a claim for greater influence in these policy realms, but also doing so with its own voice. European accomplishments in translating this voice into practice have been less than spectacular, yet there have been accomplishments, as described in the third section. Finally, the negotiations between Social Partners concerning parental leave are examined. This illustration of modest success is important because of its consecration of the Commission's specific discourse on reconciling family and work.

The Beginnings of Europe's Role

It was no accident that the 1958 Treaty of Rome allowed only the slimmest of openings to Community social policy initiatives. The first stage of European integration was a commitment to policies, such as a common market, common external tariff, and Common Agricultural Policy, designed to promote specific *national* models of development and citizenship regimes. Within these national models, social policy was a regulatory mechanism and channel for redistributing the fruits of growth, helping to consolidate post-war democratic institutions. In other words, matters of social citizenship remained the responsibility of individual member states.

However, the treaty was not totally silent on the elements of citizenship, especially equality (Collins, 1975). Free mobility of labour was the counterpart of free movement of goods and capital. The treaty enjoined national social security programs from limiting worker mobility, leading to the first social legislation in 1958 and litigation through the ECJ. In time, there was a small body of rules governing workers' rights to move across the Community, to residence in Member States, and to equal treatment in hiring and firing, remuneration and other working conditions. Article 118, on the need 'to promote improved working conditions and an improved standard of living for the workers' was the major social clause, but it established few instruments beyond proper functioning of the common market for doing so. The Commission acquired little power beyond cooperating with the member states by conducting studies, issuing opinions, and organizing consultations.[1]

Article 119 came to be a significant exception. The article states that 'each member state shall during the first stage ensure and subsequently maintain the application of the principle that men and women should receive equal pay for equal work.' This principle became the basis of virtually all the Community's subsequent efforts in the broad area of equal opportunities, as well as the areas of childcare and family policy.[2]

There was brief renewal of interest in further European integration in the early 1970s, and expanding European-level social citizenship rights was part of this phase. Preliminary guidelines for a Community social policy program were set down in 1971, followed by a Social Action Program in 1974, in which Member States pledged to adopt a number of measures over three years (Collins, 1975: 212ff). Among these were 'action for the purpose of achieving equality between men and women as regards access to employment and vocational training and advancement and as regards working conditions, including pay ... [and] ... to ensure that the family responsibilities of all concerned may be reconciled with their job aspirations.'[3] In the Program it was further noted that one cause of inequality between women and men was 'the lack of adequate facilities for working mothers' and that there was a need to give 'immediate priority to the problems of providing facilities to enable women to reconcile family responsibilities with job aspirations.'

These initiatives were both the first Community ventures towards family and childcare policy and the introduction of the idea of 'reconciliation of work and family.' Reconciliation, like many catchphrases, admits of a wide range of different interpretations. Indeed, versatility makes the term useful.[4] In its original 1974 declension it pointed to the need for public policies to help *women* reconcile work with family responsibilities. The assumption was that women would have to make the primary adjustments, but that public policy could devise programs to help them. This definition of reconciliation resembled standard welfare state discourse. It socialized the 'costs' of child-rearing as solely the responsibility of mothers. It avoided any reference to the more intractable problems due to gender roles inside and outside work. Over the years the Community's use of 'reconciliation' would change in different contexts and at different times, depending upon the general policy concerns of the moment. It would also change according to where it was used within EC and EU discussion.

The burst of social policy activity was brief. Economic difficulties and rising unemployment stimulated new preoccupation with national matters plus resistance to European solutions. Further, the expansion from six to nine Member States in 1973 led to chronic conflicts over budgets that paralysed Community decision-making. In consequence, governments increasingly subverted those social policy measures that were adopted, and few new social measures were passed by the Council of Ministers.[5] Proposals for workers' participation (e.g., the Vredeling Directive of 1980) were stopped, as well as Regulations on working time (part-time and temporary work). Perhaps the most important area of progress was workplace health and safety.

Openings for action under article 119 were broader than those in other social policy areas of the treaty, and legislation based on it was one of the few substantial outcomes. From 1973 – when few Member States had laws on equal opportunities – to 1986 five Directives were passed. The first (75/117/EEC) was on 'the approximation of the laws of the Member States relating to the application of the principle of equal pay for men and women.' It was immediately followed in 1976 by a second on 'the implementation of the principle of equal treatment for men and women as regards access to employment, vocational training and promotion' (76/207/EEC), which expanded Community purview beyond equal pay towards broader challenges to gender discrimination. Next, in 1978 there was a directive 'on the progressive implementation of the principle of equal treatment for men and women in matters of social security' (79/7/EEC), including health insurance, health and safety at work, invalidity, old age, occupational diseases, and social assistance. Finally, in 1986 a Directive 'on the implementation of the principle of equal treatment for men and women in occupational social security schemes' (supplementary pensions and other non-public social protection arrangements; 86/378/EEC) was passed, as was Directive 86/613, which extended equal treatment to the self-employed (including agricultural work).[6]

Simultaneously, the ECJ (in the first *Defrenne vs. Sabena* case, 43/75) issued a ruling on article 119 that expanded possibilities for Community action on equal opportunities (Hoskyns, 1996: chapters 4–5). The ECJ announced that article 119 was meant, first, to avoid situations in which Member States with equal opportunities legislation might suffer as a result of competition with those without it. It added, 'this provision forms part of the social objectives of the Community, which is not merely an economic union, but is at the same time intended, by common action, to ensure social progress and seek the constant improvement of the living and working conditions of their peoples' (ECJ, Case 43/75, para. 8–10; Ellis, 1994). ECJ rulings also made article 119 directly applicable throughout the Community, thereby inviting individual suits. Any employee could invoke the article against any employer. The court also widened the definition of 'pay' over time to include pay-connected entitlements, such as bonuses, sick pay, and the like.[7]

The Directives and court decisions successively expanded the scope of the principle of equal opportunities. The equal treatment Directive (76/207/EEC) was particularly important because it elaborated the concept of 'indirect discrimination.' Although the concept is not clearly defined in this or subsequent Directives, according to a 1991 Commission clarification, it 'is presumed to exist once an apparently neutral measure in fact has a preponderant effect on workers of a given sex – without there being any need to establish the intention to discriminate.'[8] While the language here reveals the link to traditional concerns – workers are the category at issue – it is not difficult to see how reflection upon indirect discrimination might stretch to matters outside the workplace. Indeed, this is what happened. This body of article 119 legislation and jurisprudence provided the legal underpinnings of Community endeavours in the areas of family and childcare policies.

The existence of the 'Equality Directives' caused the Commission to establish in 1981 the Advisory Committee on Equal Opportunities for Women and Men, while simultaneously strengthening its internal Equal Opportunities Unit, established in 1976 in Directorate General (DG) V – Social Affairs.[9] The major initial task of the Equal Opportunities Unit, through its legal staff, was to monitor the implementation of the equality Directives with an eye to bringing laggard member states to the ECJ.[10] It also was charged with preparing possible Community legislation. After strengthening the Equal Opportunities Unit, the EC produced the First Action Program on the Promotion of Equal Opportunities for Women (1982–85) designed to serve as a mandate for the unit (Com [81] 758 final). This First Action Program also prepared the equal opportunities work of the Delors Commissions.

The First Action Program on Equal Opportunities for Women brought initial Commission recognition of the connection between childcare and equal opportunities. The suggestion was made in point A7 to extend 'parental leave and leave for family reasons and at the same time to build up the network of public (childcare) facilities and services.'[11] The Commission defined its purpose to be to study 'the evolution [of facilities and services] and then propose measures for maintaining and extending [them].'[12] An initial survey by Camille Piachault, *Daycare Facilities and Services for Children under the Age of 3 in the European Community,* was submitted in 1984. Pursuant to the Action Program, the Commission also proposed Community legislation on parental leave and leave for family reasons in 1983 (Com (83) 686 final; amended as Com (84) 631 final). This Directive came as close to family policy legislation as any Commission action to that point, but it did not pass the Council of Ministers.[13]

Reconciliation and Its Declensions

What was most interesting about the Commission efforts in the early 1980s was their language.[14] The parental leave Directive provides a good example. Couched in standard welfare statist terms, it was proposed to prevent disparities between different provisions for parental leave in Member States from distorting the functioning of the Common Market (and necessitating upward harmonization under article 117) and to promote equal treatment for men and women as regards access to employment, vocational training and promotion, and working conditions (*Social Europe,* 3/91: 135). In the words of a member of the Equal Opportunities Unit, 'in the official point of view the problem of equal opportunities was mostly explained in terms of arrears ... which could be bypassed if women would get a fair chance.' It took rather more time for recognition to spread that 'equal treatment on unequals only reproduced the existing inequality between women and men' (Boddendijk, 1991: 94).

In the second Action Program of the Promotion of Equal Opportunities for Women (1986–90), prepared just prior to the first Delors Commission in 1985, the language began to change, as the EC developed its own vision of women's civil rights and social citizenship. The Commission and the broader Community returned to the concept of reconciliation and for nearly a decade moved towards more involvement in family policy and childcare areas. In its official sense reconciliation was the bridge concept that allowed the Commission to slide towards new areas whose treaty base was shakier than the solidly grounded Directives of the 1970s. The logic, however, was clear. In order for women and men to be equal in the labour market (remember that since 'pay' was mentioned in article 119, the Community's expansion had already been significant), the indirect, non-market relationships between them had to be reconciled. Inside the Commission, reconciliation took on a considerably stronger connotation. Family and work should be reconciled in ways that promoted greater equality in both realms for women. This notion pointed at power and inequality both in the work-place and in the family unit. It was a clear shift away from a traditional welfare statist vision. How far reaching it could be can be seen in later remarks by one of the Advisory Committee's leaders, who noted that pursuing equal treatment in traditional ways, 'only reproduced the existing inequality between women and men. And since most women and men start their societal career from different ... points, it must be clear that a genuine equal opportunities policy has to start from the premise that in the long run the equality of women and men is fostered by a policy by which in the short and medium run unequals are treated in an unequal way and equals are treated equally' (Boddendijk, 1991: 95). These words of an insider, at least, expressed a progressive posi-tion on gender inequality issues far from the more traditional dis-courses on family wages, reproduction, and the gender division of labour prevalent in Member State discussions. Implied was a strategy of promoting affirmative action ('positive action' in EC discourse). Actions appropriate to such words were less easy to define, however, at least in the early 1980s. Nonetheless, as different Commission and para-Commission teams were assembled, they tended to attract policy activists on the cutting edge of new conceptualization and politics.[15] At the root of these efforts was DG V – Social Affairs, trying to animate and agitate so as to open paths to future activity.[16] Much of what DG V initially did, therefore, was 'soft.' It produced reports, monitored the workings of laws relevant to equal opportunities, published, net-worked, and funded groups and activities.

The emergence of new language about reconciliation in these activi-ties, however, was no accident. Because the Commission needed enthusiastic troops for its animation campaigns, it became a welcom-ing site for practically minded feminists. Moreover, the later 1970s marked the end of the post-war boom. Average growth rates fell by half, unemployment began to rise, and the labour market position of women began to deteriorate. Unemployment, employers' search for flexibility, and the rapid growth in atypical work, often without the legal and contractual protection of full-time employment, prompted new concerns about the crumbling labour market position for women. Next, for a host of reasons – an ageing work force, the foreseeable high costs of welfare states resulting from the significant decrease in the working population, problems of productivity – demographic con-cerns reappeared on the agendas of certain Member States, particularly those that had traditionally had 'family policy' directed towards promoting higher birth rates. Pro-natalism, of course, could provide arguments for measures to remove women from the labour force altogether, and this prospect provided yet another reason for institutions that were constitutionally committed to equal opportunities to develop new ways of arguing the cause. The beginnings of European action in the general area of family and childcare policy issues thus coincided with the economic crisis.

Most important, however, discursive shifts were connected with the articulation of equal opportunities activities inside the Commission. The Equal Opportunities Unit of DG V gained more prominence as staff grew, budgets rose, and publications multiplied. It acquired new capacities in the family and childcare policy areas. One new approach after 1982 was to sponsor networks in different sub-areas to research, publicize, and organize specific matters. Thus, after preparatory work – the 1985 *Piachault Report* plus an important seminar in Rome on Parental Leave and Collective Childcare in the same year – the Commission's Second Medium-Term Action Program on Equal Opportunities made recommendations for action on childcare facilities and set up an expert Childcare Network, the sixth such creation. The Equal Opportunities Unit's growing prominence and movement into new areas is shown in the growth of networks in table 7.1.

The Childcare Network was composed of twelve national experts coordinated by Peter Moss, a British specialist affiliated with the University of London's Institute of Education. Moss's strongest commitments were to children's rights and the importance of early childhood education.[17] Thus, while he understood the logic of the Commission's movement towards childcare matters via equal opportunities legislation and jurisprudence around article 119, he saw childcare issues in quite a different light. The Commission was obliged to justify its approach in terms of labour markets and the indirect determinants of gender discrimination in the labour market, but he understood the causality in a different way: gender and other relations in the family plus early childhood education shaped societal patterns, rather than the other way around. From this point of departure, he assumed that one way to eliminate labour market discrimination would be to change gender roles in the care relationships in the family and in early childhood education. Were both male and female roles in these relationships to become more equal, particularly in the distribution of caring responsibilities, then labour market shifts could also ensue. Other members of the Network shared many of these convictions, but, like

TABLE 7.1
European networks on equal opportunities

Expert Network on the application of the Equality Directives (1982)
Monitors application of directives; gathers data on national equal opportunities legislation and legal decisions

Network on the position of women in the labour market
Focuses on increasing women's share of employment, upgrading employment opportunities, and reducing the obstacles to women's occupational integration, especially by ensuring a harmonious balance between work and family life

Network for positive action in enterprises
Affirmative action and information circulation on such matters

Steering committee for equal opportunities in broadcasting
Monitors employment in broadcasting and promotes affirmative action

Working party on equal opportunities in education (1986)
Efforts to develop curriculum and teaching in schools to promote equal opportunities

Childcare Network (1986) (Name changed to Network on Childcare and Other Measures
  to Reconcile Work and Family Responsibilities in 1991)
Collects and assesses data on childcare and runs campaign to make people aware of the importance of childcare

Network on vocational training programs for women (IRIS) (1988)
Promotes vocational training for women and access for women to existing training schemes

Network on women in the decision-making process (1990)
Analyses obstacles facing women in decision-making and devises strategies for coping with them

Network on family and work (1994)
Identifies, studies, stimulates, and disseminates exemplary practices in companies and organizations that relate to an improved balance between family life and work; information gathering and publicizing on such matters

---

Source: *Newsletter of the European Network 'Families and Work,'* December 1994, DG V

most experts, they were convinced that their ideas about childcare were informed by solid science, whose conclusions made their work in Europe very urgent. Policy experts are often advocates and activists, after all. They try to do politics as well as advise politicians.

The language of the Childcare Network's first large production, the

Consolidated Report to the European Commission on Child-Care and Equality of Opportunity (Moss, 1988) illustrated the commitment of these experts. Significantly, the first chapter is entitled 'Childcare, Gender and Inequality,' and they proceed, while presenting data about women and men's work situations, to imply that gender discrimination in the labour market is connected to the gender division of labour in the family. In subsequent chapters they support this thesis, before turning, in part 2, to a review of the history and contemporary situation of childcare services in Europe. In its first pages, the Network's discourse is displayed quite clearly, as the following citations show:

> In its Second Action Program, the Commission emphasizes that the sharing of family and occupational responsibilities, particularly the development of adequate childcare facilities ... [is] a sine qua non for the promotion of true equality at work ... The Network's starting point has therefore been to examine the current distribution of family responsibilities, especially those concerned with the care of children; and to consider ways of promoting a more equal distribution, that does not disadvantage women ...
>
> The Network has considered the distribution of responsibilities between mothers and fathers. We accept the view that 'caring for and bringing up children should be regarded as a joint responsibility of the father and mother.' We agree, too, with the Commission that sharing between parents 'is an essential part of strategies designed to increase equality in the labour market.' (Moss, 1988:1)

The report, however, is not limited to commentary on sharing between parents and on the role of childcare services. Concern is also expressed about how employment can be adapted to enable parents, fathers as well as mothers, to combine and reconcile parenthood and employment; issues such as fathers' involvement in childcare, childcare services, and employment adaptations are closely linked. The achievement of equality requires action on all three. Without proper sharing of childcare responsibilities, women with children will be at a major disadvantage in competing for jobs and may become heavily concentrated in the poorest-quality jobs. 'Mothers, or indeed fathers, should also be able to combine employment and family responsibilities with minimum stress. Policies should be directed to increasing their "job satisfaction" in both employment and parenthood. Finally, childcare services should be more than a place to "park" children while their parents are out at work ... there must be a concern with quality as well as quantity, and with ensuring that services meet all aspects of children's needs' (Moss, 1988: 3–4).

The Delors Commissions: Social and Family Policy

From 1985 to 1995 successive Commissions of the EU, presided over by Jacques Delors, seized upon and expanded Europe's small social citizenship legacy and were particularly active in equal opportunities matters. The Commission took seriously the second Action Program on Equal Opportunity, including the program's stress on the sharing of family and occupational responsibilities and the development of adequate childcare facilities, as cited above. The general assumption was that more was at issue than public policy and private-firm outlooks. Work and family had to be reconciled, and to that end the caring and rearing of children ought to be the joint responsibility of mothers and fathers.

Family Policy

The Commission's entry point into the family policy discussion came as a result of a Communication, *Problems of social security – areas of common interest* (July 1986). The connection was made via demographic trends in the Community and their implications for the future, then being discussed widely in Member States. In its Communication, the Commission suggested the establishment of high-level consultations of national officials involved in family policy (Teirlinck, 1994: 9). The 1988 Copenhagen European Council accepted this recommendation, with the French leading the field in deploying pro-natalist rhetoric (in the Commission's words, later, 'the French delegation mentioned the disturbing demographic situation in Europe and emphasized that Europe could not retain its political, economic and cultural position in the world without a renewal of its demographic dynamism'). (*Social Europe*, 1/94: 121). In 1989 the Commission wrote a specific Communication on family policy, in conjunction with Council discussion (Com (89) 363 final).

In this Communication the Commission used the setting of demographic alarm to introduce new official language. It stressed, in the first part, the socio-economic tendencies behind Europe's demographic changes, reviewing the decline of 'typical' families, increasing female labour force participation, companies' search for new flexibility, and the resort to atypical work, often done by women. The resulting imbalances between female and male participation in family life were then highlighted as important in themselves, leading to the suggestion that it 'would therefore seem advisable to examine the effects of different forms of work organizations and the status of workers on their family and social life, in particular the balance between work and family life. The problem of sharing family and occupational responsibilities and the care of children, particularly in connection with the integration or reintegration of people who have left the labour market, will ... become more acute.'[18]

This stretching of the traditional trade and market mandate then led to the suggestion that the Community should become more involved in a key component of family policies: childcare facilities. The second part of the Communication was entitled, 'Recognition of the role of the family and action in its favour by the public authorities,' and listed, among other things, was a series of precedents that might allow the Commission and the Community to become more active in such areas. The number of citations to the work of various members of the Childcare Network indicated the growing influence of its work.

In the conclusion of the Communication, justifying new Community action in the family and childcare policy areas, the Commission noted that 'The legitimacy of Community interest is based not on ideology but on the acknowledgement and methods of a Community action at family level; the appropriateness of such Community interest is based less on ideological grounds but more on such objective facts as the economic role of the family, the importance of family as the touchstone of solidarity between generations, the irreversible desire for equality between men and women, and the wish of women to have complete access to working life.' Repetition that ideology was not the centre of new Community concerns, followed by several claims that some might interpret as 'ideological,' reveals some Commission discomfort. Family and childcare policy areas were a tightrope for the Community.

Substantive suggestions were made about future Community action, such as continuation of actions seeking to inform and increase awareness, particularly through the production of regular information on demography and measures concerning families (with greater use of the existing network of experts). The Community should also begin to take into account the family dimension in the establishment of appropriate Community policies, a first step towards the 'mainstreaming' of such matters.[19] Finally, there should be regular concertation at Community level, centring on '(i) the impact of other Community policies on the family, notably on child protection; (ii) reconciliation between professional life, family life and the sharing of family responsibilities; (iii) measures taken in favour of certain categories of family, notably single parent and large families; (iv) attention to the most deprived families.'[20]

The Commission's Communication to the Council of Ministers and the Social Affairs Council's response is interesting. The Childcare Network advocated reconciliation, so as to change the gender division of labour in family care work. The Commission toned down this recommendation and tried to reformulate it to fit its own mandates, but it also used it at critical points. The purpose of this Communication was to make a case for greater Community involvement in the family policy area. The Social Affairs Council's response to the Communication, although it took up some of the Commission's discourse (most notably, parts of the 'ideology' paragraph), was significantly watered down in terms of reconciliation. The Council agreed to limited Community involvement in information gathering and circulation on key issues concerning families; to 'inclusion of the family dimension in the establishment of appropriate Community policies, for example, in the freedom of movement of persons and equality between men and women' to a much more intensive exchange of information at Community level concerning the impact of Community policies on family; and to measures to implement equal opportunities (particularly on access to the labour market, plus the possibilities of limited action on family matters) (*Social Politics*, 1/94: 128–9). In 1988 a European Observatory on National Family Policies for gathering data was also created.[21]

The Social Charter

The social policy focal point of the Delors Commissions, and of the social citizenship commitments in European integration more generally, was the 1989 Charter on the Fundamental Social Rights of Workers (*Social Europe*, 1/90). The Social Charter was a 'solemn Declaration' with no direct constitutional standing in itself. Instead, it was designed to set out the maximum possible scope within existing treaty bases for European-level social policy action. It should be read as a set of proposals for European social policy action. At a deeper level, however, it was also a blueprint for what the Delors Commissions believed *could* be squeezed out of treaty wording on social policy matters, were the

Council of Ministers willing to cooperate. Point 16 of the charter began as follows: 'Equal treatment for men and women must be assured. Equal opportunities for men and women must be developed. To this end, action should be intensified to ensure the implementation of the principle of equality between men and women as regards, in particular, access to employment, remuneration, working conditions, social protection, education, vocational training and career development. Measures should also be developed enabling men and women to reconcile their occupational and family obligations.' The last phrase in point 16 is particularly interesting. The Commission believed that existing treaty stipulations would allow European-level action to equalize treatment of men and women not only in work and in the labour market, but also in the social conditions of family and child rearing that affected entry and position in the labour market.

In the Action Program that followed the Social Charter forty-seven different Community instruments in social policy were proposed, an exhaustive list of all of the measures that the Commission judged were legally possible under the pre-Maastricht Treaty, and all had been submitted by the end of 1991 (Com (89) 568 final). The Commission knew full well, however, that only those that could be dealt with under qualified majority decision rules (essentially workplace health and safety issues) would pass the Council of Ministers. The United Kingdom, and on occasion other countries, would block the remainder. The fate of the most important Social Charter Action Program initiative is summarized in table 7.2. In addition, the Commission reintroduced the Directive on Parental Leave, which became the first measure to be successfully bargained by the Social Partners in 1994 (see below).

Of the several Action Program Directives directly or indirectly pertinent to reconciling family and work, only one of the three concerning atypical work passed, although a second later became subject to negotiation between the Social Partners. The European Works Council Directive was eventually passed under the Maastricht Social Protocol and would provide an important precedent for other areas, including childcare. The only significant Directive passed in the immediate area of family policy was on the 'Protection at work of pregnant women or women who have recently given birth,' proposed in September 1990. The Council resolution (October 1992) watered down the Commission's proposal, particularly in the realm of compensation, but it nonetheless granted the right to a minimum of fourteen weeks' paid maternity leave, with the level of pay at least equivalent to sick pay

TABLE 7.2
The most important social action program measures

Proposal	Introductory date	Result
Atypical work 1: Working conditions	June 1990	Resubmitted under Maastricht Social Protocol, agreed by social partners 1996, passed 97/81/ EC
Atypical work 2: Distortion of competition	June 1990	None
Atypical work 3: Health and safety (qualified majority – qm)	June 1990	Adopted 6/91 (91\383\EEC)
Working time (qm)	September 1990	Adopted 11/93 (93\1041\EEC)
Pregnant workers (qm)	November 1990	Adopted 11/92 (92\85\EEC)
European works councils in transnational corporations	February 1991	Adopted 9/94 (94\45\EEC)
Explicit employment contract	January 1991	Adopted 11/91 (91\533\EEC)
Updating of 1975 directive about collective layoffs	October 1991	Adopted 8/92 (92\56\EEC)

Source: See *Social Europe*, 3/94: 108–14, annex 1

(*Social Europe*, 3/91: 148ff.). Despite the watering down, passage of the Directive was very important in a number of Member States where such protection was minimal.

In the pertinent softer sections of the Action Program there was a review of the EC's general involvement in equal opportunities matters, signalling the preparation of the Third Equal Opportunities Action Program (1990–94). An earlier proposal from 1988 on 'the burden of proof in the area of equal pay and equal treatment for women and men,' which had been folded into the Action Program, also remained on the Council table.[22] A Directive 'On the protection of pregnant women at work' was announced. Also listed were a 'Recommendation concerning child care' and a 'Code of good contact on the protection of pregnancy and maternity' (*Social Europe*, 3/91: 119–20). The Third Action Program, itself, contained a predictable list of goals on equality in pay and work, access to the labour market, and broader anti-discrimination efforts (*Social Europe*, 3/91: 161–76). The most important new program included was New Opportunities for Women (NOW), financed by the European Social Fund and designed to help women to start a small business or acquire training. NOW also involved considerable support for the development of childcare facilities and training in the childcare area.[23]

When specific childcare matters were raised in the Third Equal Opportunities Program, they were couched in the reconciliation of working and family life discourse developed by the Equal Opportunities Unit and the Childcare Network. The major paragraph is worth reading in this respect: 'It has become apparent during the course of recent years that the insufficiency of childcare provision constitutes a barrier to the occupational integration of women with children on the labour market and that, in order for such women to be properly integrated, considerable progress in the reconciliation of working and family life needs to be made. This situation also requires that men – as well as women – should be able to benefit from the full range of measures directed towards the reconciliation of working and family life and thus be enabled to take on a fair share of family responsibilities.' At least in its assigned area, therefore, the approach of the Childcare Network had made breakthroughs. The actual work of the Network was given a more precise mandate in the Third Action Program: to reinforce the NOW initiative, monitor developments, evaluate policy options, collect and disseminate information, and establish criteria for the definition of quality in childcare services.

Perhaps the major result of the Third Action Program in the family and childcare policy area, which the Childcare Network influenced, was a Council Recommendation of 1992 on childcare (92/241/EEC). This was a classic example of soft law, a series of solemn commitments and injunctions without legislative constraint to make them effective. The 'whereases' in the Recommendation's preamble give a good sense of the claims that the Commission had assembled by 1992 to justify activity in the childcare area. It began with article 16 of the 1989 Social Charter, the Third Action Program, and the 1989 Commission Communication on family policies, then set out a range of socio-political reasons to support more action. The reconciliation vocabulary was important throughout the 'whereas' introduction, including: 'Whereas child-care methods, parental leave and maternity leave form part of a whole which enables people to combine their family responsibilities and occupational ambitions ... Whereas the reconciliation of occupational, family and upbringing responsibilities arising from the care of children has to be viewed in a wide perspective which also takes into account the particular interests and needs of children at different age levels, where it is important, to achieve this, to encourage an overall policy aimed at enabling such reconciliation to occur.'[24]

The practicable parts of the document, however, reverted to more standard welfare state discourses. The Commission underlined shortages and deficiencies in childcare provision in Member States, noted that better services could facilitate freedom of movement of workers and mobility in the European labour market, and concluded with reference to ways that the reformed Structural Fund policies (primarily NOW) contributed to equal opportunity. But reconciliation discourse had made inroads even in such welfare statist pronouncements. Areas of initiatives for Member States included the provision of childcare services; special leave for employed parents with responsibility for the care and upbringing of children; and making the environment, structure, and organization of work responsive to the needs of workers with children. Finally, Member States should promote initiatives to enable women and men to share their occupational, family, and upbringing responsibilities arising from the care of children. Along with exhortations to Member States to promote 'best practice' childcare, it was also recommended in article 16 that 'Member States should promote and encourage, with due respect for freedom of the individual, increased participation by men [in childcare], in order to achieve a more equal sharing of parental responsibilities between men and women and to enable women to have a more effective role in the labour market.'

Nested Narratives, Multiple Motives

On the face of it, it would seem that we are recounting a simple story of the Childcare Network and the DG V acting together to generate momentum over the late 1980s and achieving some success in the early 1990s in promoting a new way to represent social citizenship, work, and gender relations. The success was primarily in words, in the ways in which childcare and family issues were discussed in Commission documents. This success was notable, however, during a period when various discourses, sometimes couched in different languages of reconciliation, were used by Member States, where high unemployment and demographic concerns prompted new longings to remove some women from the labour force and persuade them to return home to produce children and engage in domestic labour. Eventually, the DG V discourse shaped a Council Recommendation to open the door to greater European activity in childcare through soft Community law.

The story lines get more complicated, however, when one reflects on the institutional process. The Council Resolution was the high point of a long narrative. The Childcare Network had spent five years working to legitimate its version of reconciliation discourse and vocabulary. The job ostensibly involved data gathering and presentation of expert opinion and analysis,[25] but it was also advocacy work. Both were supported and encouraged by the Equal Opportunities Unit. More generally, however, the Commission itself felt constrained to use a less progressive discourse, a more standard welfare statist one, when it issued general social policy pronouncements. Over time, however, the Childcare Network's formulations 'colonized' the Commission's general pronouncements when they concerned childcare per se. In consequence, when dealing with women's issues in general, the Commission tended to use article 119 and equal opportunities language, with a more traditional welfare state / labour market inflection, and then to switch to reconciliation language on childcare and family policy matters. This dichotomy sometimes made for strange reading, but it must be regarded as a success for the Childcare Network and the Equal Opportunities Unit.

The Council of Ministers was a politically conservative body heavily grounded in Member State concerns and increasingly wary of Commission attempts to prod the members toward reforms. Meeting as the Social Affairs Council, it considered social matters relatively infrequently, and it used very spare language, as demonstrated in its documents. The 1992 Recommendation is perhaps the most important exception to the Council's discretion on childcare matters in the Community's history.

The Network on Childcare (so called after 1991) continued its work after the council Recommendation, focusing on three of the Recommendation's reconciliation measures: services for children, leave arrangements for parents, and increased participation by men in childcare. Beyond its annual reports and networking activities, it produced a wide range of other materials.[26] It showed no inclination to tone down its commitment to reconciliation, as shown in the first paragraph of the Network's 1993 *Report*:

Reconciliation of employment and family life is necessary if women and men are to have equal opportunities in the labour force ... 'Reconciliation'

– harmonizing employment and family responsibilities so that they co-exist with the minimum of friction, stress, and disadvantage – is a broad concept. It covers:

• men as well as women, since both have family responsibilities
• the life course, since men and women have family responsibilities – caring for others, sustaining relationships, looking after the home – throughout their adult lives
• a wide range of measures ... the upbringing of children, services for children, leave arrangements for parents, making the workplace more responsible to the needs of employer parents and promoting increased participation by men in the care of children. (Moss, 1994:1)

In the light of the shift of emphasis in Community social policy – a retreat, in fact – that ensued in the days of recession and anti-Europe backlash after Maastricht, the Network tried to translate reconciliation into the new employment and job-creation concerns of the 1993 *Green Paper on Social Policy* and the Commission's *White Paper on Growth, Competitiveness and Employment: The Challenge and Ways Forward into the 21st Century*.[27] In the words of the 1993 Network Report:

Reconciliation can contribute to reducing unemployment in two ways. First, it can create new jobs; the Commission's White Paper ... proposes that 3 million jobs could be created through the development of a 'social economy' which includes services for the children and the old. Second, a more equal allocation of care and employment – the 'social work-load' – could produce the double benefit of reducing stress on employed parents (and other carers) and increasing employment.

Reconciliation requires the re-allocation of work between men and women. As more mothers are employed, fathers need to assume a greater share of family responsibilities and reduce their long hours of employment ... Reallocation across age groups is another dimension. An important structural change occurring within the labour market is a concentration of paid work within the 25–49 age group ... This age group is also heavily engaged in unpaid caring work ... At the same time, employment is also falling among the under 25s and over 50s ...

The challenge is to re-allocate the 'social work-load' between women and men and between women and men and between different age groups – and in the process to reduce unemployment ... spreading the social work-load more evenly by: providing opportunities to reduce working hours (not necessarily on a permanent basis but at time of their lives when men and women choose to do so); encouraging more equal sharing of family responsibilities between women and men; and creating more jobs to compensate for the reduction in working hours and by the development of 'care' services.'[28] (Moss, 1994:4)

Behind this level, however, lay another. The Delors Commissions developed complex approaches in their efforts to generate support for their own strategies, while casting nets to prepare the ground for future Europeanizing spillover (Ross, 1995). Across a range of policy areas where Europe had tentative, limited standing to act – social policy, of course, but also industrial relations matters, the environment, industrial policy – it sought to mobilize support for new initiatives from existing and potential interest groups, including non-governmental organizations (NGOs) and social movements, experts, policy activists, and intellectuals. The unspoken idea was to provide strong incentives to such groups and individuals – usually in the form of Commission encouragement, an official imprimatur, and some financing – to shape a new European focus and new activities. Through this approach of seducing interest groups and intellectual communities towards Europeanization, the Commission obviously hoped to gain precious political support for its own actions. It also sought to use these groups to generate broader awareness and mobilization in policy areas where the Commission hoped to advance. However one might evaluate the contents of the policy goals that the Commission sought to promote through such animation, it sought to instrumentalize external groups for a number of its own purposes while promising these groups some policy payoffs.[29]

Something similar was going on in the childcare area. The Network on Childcare gathered and disseminated a wide range of comparative information, held numerous meetings and seminars, developed extensive contacts in Member States, and, in general, agitated around the issue. The payoff for the Commission was the use of the Network as information gatherer and disseminator of a message about Commission support for broader European activity in childcare. It also hoped to generate sympathy for itself in feminist-policy intellectual and activist circles and to test the waters about an ultimate extension of activities in the childcare area.

When the Commission handed a variety of balls to various experts, advocates, and interests in different policy areas and encouraged them to run with them, it had to anticipate that the games that ensued would not be completely controllable. This was the case with the Network on Childcare and a number of other such operations. One very important consequence in the equal opportunities area was the adoption by the Commission, itself, of the discourse of reconciliation – a product of activist-Commission interaction – upon which we have focused. In many similar cases, those running with the ball were later judged by the Commission, itself, or the Council, to have run too far and too fast for the crowd to follow. This was what happened, in part, to the Network on Childcare. Before we turn to this story, however, a detour is in order.

Parental Leave: Detouring to Family Policy through the Maastricht Social Protocol

What good is the creation of a discursive legacy around reconciliation if it has little repercussion on policy? Since one never knows which discursive trend will be taken seriously in an uncertain future and because there are always a vastly larger number of discursive constructions available than will ever become important in policy terms, the question is pertinent. In this case, however, it is possible to say more. Through a very complicated chain of events the reconciliation discourse made contact with the Commission's 1983 proposal for a directive on parental leave which surfaced again in 1994. Rather than leading to Community legislation, however, it became the arena for the EU's first experience with Euro-level collective bargaining under the Maastricht Treaty's Social Protocol.

From Social Dialogue to Parental Leave

The Single European Act included a new article 118B stating that 'the Commission shall endeavour to develop the dialogue between management and labour at European level which could, if the two sides consider it desirable, lead to relations based on agreement.' The launching of social dialogue by Jacques Delors predated this act. Delors was a devoted promoter of confidence-building discussions of the social dialogue kind and believed that over time they could encourage the leaders of labour and capital to develop new trust. There was considerable distance to travel. The initial Val Duchesse discussions in 1985 among the UNICE (Union of Industrial and Employers Confederations of Europe), the ETUC (European Trade Union Confederation), and the public-sector employers' association, the CEEP (*Confédération Européenne des Employeurs Publics*) began in conflict and fizzled out quickly. Social dialogue was launched again in 1989 in the new context of Social Charter élan, but the same problems prevailed. By 1990 the setting had begun to change. The Community's decision-making powers were growing as a result of the single-market program, and interest groups, even those tightly bound to the nation state, such as labour and capital, had to adjust. The Commission's own efforts to accelerate these adjustments were important. With the inauguration of the Social Action Program, it opened an extensive campaign to provide incentives (favourable Euro-level policies, regulations, and support) that might bring the Social Partners to Europeanize further, perhaps even to bargain on important issues at European level.

This initiative, however, did not lead immediately to progress. UNICE's position was to refuse anything remotely resembling Euro-level collective bargaining. It could always count on the United Kingdom, and other Member States on certain issues, to block European social legislation, including treaty changes that might make bargaining more feasible. The Maastricht year of 1991 changed the setting. The Commission put an ingenious proposal on the table to change article 117 of the treaty. The goal was to expand the range of social policy matters that the Community would be able to treat both by granting it new areas to work in and new possibilities for qualified majority decisions in Council. The proposal included a clause that would allow the Commission to announce its intention to act in a specific area. The social partners would then have a short period to decide whether to negotiate a bargain or to accept legislation. Council approval could grant any bargain full legal status.

The Commission's proposal was shrewd. In essence, the Commission could threaten the Social Partners by saying, 'negotiate, or we will legislate.' The hope was to generate a Euro-level industrial relations system (Ross, 1995: chapters 3–6). The proposal eventually ended up as the core of the Maastricht Social Protocol.

Use of the Social Protocol was delayed by difficulties in the ratification of Maastricht, which did not occur until autumn 1993. With one remaining year in power, the Delors Commission had to choose its strategic opening carefully. Its first step was to define how the Social Protocol procedure would work. Two possible approaches to social matters existed. The Commission could choose on a case-by-case basis (excepting only health and safety proposals, where the old qualified majority procedures would continue). Under the Maastricht Protocol there would be two six-week preliminary consultations between the Commission and the Social Partners about the general area for potential legislation and subsequently the potential contents of such legislation. The Social Partners could then either deliver recommendations to the Commission for its legislative task or 'inform the Commission of their desire to embark, in the context of their bargaining independence, upon a process of negotiation which could lead to a direct agreement between the parties.'[30] In the case of failure, the Commission would then begin the legislative process.

The Commission's first choice to test the Maastricht arrangements was the European Works Council Directive.[31] The test failed, however, when the social partners could not agree, leading in 1994 to a full Council Directive. The Commission then decided to use the Maastricht Protocol again in early 1995 to deal with parental leave. In February 1995 the acting director general of the Commission's DG V officially informed the Social Partners of the Commission's intention to act in the area of 'the reconciliation of professional and family life' under the Maastricht Social Protocol and invited them to begin consultation procedures. Most significant in the DG V document was the use of reconciliation discourse. In its initial paper 'to seek the views of management and labour on the issue of reconciliation of professional and family life,' the Commission began by noting that 'reconciliation is a concept which is still developing within the EU.'[32] The first context for such development was 'equal opportunities: there will be no substantial progress towards greater equality between men and women until a comprehensive reconciliation policy is put in place for all workers. It will be instrumental in relieving women in particular from unreasonable and conflicting demands in their working and family lives.' The second context was the changing labour market, where 'enabling workers to reconcile their family lives with their work obligations will allow more women to become economically active.' Next, in the family realm, 'reconciliation aims to uphold family relationships and responsibilities ... Men should be able to take a greater part in caring commitments.' The final context was that of training and education: 'It is submitted, therefore, that a policy rooted in equal opportunities has developed into one focused on quality. Quality of family life, quality of working life, and quality of human resources.' The Commission's justification for reconciliation could have been borrowed directly from documents of the Equal Opportunities Unit and the Network on Childcare, including an explicit invocation of the 1992 Council Recommendation on Childcare.

The first stage of consultation, designed to elicit the Social Partners' general views on the desirability of Community action, ended in agreement.[33] The second six-week consultation period ended with the opening of what the ETUC called, in its press release of 7 July 1995, 'the first European negotiations.' The organizations quickly alerted their constituents and sought mandates. The negotiations, chaired by Madame Walgrave, president of the Belgian National Labour Council, were given six months to conclude.

Reconciliation of work and family life was an opportune theme for negotiation. Since the UNICE and business wanted to avoid Euro-level legislation, the UNICE was all in favour of reconciliation, as long as it was voluntary. The ETUC wanted negotiations in principle and thought that success on this issue could help with its significant female constituency. Moreover, many Member States already had in place parental leave arrangements, which were often more generous than those the negotiations were likely to produce, thereby lowering the costs of bargaining for business.[34] The ultimate goal was a framework agreement, declaring the general desirability of parental leave and setting out minimum conditions. Specific agreements on parental leave would then be negotiated nationally by the Social Partners to take into account particular national industrial relations and family policy practices. In some cases national legislation higher than the minimum conditions in the framework agreement would be enough.

Discussions were focused on the minimum standards in the proposed framework agreement. The most profound issue was whether parental leave would be regarded as an individual right available to everyone employed, or whether access would be restricted. The ETUC insisted on the former, while the UNICE wanted it only for firms with more than fifty employees. Everyone seemed to agree that the correct length for a leave was three months, but there were disagreements about remuneration and continuation of social protection during this period. There was agreement that this leave should be non-transferable (particularly from husband to wife), but also some discord over the age limits of children for whose care the program was mainly designed. The ETUC wanted the leave principle extended to 'ascendants' (the elderly) as well as 'descendants' and to family crises as well.

Employers initially refused to agree to anything implying greater costs to them. There were also disagreements on criteria for eligibility (how long on the job, full time vs. part time, what to do with small firms, how long the notification period should be). Everyone felt, however, that no leave arrangements under a framework accord should lead to a lowering of existing standards in member states. Both the ETUC and the UNICE also insisted that both public and private sectors be covered.[35] The first draft of a final accord was circulated on 28 September 1995. The major remaining differences were on the question of the 'individual right,' whether leave would be for care of dependent elderly parents and family emergencies, how universal (ETUC) vs. flexible (UNICE) minimum requirements would be, and whether sectoral negotiations should follow (ETUC for, UNICE against).[36] The critical outstanding issue was the level and nature of remuneration.

A framework agreement was finally reached in December 1995. The ETUC called it 'the first European collective bargain.' Reconciliation language was prominent throughout the 'General Considerations' prefacing the accord. The content of the agreement is worth reviewing. The ETUC won on two major points. First, parental leave was recognized as an individual right for women and men workers with natural or adopted children, to last a minimum of three months and to be taken at any point that could extend to the child's eighth year. Parental leave was non-transferable, so as to promote equal opportunities between men and women; fathers could not transfer it to mothers. The bulk of specific arrangements (how the three months was to be taken, whether eligibility was subject to a minimum seniority, specific conditions for adoption, notification times, justifiable reasons for employer postponement, the rules for small firms, etc.) were to be negotiated. National laws to safeguard the new right were to be passed to prevent victimization and ensure return to work for leave-takers. The second ETUC victory was provision for emergency leave in the event of family illness and accident. The UNICE's big victory was that there were no minimum remuneration requirements. The agreement also stipulated that the negotiated minimum standards could not be used as an excuse to lower existing national standards. The Council of Ministers then passed a Directive (96/34/CE) that made the framework agreement official Community law (EC OJ, no. 145, 19/6/96: 5–90).

The parental leave episode is illustrative of our general story. The discourse of a small group of experts and advocates inside a slightly larger bureaucratic unit within the European Commission, itself a grouping of experts and advocates, had found its way to collective bargaining on a European level, as it had earlier found its way to the 1992

Council Recommendation. How significant this development was is difficult to evaluate. The parental leave deal was not a particularly beneficial or eventful one for many European workers, many of whom already had a better arrangement in place nationally. For those who had no such arrangements the deal was very positive, even though its minimum standards were ... minimal. Whether these minimum standards would have included consecration of parental leave as an *individual* right and whether the non-transferability of parental leave would have been included without the long story that we have reviewed is doubtful.[37]

The story, however, is sinuous. Three additional pieces of legislation have since passed, related directly or indirectly to family policy and childcare, two negotiated between the social partners and then regularized by council decisions. The first prevents discrimination against part-time workers while simultaneously facilitating part-time work arrangements – a trade-off to the UNICE and also an opening to greater female labour force participation (see 97/81 EC, 15 December 1997). The second regulates short, fixed-duration labour contracts (see COM 1999, 203 final), also works to make female labour market participation more equitable and predictable. In neither case, however, was article 119 (which became article 141 in the Amsterdam Treaty) or equal opportunities invoked. The third directive (97/80 EC 15 December 1997) on the 'burden of proof' in cases of discrimination based on sex passed as a Commission proposal after the Social Partners failed to reach agreement. It did invoke article 119, but in a completely straightforward way, to justify placing the burden of proof on employers called upon to respond judicially in matters of sexual discrimination in the workplace.

Concluding?

The European Union began with very few social policy commitments, none in the area of family and childcare policy. The near-chance inclusion of article 119 in the Treaty of Rome prompted both litigation and legislation in the general area of equal opportunities. The Commission and other actors seized upon the ambiguities of article 119 to stretch the concept of equal opportunities to cover labour market discrimination and more. By the 1980s social structures that contributed to gender discrimination at work were in article 119's sights, at least in discursive terms.

In the early 1980s the Commission began institutionalizing its equal opportunities work in the small Equal Opportunities Unit within the Employment and the Labour Market directorates of the Social Affairs division of the bureaucracy. This institutionalization created an enclave of administrators with their own interest in moving programs forward into new territories. Furthermore, the constitution of networks, including the Childcare Network, installed well-connected experts and advocates who sought to broaden definitions of equal opportunities to include childcare and family policy matters. Everyone in this little Brussels-centred community wanted to involve policy intellectuals, social movements, and interest groups favouring such a broadening in the Commission's activities. In time, the team evolved particular ways of framing its concerns, the 'reconciliation discourse,' as we have called it. Reconciliation provided a useful vocabulary, because it had a long history in debates about equal opportunities and was sufficiently plastic to admit different declensions, of which there were many already on the field in the 1980s and early 1990s. Declensions that reconciled family with work at the expense of women – whose removal from the labour market to the household might ease unemployment statistics and promote a rise in birth rates – were on the rise. Others had standard welfare statist implications, seeking reconciliation between family and work by promoting more extensive childcare arrangements that allowed women to subcontract part of their family 'duties' and work. These arrangements would ease, but not really confront, the matter of women's dual responsibilities in the labour market and at home while doing little to promote the renegotiation of responsibilities in family life between men and women. The discourse of the Childcare Network was different, even if it used many of the same words. Its core notion was that the reconciliation of employment and family life was necessary if women and men were to have equal opportunities in the labour market.[38]

The refining of a political discourse, itself, is an interesting process. More interesting, however, is the permeation of policy by such a discourse. This process actually occurred, albeit in a small way, under the Delors Commissions. The *White Paper on Completing the Internal Market* (1985) brought enhanced willingness to pool and marketize a number of dimensions of economic policy. Little of market building, save the reform of the Structural Funds of 1987–88, would bring market corrections in social policy. The Delors Commissions and their allies strategized that pressure for market correcting in social policy realms would grow as the single market became a reality. The 1989 Community Social Charter on the Rights of Workers, the Action Program that followed it, and the Social Protocol of the Maastricht Treaty were vehicles to channel these pressures.

Europe began seriously to stretch its social policy ambitions only after 1989. From that point it became permissible at least to discuss Euro-level action. Efforts thereafter were larger but the accomplishments modest. The introduction, by DG V, the Equal Opportunities Unit, and the Childcare Network, of reconciliation discourse into policy documents and proposals, in particular, into the Council Recommendation on Childcare of 1992, was made possible by this changed atmosphere. On the matter of parental leave, in which Euro-level collective bargaining became feasible under the Maastricht Social Protocol, genuine policy action incorporating this discourse actually happened.

The parental leave issue was thus a laboratory for a number of different experiments. The contrast between the earlier discourse on parental leave (from 1983) and that which the Commission enjoined to the Social Partners, which, watered down, emerged in the negotiations, is significant. Finally, the ways in which the Social Partners defined their approaches is an important indicator of general attitudes. The ETUC, although an unusually enlightened union organization, is, like most union organizations, not easily open to discourses like those of the Commission's. Since unionism has been defined by a male blue-collar heritage that in many countries presumed a male breadwinner model for the family, the Commission's notions of reconciliation implied new territory. The ETUC bravely embraced the word *reconciliation* and insisted upon making parental leave an individual right that could not be transferred (offloaded?) from men to women, but how far this attitude went towards adopting the deeper logic of the reconciliation discourse is unclear. The UNICE, the employers' negotiator, had no difficulty in embracing all that was heart-warming in reconciliation as long as it did not involve obligatory new constraints and costs for its constituents.[39]

In the 1990s context, marked by renewed demographic fears and continually rising unemployment, the discourse of reconciliation was progressive. It was redefined slightly and then presented as, first of all, a source of job creation in the social economy (services for children and the elderly), following recommendations in the Commission's 1993 *White Paper on Growth, Competitiveness and Employment* (which the Equal Opportunities Unit influenced). DG V's reconciliation discourse thus became a legitimate policy discourse on the European level. It may have been past its prime, however, and the extent to which it has further permeated areas of European policy beyond parental leave has been limited. Further action on the atypical work and 'burden of proof' Directives did occur, but however significant these measures may turn out to be in better regulating part-time work and sexual discrimination in the workplace, they were not argued for in reconciliation terms.

The more significant change is that in the second half of the 1990s the Commission backed away in general from new legislative social policy initiatives. This reluctance was not simply because the big legislative mandates of the single-market period were carried out or because of perceived public opposition, even though there was plenty. More deeply, it represented a fundamental change of emphasis for the EU. In issue terms, mass unemployment, low growth, and the creation of Economic and Monetary Union (EMU) eclipsed almost everything else. Quite as important, Member States and their electorates became more wary and defensive about new EU incursions into their dwindling stock of sovereignty, most of which involved matters of social citizenship. There was also backlash against the Commission after the activism of the Delors years. The timid Santer Commission (1995–2000) thus decided to lie low.

House intellectuals in the Commission acknowledged that anything innovative in the social policy area would have to await Member States' perceiving new needs arising from the workings of the single market and EMU. Their perhaps vain hope was that eventual needs to harmonize different national policies in the social protection and taxation areas and to confront common new problems of welfare state reform and labour market policies would reopen the dossier.

The Fourth Action Plan on Equal Opportunities nonetheless continued much of the familiar analysis into the later 1990s. It directly addressed matters of women's citizenship by examining Member State legislation on social rights. The Commission narrowed this to specific, although rather important, areas in which it would work to individualize rights by working through the ECJ and member states. It proposed new legislation, for example, in equal treatment in social security, plus extensive research on the area (Com (95) 381 final: 24). Individualizing rights, were it successful, would make enforcing equal opportunities and reconciliation matters considerably easier for individuals and would build up a new body of jurisprudence.[40] Very little actually followed.

These programmatic projections, some quite promising, were not the most important issues about the Fourth Equal Opportunities Program. The period of preparation and passage of the Fourth Program coincided with institutional changes that foreshadowed a larger shift in the Commission's work. First, the European Council intervened at the end of 1995 to cut the Unit's budget in half. This action, prompted by German annoyance at alleged lapses in 'subsidiarity' in the Commission's social policy programs, particularly in the poverty and equal opportunities areas, was essentially a manifestation of Member State disgruntlement with Commission activism. Next, the director of the Equal Opportunities Unit during the period of the Third Program was abruptly removed. All these developments amounted to a shutdown of the 'reconciliation shop.'[41]

This small upheaval revealed a major change in the EU and the Commission's approach to most social policy matters, coinciding with the approach of EMU. EMU was designed to achieve a number of objectives. Not the least important of these was the creation of a new policy-making context to prod Member States to undertake 'structural reform' in social policy. This followed general élite consensus that Europe's social protection programs and labour markets created rigidities that were barriers to competitiveness. In consequence, Member States have had to begin renegotiating dimensions of their basic social compacts to protect themselves against the negative consequences, in terms of competitiveness, of failure to change in the face of EMU.

As the EU began the new millennium, therefore, the Commission had shifted from its earlier role as drafter of regional regulatory legislation to that of a 'facilitator' of more effective Member State strategies. In this new role it seeks to provide good ideas and set guidelines and benchmarks for national targeting and emulation. The previous, Delorist model of setting regulation in a supranational state-like way has given way to one in which EU institutions, the Commission in particular, are facilitators for disseminating 'best practices.'

This shift is likely to diminish the kinds of supranational prodding to change that we saw in the 'reconciliation' period of 'soft' and 'hard' EU-level intervention. The most significant index of this reduction can be found in the substantial recasting of equal opportunities activity. In 1996 the Commission issued a Communication (Com (96) final, February 1996) on 'incorporating equal opportunities for women and men into all Community policies and activities.' This shift towards a strategy of 'mainstreaming' pointed to new and systematic efforts to see that equal opportunities goals were included in all of the Commission's policy areas. This commitment was then enshrined in new Preamble Articles to the Amsterdam Treaty.

'Mainstreaming' policy and 'rights' have thus become the major focus of EU equal opportunities efforts. It is too early to say very much about the effectiveness of this change. The Commission's shift from legislator towards facilitator of best practice in employment matters, however, may open up new opportunities. In the Commission's own first review of 'mainstreaming' it notes 'a number of policies ... singled out for specific attention.' Among them, 'the equal sharing of work and family responsibilities between women and men needs to be encouraged as part of schemes promoting part-time work, flexibility and new forms of work organization' (European Commission, 1998: 2). This focus may mean, therefore, that the 'reconciliation' discourse will be heard more clearly in those areas where the Commission has legal responsibility for action, even though most parts of the Commission have a great deal to learn before this can happen seriously (see Pollack and Hafner-Burton, 2000, for a preliminary evaluation). It is likely to be heard most clearly in those particular areas, such as employment policy, where DG V, itself, has responsibility. In general, the European Union's direct activism on childcare matters, limited in scope though it has been, will probably be even more restricted in the future. If mainstreaming is successful, however, there may be considerably more indirect activism, with reconciliation language and priorities inserted into the workings of a range of Euro-level policy areas.

NOTES

1 There was, however, some new scope available in the areas of health and safety, catalogued in Byre (1992: chapter 10).
2 On article 119 see Vogel-Polsky and Vogel (1991), Byre (1992: chapter 8), and Hoskyns (1996: chapter 3).
3 The Social Action Program is in the *Bulletin of the European Community*, no. 10, 1974. The Social Action Program appears in the Council Resolution of 21 January 1974.
4 The first use in international documents has been traced to the International Labour Organization (ILO) in its 1965 recommendation (no. 123) on family policy (Junter-Loiseau and Tobler, 1995).

5 For a rapid review, see Teague (1989: chapter 4).

6 Useful, brief summaries of all legislation in this area can be found in European Commission (1994: 153–92).

7 For greater detail see Blanpain and Engels (1993: chapter 4) and Weatherill and Beaumont (1993: 544–60). The ECJ ruled in 1990, in the so-called Barber Case, that pensions fall within the equal pay for equal work principle.

8 See *Social Europe*, 3/91:79. Indirect discrimination exists if 'it can be proven that a rule applicable to both men and women workers in fact prejudices many more workers of one sex than of the other' and is illegal 'unless it can be justified with reference to reasons having nothing to do with sex discrimination.'

9 There is a brief review of these early activities in European Commission (1988).

10 The unit provides a very useful description of itself in 'The Equal Opportunities Unit' (DG V/B/4) which is updated periodically.

11 There is a brief review of these early concerns in European Commission (1988).

12 This citation and much of this paragraph are borrowed from Moss (1988).

13 The text of these actions is in *Social Europe*, 3/91, annex.

14 Hoskyns (1996: chapters 6–8) reviews the politics behind much of the renewal of activity.

15 This was not unusual for the Commission. It happened in the early 1980s in the realms of technology and research and development policies, the environment (DG 11 was perceived from the outside as a 'Green' enclave), in industrial relations, and so forth.

16 The Commission and the Equal Opportunities Unit were careful about keeping in constant contact with the Women's Rights Committee in the European Parliament.

17 The information in this paragraph is based on an interview, conducted by the author, with Peter Moss.

18 The communication is available in *Social Europe*, 1/94.

19 'Mainstreaming' was a notion then gaining ground in the Commission to ensure that various market-controlling Community commitments would be taken into consideration across the entire range of policies. In the early 1990s there was a rush to make the inclusion of environmental criteria, consultation with the Social Partners, and equal opportunities issues obligatory in the formulation of all EC/EU policies.

20 The communication is reprinted in *Social Europe*, 1/94: 126–7. The council's response appears on 128–9.

21 Among other things, the Observatory on Family Policies publishes an

annual report on trends in national family policies. See also Dumon (1994: 38–41).

22 The proposed Directive would make employers sued for unequal treatment responsible for providing proof that no such had occurred (*Social Europe*, 3/91).

23 NOW would allow the Commission, in structural funds areas, to support the provision of childcare facilities, particularly in zones of industrial concentration; the operational costs of childcare facilities related to vocational training centres; and vocational training for childcare workers. *Women of Europe* (supplement 34, 1991) contains a good review of these matters.

24 The Council Recommendation on Childcare (31 March 1992) is reproduced in *European Community Acts on Equal Opportunities* (Brussels: DG V/A/3, Equal Opportunities Unit; document reference V/2162/94).

25 A list of the Network's publications through 1992 includes *Childcare and Equality of Opportunity* (1988); *Structural Funds and Childcare: Funding Applications and Policy* (1989); *Childcare in the European Communities 1985–1990* (1990); *Childcare Needs of Rural Families* (Seminar Report, 1990); *Childcare Workers with Children Under 4* (Seminar Report, 1990); *Quality in Childcare Services* (Seminar Report, 1990); *Men as Carers for Children* (Seminar Report, 1990); *Mothers, Fathers and Employment* (1990); *Quality in Services for Young Children: A Discussion Paper* (1991). All are published in both English and French by the European Commission, DG V/A/3, except the third, which was published by DG X's Women's Information Services in English only.

26 They include *Mothers, Fathers and Employment, 1985–1991* (1993); *Structural Funds and Childcare with Special Reference to Rural Regions* (1993); *Monitoring Childcare Services* (1994); *Men as Carers: Towards a Culture of Responsibility, Sharing and Reciprocity between Women and Men in the Care and Upbringing of Children* (1994); *Leave Arrangement for Workers with Children* (1994); *Challenging Racism in European Child Care Provision* (1994); *Childcare Services for Rural Families* (1995); *Family Daycare in Europe* (1995); *Men, Media and Childcare* (1995); *The Costs and Funding of Services for Young Children* (1995); *School-Age Childcare in the European Union* (1996); *Quality Targets in Services for Young Children* (1996); *Fathers, Nurseries and Childcare* (1996); *Men as Workers in Childcare Services* (1996); *A Review of Services of Young Children in the European Union, 1990–1995* (1996) The Network also produced a videotape in 1995 entitled *Can You Feel a Colour?* about high-quality childcare services in Italy and Denmark.

27 The 1993 Green Paper was meant to be used to consult interested groups, in preparation for a social policy White Paper to appear in 1994. The White Paper was Jacques Delors's last major attempt to set the agenda and still

shapes thinking today.

28 In contrast to the elabourate and thoughtful reflections of its earlier publications, the Network on Childcare's *1994 Annual Report*, published in 1995,
was remarkably terse. Its seventeen pages were devoted to relatively flat
descriptions of its recent publications and little more. As we will see below,
at this point its existence was at stake and the handwriting on the wall was
ominous.

29 The best example of this approach is to be found in the Commission's
multi-purpose work with the ETUC in social dialogue. By providing the
ETUC with recognition and substantial funding, it hoped to gain labour
support for other Commission initiatives, strengthen labour's commitment
to Europe, and prod both labour and the employers towards Euro-level
bargaining (Martin and Ross, 1994).

30 The negotiating process would then have four possible outcomes: bargained agreement plus a request to the Council to grant it the force of law,
bargained agreement to be implemented by the bargaining parties and the
Member States, request to the Commission to extend the negotiating
period, or failure to reach agreement.

31 The Council passed the Directive on 22 September 1994 (94/45/EC).

32 This document is available in Director-General of Commission DG V,
Reconciliation of Professional and Family Life, internal document (Brussels,
autumn 1994).

33 There were six questions. Is action in the area appropriate? Should it be at
Community level or elsewhere? How should action be undertaken (legislation, contracts, recommendations, codes of conduct)? What should the
main elements of the action be? And, oddly, 'in what way can the new
technologies and the information society contribute to improved possibilities for the Reconciliation of Work and Family Life?' (reflecting one of
the commission's parallel concerns). How should costs and benefits be
balanced? These questions are taken from an unpublished Commission
Document, 'On Reconciliation,' 6.

34 For a summary of parental leave provisions in place in 1992 see the
Network on Childcare's *1992 Annual Report*, 15.

35 Most of this information is taken from internal ETUC documents, in
particular that dated 12 September 1995.

36 See *ETUC Internal Bulletin* (27 September 1995) and the unpublished
'Framework Agreement on Parental Leave, First Draft' (28 September
1995).

37 After the parental leave deal, the Commission started the bargaining
procedure on two 'atypical work' directives of considerable significance for

families and equal opportunities. The first was on 'flexible working time and worker security' (types of work other than full time and permanent). It was aimed at guaranteeing workers in 'new formulae of work' the same rights and treatment as workers with full-time permanent jobs. The Commission presented the issue as a trade-off, granting to employers more flexible work and to unions the need to 'organize' and regulate such work. The basic principle was 'non-discrimination' between full- and part-time or other atypical work. The ETUC and the UNICE agreed to negotiations concluded in spring 1997 with the second 'European collective bargain.' The atypical work agreement was an important step because it concerned a more controversial high-stakes matter than parental leave. See Commission of the European Communities, *Proposal for a Council Directive concerning the framework agreement on part-time work concluded by UNICE, CEEP and the ETUC*, Brussels, 23 July 1997, COM (97 392) final.

38 As elaborated by Peter Moss, coordinator of the Network of Childcare, the challenge of reconciliation is to allocate the 'social workload between women and men and between different age groups' (Moss, 1994: 6).

39 The priorities that the ETUC gave to 'women's issues' as opposed to, say, 'women as workers issues' are relatively low, although perhaps nowhere nearly as low as the priorities of some of their more important constituents (the German DGB, for example). There has been some difficulty over this point in the recent internal life of the organization. The UNICE, the employers' organization, has a better record on in its own operations and its discourse, but the UNICE is rather prone to genuine cheap talk, because its basic political position is that there should be *no* European-level political regulation of any key labour market matters.

40 The most significant innovation in the Fourth Program was a shift towards 'mainstreaming' equal opportunities matters in all areas of European-level policy, modelled on mainstreaming in the structural funds. Adoption of mainstreaming would mean that every measure proposed to the Council or taken by the Commission would have to take equal opportunities and reconciliation into account. A commissioner-level committee to oversee mainstreaming is already in place. Genuine mainstreaming, however, must involve major changes in process and outlook in the most powerful administrative agencies of the Commission and the Council, not to speak of its implications for member states. What will happen, therefore, is uncertain.

41 There is an irony in this situation. The social affairs commissioner, Padraig Flynn, had been raked over the coals by the European Parliament during its 1995 discussion – the first such – of the qualifications of the new commissioners for their assignments. The general tenor of the Parliament's objec-

tion to Flynn was that he had no sympathy at all for equal opportunities. This disapproval did not stop his appointment, but it did lead to the creation of a 'supervisory board' of five commissioners (all women) in this area.

Chapter Eight

Comparing Childcare Programs: Commonalities amid Variety

Jane Jenson and Mariette Sineau

As documented in detail in the previous chapters, the citizenship regimes of each of the four countries have been challenged by the economic and social changes of the last two decades. It was described in chapter 2 how, by the end of the 1990s Belgium, France, Italy, and Sweden were responding to the pressures that had made the discourses and practices associated with the post-war compromise, its institutions, as well as its employment and family programs difficult to sustain. New policy dynamics have taken hold everywhere. As documented in chapters 3 through 7, in all countries as well as in the European Union the crumbling of paradigmatic assumptions about the state and citizenship also induced a rethinking of ideas about equality, particularly gender equality. The legitimacy of women's work as well as the notion that a central policy goal was promoting women's equal labour force participation, lost ground. The effects, as we have also seen, were profoundly significant for the ways that thinking about childcare policy and mothers' employment intersected.

Here and in chapter 9 we compare these changes and examine the challenges they constitute for women's equality. In this chapter we provide an overview of the situation in our four cases: a detailed comparison of the patterns of provision, first, of publicly financed and provided care and then of privately provided care. In chapter nine we conclude the book by providing a summary of the patterns and direction of change.

Work and Family: A Variety of Policy Mixes

We begin with a characterization of the four cases, based on a consideration of the economic and demographic context (presented in chapter 2) as well as on the ways that public policy has addressed the relationship between work and family, as revealed by the detailed case studies.

Childcare and employment policies have always been closely linked in Sweden, as an expression of the policy commitment of promoting gender equality in labour force participation patterns. The result for Swedish women has been the achievement of the highest labour force participation rates by women, including mothers, of our four cases. Moreover, having overcome its earlier tendencies to decline, the birth rate is high in Sweden. In part, these two social trends depend on a substantial commitment to part-time employment and acceptance of gender-segregated labour markets. Swedish women's capacity to maintain their labour force participation and the birth rates also results, however, from the way family policy and labour market policies have been articulated. The Swedish approach is best characterized as a child-centred policy coupled to a policy of gender equality (Hantrais and Letablier, 1995: 44).[1] The effects of economic crisis appeared in Sweden much later than in the other three countries, and as yet they have not called these two policy goals into question. The post-war 'Swedish model' has only recently been shaken by new challenges, which may lead to its disappearance. Thus, in recent years, the proportion of public expenditures devoted to childcare has continued to rise. As documented in chapter 6, however, recent measures suggest that the winds of change may be about to alter even Swedish policies.

Belgium and France are similar in many ways and differ from Sweden in their conceptualization of this link between family and employment policy. Women's labour force participation is relatively high, but birth rates are still dropping, although they remain above the European average. Both countries accept the legitimacy of collective responsibility for child development and are very generous, therefore, when it comes to paying for childcare services. This commitment can help to account for the fact that in the last forty years women's behaviour has altered. Rather than leaving the labour force upon first becoming a mother, a woman now tends to keep her job at least until the birth of a third child. Nonetheless, shortages of publicly funded childcare services remain problems in both France and Belgium, and policymakers have responded to the temptation by developing policies that will encourage mothers to care for their own children rather than remaining in the labour force. Such initiatives have been presented in the name of 'choice.' Choices, therefore, are to be made not only among different forms of childcare – group based, family day care, or the several types of privately provided care – but also between parental and non-parental care. Over time, these policies have also paid less attention to the consequences for gender equality. The goals of fighting unemployment by promoting the creation of any job, even low-paid jobs in personal services, and by encouraging work-sharing have diverted attention from the unequal gender results that such relationships to labour markets are likely to incur.

The Italian model stands at another pole. The birth rate in Italy is among the very lowest in Europe, and women's labour force participation rates are low and their unemployment rates are high. Thus far, the reconciliation of work and family life seems to be managed through a reduction of family size (Hantrais and Letablier, 1995b: 54). More than in any of our other cases, moreover, childcare remains the responsibility of the family, both in political discourse and in everyday life (Sgritta and Zanatta, 1994; see also chapter 5). Since 1945 the Italian state has demonstrated little interest in providing childcare services for the under-threes, while labour market structures promoting private provision are barely developed. Therefore, care by relatives – whether grandmothers or an employed mother – remain the most frequent solution to the childcare dilemma (Dumon, 1991: 123). Even at the beginning of the twenty-first century, the childcare problem still is 'solved' by family solidarity rather than by state intervention.

All of these policy patterns, and the representations of working mothers that underpin them, have shaped the patterns of childcare provision in the four cases. All the case studies testify to the fact that changes to citizenship regimes included alterations in the services available for young children and the patterns of public funding. As we document in the rest of this chapter, not all the goals of the new programs were the same. In some cases the aim was to encourage more parental care, while for others it was to expand the variety of non-parental care available. Some policy initiatives have required continued or expanded investment in publicly provided care, while others have sought to use public funds to foster a private market in personal services, including childcare services. Sometimes policy-makers have tried to build pro-natalist goals into program design, while others have focused almost exclusively on the interface between childcare provision and employment. Given the huge variety of policy goals as well as program design that might shape any particular service for the under-threes, we have divided the discussion in this chapter between pub-

TABLE 8.1
Publicly financed and provided childcare services

Country	Year	Under-3s	3–6
Belgium	1993	30*	95
France	1993	23*	99
Italy	1991	6	91
Sweden	1994	33	72**

*The measure is of 'places available,' with the exception of two-year-olds in pre-primary schooling. All the other figures measure the percentage of the age cohort attending school or in a publicly financed service.
**Age range 3–7
Source: EC Childcare Network, 1996: 148–50

licly financed and provided services and privately financed childcare, whether the care work is done by parents or by someone employed by them.[2] The primary information source beyond our own case studies is the European Commission Network on Childcare.[3]

Publicly Financed and Provided Services for Young Children

In table 8.1 information is presented for the four countries about publicly financed and regulated services in organized family day care as well as in group settings, such as schools, childcare centres, or day nurseries. It excludes care by babysitters in the child's home and self-employed childminders.[4] In the next section of the chapter we compare such forms of provision.

Adopting the distinctions of the Network on Childcare, we examine *services* that are directly supported with public funds. We treat as 'privately funded' all forms of care in which parents are responsible for covering the costs, even if the *parents* receive some form of public support, such as tax credits, in order to help defray these costs. To qualify as 'publicly financed,' more than half of the total cost of the service must be covered by public funds. It is usual in member states of the European Union for a public agency to cover approximately 75 to 100 per cent of the cost, while parental fees account for the rest.

Use and Access to Services

In table 8.1, we see clearly that the age of the child as well as its country of residence determine whether parents have access to services for pre-schoolers. The over-threes have much better services than do the under-threes. Even if compulsory education does not begin until age six, in Belgium, France, and Italy pre-primary schools (*kleuterschool; école maternelle; scuola materna*) or other educational institutions provide a place for well over 90 per cent of the 3–6s. In Sweden, coverage is much lower for the older group; the country ranks seventh out of the fourteen countries surveyed by the Network on Childcare. Only 72 per cent of children aged 3 to 6 attend a publicly financed service, in large part because in Sweden the educational system plays virtually no role in providing services for children under the age of 7, the age at which school attendance becomes compulsory (Network, 1996: 132).

Focusing on the group with which this book is concerned, the under-3s, we learn from table 8.1 that nowhere does more than one child of every three have access to a space in a publicly financed service. Of the four countries examined here, Sweden and Belgium have the highest rate of provision, with spaces for at least 30 per cent of the children in the age cohort. In France, often presented as one of the leaders in this area, only 23 per cent of the under-threes have access to a publicly financed space. Italy trails far behind, with a mere 6 per cent of its children in a publicly funded childcare service.

These data have to be interpreted in combination with information about other programs, especially those for parental leaves and supporting private services, both of which we discuss in the next section. For example, demand for non-parental childcare for infants is very low in Sweden, because generous paid leaves mean that most parents provide their own care until the child is about 12 months old. Indeed, in 1995 only 3 per cent of children aged between 3 and 12 months received non-parental care (that is, 155 children). As infants become toddlers, however, the use of publicly funded care rises rapidly. Thus, 42 per cent of 1-year-olds were receiving non-parental care in 1995 (Network, 1996: 116).

There are also wide geographical and socio-economic variations in access to childcare. Such services are the responsibility of regional governments or municipalities. Therefore, availability is a function of differences in their preferences for providing certain kind of services as well as in their tax bases. All do not have either the same inclination or the same resources to invest in services for young children.

The financial imperative is important in Sweden, for example, where 'behind the "average" figures hide great disparities' (Daune-Richard, 1998: 53). Changes to state funding practices and decentralization (described in chapter 2, above) have widened the gap between richer and poorer communities and between urban and rural ones, despite the formal requirement imposed by Stockholm that municipalities provide all children with a place in day care. Geographical, cultural, and economic differences also characterize Belgium. For example, in the mid-1990s the Francophone provinces of Hainaut, Liège, and Namur had less than 100 spaces in day nurseries (*crèches; kinderdagverblijf*) or family daycare (*services de gardiennes encadrées; dienst voor opvanggezinnen*) for every 1,000 young children, while the numbers rose to 149 in Antwerp and 189 in the Brabant – Flemish provinces that include major urban centres. Indeed, day nurseries are, in general, concentrated in urban areas (Network, 1996: 25). In Italy, where the national average is spaces for merely 6 per cent of infants, differences between the north and the south are extremely pronounced. In certain northern Regions, day-care centres (*asili nido*) have spaces for about 30 per cent of children aged 3 to 36 months, while in other Regions, especially in the south, day nurseries do not even exist (Network, 1996: 74). France's day nurseries (*crèches*) are concentrated in Paris and its suburbs. Indeed, 46 per cent of the country's total spaces are in Ile-de-France, the region that includes Paris and five other departments. Thus, over 33 per cent of Parisian children whose mother is employed (and 25 per cent in the nearest suburbs) attend a day nursery (Desplanques, 1993: 332). These levels surpass the national average for availability of *all* types of publicly funded childcare spaces (table 8.1).

A Variety of Structures

Services for the under-threes can be found in a wide variety of settings, as documented in table 8.2. This leads us to make two basic observations. First, the degree of structural variety is not the same across the four countries. Second, responsibility for services for young children is often shared between welfare and educational institutions. The latter, however, do not absorb children at the same age. In France, pre-primary education begins at age 2, while in Belgium, it is 30 months. Italian children do not start school until age 3, whereas in Sweden, it is only since 1993 that six-year-olds may attend pre-primary school – if their parents choose to send them and there is a place available.[5]

TABLE 8.2
Distribution of publicly financed childcare services available, children 0–3

BELGIUM: Spaces available for 30 per cent of children under 3

Type of Service	Number of places	Per cent of places	Percentage change 1988–93
French-speaking community			
Pre-primary school (*écoles maternelles*)	23,211	54	+10
Day-care centres including: day nurseries (*crèches*) 0–36 months; school-based centres (*prégardiennat*) 18–36 months; community centres (*maison communale d'accueil de l'enfance*) 0–72 months	10,320	24	+17
Organized family day care (*services de gardiennes encadrées*)	9,066	21	+56
TOTAL publicly financed services	42,597	100	+19
Flemish-speaking community			
Pre-primary school (*kleuterschool*)	39,650	56	
Day-care centres including: day nurseries (*kinderdagverblijf*) 0–36 months; school-based centres (*peutertuin*) 18–36 months	11, 493	16	+23
Organized family day care (*dienst voor opvanggezinnen*)	19,134	27	+78
TOTAL publicly financed services	70,277	100	

The institutional variety in publicly funded services varies widely from one case to another. Italy is at one end of the spectrum: because children must be three or older to enter pre-primary school, day nurseries (*asili nido*), which are officially part of the welfare system, provide the only full-time, publicly funded care for infants and toddlers whose parents are employed.[6] In recent years, local authorities, especially in

TABLE 8.2—(*Concluded*)
Distribution of publicly financed childcare services available, children 0–3

FRANCE: Spaces available for 23 per cent of children under 3

Type of service	Number of places	Per cent of places	Percentage Change 1988–93
Pre-primary school (*écoles maternelles*)	250,000	49.8	+14
Community day nurseries (*crèches collectives*)	118,500	23.6	+32
Organized family day care (*crèches familiales*)	65,000	13.1	+15
Parent cooperative day nurseries (*crèches parentales*)	8,500	1.6	–
Drop-in centres (*haltes-garderies*)	60,000 (Each space can accommodate five children.)	11.9	+41
TOTAL publicly financed services	502,000	100	

ITALY: Spaces available for 6 per cent of children under 3

Day nursery (*asili nido*)	91,655	+/- 100	2
TOTAL publicly financed services	91,655	100	

SWEDEN: Spaces available for 33 per cent of children under 3

Day-care centres (*daghem*)	84,000	73	33
Organized family day care (*familjedaghem*)	31,516	27	decreasing
TOTAL publicly financed services	115,516	100	

northern and central Italy, have created a new service called the *nuove tipologie*. These are drop-in centres furnishing children and their primary caregiver – whether parent, grandparent, or babysitter – a place for play and other social activities. They may also provide care for children whose parents work part time. When they choose to provide such part-time care, they begin to resemble the drop-in centres (*haltes-garderies*) that have blossomed in France (table 8.2). Because of their relative novelty and the fact that they are primarily play centres, dedicated to socialization rather than providers of day care, however, their spaces were not counted in the EC Network on Childcare survey.

Sweden also provides a limited variety of services, as documented in table 8.2. All childcare is regulated by the agencies of the health and social affairs national bureaucracies, although it is supervised and delivered by local authorities. The educational system has no responsibility for the under-threes.[7] Two types of institution provide 90 per cent of publicly funded care: municipal childcare centres and organized family day care. Since the beginning of the 1990s, however, there has been a 'substantial development of private but publicly funded services,' organized by parent cooperatives, non-profit organizations, companies, and so on. The day-care centres in this category receive state subsidies if they follow the same rules as the municipal centres; this means that they are tightly regulated (Vielle, 1994: 73). About 10 per cent of all spaces in childcare centres now are privately provided (Network, 1996: 112). The overwhelming majority of parents seeking non-parental care still must choose, however, between a municipal childcare centre, serving between fifty and sixty children, or organized family day care. Moreover, use of the latter has declined significantly in the last decade, as more children are placed in day-care centres, which clearly have become the norm.

The picture in France and Belgium is different. Both have a wide variety of different types of institution delivering publicly funded childcare services. On the one hand, each provides a large and rising number of spaces in pre-primary education for 2-year-olds.[8] In both countries, schools provide half or more of all publicly financed spaces for children under 3 (table 8.2). The rest are funded through the social protection branches of the state.

In France, there are three kinds of care in group settings: community day nurseries (*crèches collectives*) with 23.6 per cent of the spaces; organized family day care (*crèches familiales*), providing 13.1 per cent of the places; parent cooperatives (*crèches parentales*), which provide a mere 1.6 per cent of spaces. The type of service that has expanded most in France is the drop-in centre (*halte-garderie*). Because spaces are used part time, usually providing only occasional care, they can serve many children. Experts calculate that the 60,000 spaces actually provide for 325,000 children. As shown in table 8.2, calculated on a full-day basis, these drop-in centres provide only 11.9 per cent of spaces, although there has been a 41 per cent increase in the last decade. Calculating differently and counting the number of children in each type of publicly funded service, we find that drop-in centres provide services to fully 42 per cent of all the children using a publicly financed service.

The situation in Belgium is perhaps the most diverse of all, in part because of the distinctions across the two major linguistic communities. Schools provide even more places than they do in France: 54 per cent of all the publicly financed spaces available in the Francophone Community and 56 per cent in the Flemish-speaking Community.[9] In addition, as documented in table 8.2, parents have available a wide variety of choice in type of day-care centre. The age range of children accepted as well as the types of family served, the details of governance, and other arrangements of the institutions vary within each community as well as across them (see chapter 3, above, for more details).

Cost and Financing

Cost-sharing also varies across countries. In France and Belgium, where the school system provides one of every two places, education authorities cover the bulk of the costs. In Belgium the departments of education of each Community pay the entire cost. In France, the Ministry of National Education (65 per cent) and local authorities (35 per cent) share costs. In neither case do parents pay for pre-primary schooling.

With respect to services integrated into the system of social protection, sources of financing also differ across cases. In Italy, financing is decentralized, being covered by local authorities and regional governments. In Sweden, services are partially financed by a block grant for social spending from the central government, and the rest is covered by local authorities. In 1993 the former financed 35 per cent of the costs and the latter 52 per cent (Network, 1996: 115).[10] Over recent years Stockholm's contribution has fallen off, and local authorities have had to cover a higher proportion of the costs, an adjustment linked to changes in the way subsidies are managed and transferred from the state to the local authorities, as we described above. In France, public funds come from the local governments and the CAF (*Caisses d'allocations familiales*), which exist in each Department. The role of a CAF is twofold. It both finances childcare services and has responsibility for encouraging other public and private agencies to expand their commitments to services. In 1993, on average, all the CAFs were responsible for 23 per cent of the costs of community day nurseries and organized family day care, and 22 per cent of those of drop-in centres. Local authorities covered more: 34 per cent of the costs of day nurseries and family day care and 47 per cent of those of drop-in centres.[11] Financing of the Belgian system is primarily the responsibility of agencies in each Community. The most important are the ONE (*Office de la naissance et de l'enfance*), accountable to and funded by the Ministry of Culture and Social Affairs of the Francophone Community, and the K&G (*Kind en Gezin*), overseen by the Ministry of Culture, Family and Welfare in the Flemish-speaking Community. On average, in 1987 the ONE covered 48 per cent of childcare services while in 1994, the K&G was responsible for 56 per cent of total costs in its Community. Other sources of funds are local authorities, non-profit organizations, regional governments, and federal family allowance funds and job promotion programs (Network, 1996: 28).

Parents' costs also vary widely. Italy and Sweden demand the smallest proportional contribution from parents. The parental part of total costs is 12 per cent and 13 per cent, respectively. In Sweden, however, the proportion covered by fees is increasing, since local authorities have to make do with smaller budgets and lower revenues (Network, 1996: 115). Moreover, as described in chapter 5, recent reforms in Italy set a 30 per cent limit on the parental contribution, suggesting that pressures to increase their part of the service had been mounting. Fee levels and proportional contributions also vary from one locality to another, owing to differences in local tax revenues (Broberg and Hwang, 1991, 1992). In Belgium, in the Francophone Community, the parental contribution is slightly higher, at 17 per cent, while in the Flemish-speaking Community, parents cover fully 30 per cent of the costs. France also relies substantially on fees to finance its public services. For drop-in centres, 23 per cent of costs are covered by fees, while the statistic is 28 per cent for the day nurseries and organized family day care.

Despite these differences in proportion, all four cases share one important characteristic: actual fees paid are calculated on a sliding scale, geared to family income and number of children. Priority access to spaces may also be given, as it is in Italy, to low-income and single-parent families (Dumon, 1991: 121). Moreover, in France and Belgium, where the proportion of costs covered by parents is highest, the actual costs to parents are somewhat lower than is apparent at first glance. The tax systems in these two countries allow parents to claim tax credits for fees paid. In Belgium, families with at least one working parent and a child in a centre or family day care can deduct 80 per cent of the cost, up to a daily maximum. In France, parents may deduct 25 per cent of expenses related to care outside the home of a child under 7, up to an annual maximum.[12] To be entitled to this tax deduction, both parents in two-parent families must be employed, and at least one full time (Vielle, 1994: 75). In this way, the redistributive effect that might come from linking fee scales to income is attenuated.

Despite paying lower fees and having access to other forms of financial assistance, working-class and low-income families, at least in France and Sweden, tend to use day nurseries and family day care much less than better-off families do. In French studies in the early 1990s it was found that of the employed mothers of children attending such institutions, 19 per cent held management positions, 11 per cent were office workers, and only 5 per cent were blue-collar workers (INSEE, 1992: 70–1). Other, often informal, forms of care were preferred by the low-income or working-class parents. In Sweden, as well, it is middle- and upper-middle-class parents who send their children to childcare centres, while working-class parents tend to prefer family day care or informal care arrangements (Jacoby and Näsman, 1989).

General Trends

In order to understand the ways that different publicly financed and provided childcare services have evolved, we must consider the two types of variation documented in table 8.2. First, the increase in the number of spaces available has not happened at the same pace everywhere. Indeed, in Italy over the five-year period, there was quasi-stagnation in the number of available spaces. In contrast, in the other three cases there was some significant increase in places in at least one of the services provided. A second observation, then, is that the rate of increase varies across types of service, as well as across countries. For example, in Belgium, the rise in the number of spaces was very pronounced for organized family day care; neither the childcare centre nor the pre-primary education category increased nearly as fast. In France, it was the drop-in centres that took off, while community day nurseries followed, not far behind but clearly in second place. The rates of increase in both pre-primary education and family day care lagged far behind these two kinds of services. In Sweden, for a corresponding period, places in childcare centres rose at the same rate as in France, while places in family day care actually fell off.

The message of such comparisons is that, at least for the three countries where the number of places was climbing, the services targeted are quite different. In Belgium, organized family day care is preferred, along with pre-primary education. In the Francophone Community, the result is that 75 per cent of the places for under-threes in publicly financed care are in one of these two institutions, while the corresponding figure is fully 82 per cent in the Flemish-speaking Community. In France, in contrast, it is pre-primary education plus community day nurseries that provide places for almost three of every four children in publicly provided care. Finally, in Sweden, with no places in the school system, the same percentage of places is allocated to childcare centres.

Privately Provided Childcare

A second type of childcare that is available in these four countries is privately provided, inside or outside the child's home. Sometimes parents or other relatives are the caregivers, while at other times, care is a personal service provided by someone employed by the parents. In this category, then, are two main forms:

1. Non-parental care. This might be provided by a babysitter or by a childminder with some training. It is often subsidized by the public treasury. Family members, especially grandparents, also often provide care.
2. Care provided by a parent who is either on leave from the labour force or a stay-at-home parent.

Although it is hard to come by reliable and comparative statistics on privately provided services, some of the available data are presented in table 8.3. Belgium is absent from the table because no reliable information was available. The Swedish data are the most detailed, being based on an annual survey of childcare needs. We see that among all children aged 0–6, fully 49 per cent receive a form of privately provided care, with the largest category (22 per cent) being parents caring for their young children while they are on parental leave. A further 15 per cent are looked after by a parent who is not employed (although

TABLE 8.3
Who cares for the children

FRANCE*: Children 0–3**

Privately provided care
    Relative or babysitter at home   13%
    Self-employed family day-care provider   22%
    Non-registered childminder   22%

Publicly provided services   42%

---

*These statistics are for 1993 and describe the situation
for children 0–3.
**This is measured in 'places' and provides percentages
of children in some form of non-maternal care.
Source: Network, 1996: 65

ITALY*: Children of employed mothers

Privately provided care
Relative
    Mother   27%
    Father   2%
    Other relative   48%
Paid caregiver in home   15%

Publicly funded service   10%

---

*These statistics date from 1986–87, in fourteen regions;
they are for children under 3.
Source: Network, 1996: 78

SWEDEN*: All children 0–6

Privately provided care
Relative
    Parent on parental leave   22%
    Unemployed parent   6%
    Non-employed parent   4%
    Parent working/studying   5%
    Parent is a day-care provider   2%
Parent cooperative centre   4%
Private 'arrangements'   6%

Publicly funded services   51%

---

*These statistics are for 1994. They are for children 0–6.
The 'child' is the unit of measurement.
Source: National Childcare Needs Survey, provided by
Gunni Kaerrby

among them are a small number whose parent is employed but is not using any form of non-parental care). This system of classification puts under the 'private' heading day-care centres organized by coopera- tives of parents, although we discussed them, above, as a form of pub- licly funded care.

In a French study it was found that fully 54 per cent of all children aged 0–3 were cared for by their own mothers, some of whom were on parental leave (Desplanques, 1993: 330). In this table, however, we con- sider only a subset of children, those in some form of non-parental care. Of these children 58 per cent receive privately provided care. In the French data, the importance of self-employed day-care providers (*assistantes maternelles agréées indépendantes*) is clear; they look after 22 per cent of the children. Their portion of the market for personal ser- vices is matched, however, by non-registered childminders who care for children in their own homes. Finally, in France, well over one in every ten children are cared for by a babysitter or a relative in his or her own home.

In Italy, the data are even more partial. The findings of a survey of fourteen regions that analyses the situation of children whose mother is employed are presented. Here, we find the highest level of privately provided care. Most striking is the observation that relatives are by far the most common caregivers. Fully 48 per cent of these children are cared for by a relative, while a further 27 per cent are cared for by their *employed* mother. Only 15 per cent of children have a babysitter.

In the following subsection we examine in more detail these privately provided services, looking first at non-parental care and then turning to two forms of parental care – leaves and stay-at-home mothers.

Privately Purchased Childcare

By 'privately purchased' childcare we mean services provided by babysitters or childminders hired by parents. In contrast to the pub- licly funded services described in the previous section, these forms of care receive no direct infusion of public funds. Nonetheless, as we will see, they are often heavily subsidized through tax deductions or employment programs. The distinction might be understood as fol- lows. In publicly funded services, the service itself receives the funds. Thus, a childcare centre receives a municipal grant, while an organized family day-care provider is employed by a local government or other public agency. In the case of someone purchasing a private personal service, if any public subsidy exists, it goes to the consumer – that is, the employer – as partial compensation for the cost. Such private arrangements may range from hiring a neighbour, friend, or babysitter with no formal training to employing a qualified childminder whose credentials and workplace are regulated. In both Belgium and France, the latter is an important segment of the private market in services.

It is difficult to draw reliable conclusions about these personal services because, as we have just indicated, the data are so fragmentary. Nonetheless, it is possible to make the following cautious observations. In Sweden, the market for personal services is the least developed, although, as described in chapters 2 and 6, its enlargement is a government priority. As we saw above, some limited privatization is occurring, but even private services still are often provided in group settings, such as alternative day-care centres, and are publicly funded. Self-employed childminders do offer their services, but the market remains very limited. In Italy, where care by relatives is clearly the norm, the job market for self-employed childminders is also very small. To the extent that it exists, it is in the large cities of the north and their suburbs. Recent changes, as outlined in chapter 5, seek to promote childcare in homes, by regulating and setting standards for childminding, thereby improving quality of services.

Privately purchased services are both popular and on the increase in France. The number of self-employed daycare providers (*assistantes maternelles agréées indépendantes*) has increased since 1988 for two reasons. Programs that seek to expand the number of such spaces focus on improving the training and credentials of childminders. Second, employment policy has generated a series of measures, explicitly intended to encourage parents to become employers of childminders, either self-employed day-care providers or babysitters. They are the Allowance for Childcare at Home (*Allocation de garde d'enfant à domicile*; AGED) instituted in 1986 and the Subsidy for Hiring a Childminder (*Aide à l'emploi d'une assistante maternelle agréée*; AFEAMA) of 1990. By 1995, 16 per cent of the CNAF's expenditures on young children (*entretien-naissance jeune enfant*) went to these programs (Boissières, 1996: 50). There were 46,500 recipients of an AGED by the end of 1995, while those using the AFEAMA had reached 321,000 (Meunier, 1996: 61).

In Belgium, private services are less developed than in France, but as in the Hexagon, they are subsidised via tax advantages. Parents using a childminder can deduct 80 per cent of the cost, up to a daily maximum. Some types of private services are on the increase, while others are declining. For example, in the Francophone Community, the ONE found that between 1988 and 1993 there was an increase of 95 per cent of places available (from 2,335 to 4,555) in private day-care centres (*maisons d'enfants*), while the number of self-employed family day-care providers fell by 44 per cent. In the Flemish-speaking Community, on the other hand, there were 12,586 places provided privately by regulated self-employed daycare providers (Network, 1996: 29).

Parental Leaves

The next form of private provision, paid parental leaves,[13] also is subsidized by public funds or employer contributions sanctioned by law. Parental leaves exist in all four countries, although, as we will see, the conditions of access and level of payment vary widely.

In the early 1980s the European Community identified parental leaves as an important institutional support for its commitment to promoting gender equality at work. Then, in 1986 the Commission's Equal Opportunities Unit created the Childcare Network and targeted leaves for workers with children as one of its four priorities (Network, 1996: 4–5). In a Recommendation on Childcare adopted on 31 March 1992, the Council of Ministers called for parental leaves to be available in all the member states. In chapter 7 we documented in more detail the history of the European Union's actions for promoting the reconciliation of work and family life, including the 1995 Directive on parental leaves.[14]

Most member states did not wait for European action to launch their activities in this domain. Parents in three of our four countries (France, Italy, and Sweden) already had a statutory right to parental leave well before the EC turned its attention to the matter. Sweden created its first program in 1974, and France and Italy followed in 1977. Belgium had no guaranteed parental leave until after the EU directive was passed. In 1998 it instituted paid three-month guaranteed leaves, resulting from a combination of law and collective agreements (European Commission, 1999: 121–2). Earlier, however, Belgium had instituted the Voluntary Career Break in 1985. This wide-ranging program, whose goal is combating unemployment by encouraging work-sharing, makes it possible for employees to take paid leaves for any number of reasons (Vielle, 1994: 85). High on the list is child-rearing (see chapter 3 for details).

Parental leaves, even where they exist, are not necessarily accessible to all parents. In Belgium, for example, the Career Break is the functional equivalent of a paid parental leave. If the Career Break is the functional equivalent, it is regulated differently, depending on where the parent works. In the private sector, a general collective agreement binding employers and unions covers all workers, but the specific conditions of access may vary across industries, according to the collective agreements negotiated within each (Network, 1994: 17–18). Moreover, unless labour-management negotiations formally eliminate the requirement, the employer must grant permission for any employee to take leave. The bulk of public sector workers do have the right to a Career Break, although those in senior positions must request permission and may be refused if management decides it would be too disruptive (Network, 1994). Unemployed workers also may take a Career Break, which implies that, for family or other personal reasons, a person might take leave from the unemployment insurance system and the requirement to be seeking work (Vielle, 1994: 85–6).[15]

In France, as well, until passage of the Family Law of 1994, access to unpaid parental leave (congé parental d'éducation) depended on the size of the firm or other conditions related to employers' needs. Moreover, paid parental leave (allocation parentale d'éducation) is available only in limited circumstances and depends on the birth order of the infant. It, too, is available to unemployed parents.

As revealed in table 8.4, parental leaves vary widely. First, they are of diverse lengths, and in all cases they can be taken either full time or part time.[16] In Belgium, a paid Career Break may last up to twelve months full time, with the option of renewing it up to five times. The leave may also be taken on a part-time basis, for a period from six months to five years. Because the right is an individual one, either parent may take leave, and nothing excludes both from being on leave simultaneously. In France, unpaid parental leaves may last up to thirty-six months, and they can be taken only if the child is under 3, a provision that contravenes the EU Directive's guarantee until age eight.

In both France and Sweden, either parent may take a leave, but only one parent may be on leave at a given time.[17] In Sweden and Italy, however, each parent must use at least thirty days. If one of the parents does not go on leave for at least one month, the family's total eligibility is reduced. In Sweden, paid leaves can last up to a total of fifteen months and may be taken any time up to the child's eighth birthday (or the end of the first grade). Indeed, given the flexibility in schedul-

TABLE 8.4
Parental leaves

Country	Benefit	Created	Duration	Benefit level	Use	Individual or family	Part-time possible	Level of use
BELGIUM	Career Break	1985	6 to 12 months, renewable up to 5 years	low – tied to rates for unemployment insurance	Any reason, including care of children	Individual benefit	yes	87 per cent female recipients (1995)
	Break from unemployment	1985	6 to 12 months, renewable up to 5 years	low – tied to rates for unemployment insurance	Any family reason, including care of children	Individual benefit	no	98 per cent female recipients (1995)
	Parental leave	1998	3 months, paid	flat rate – 20,000 BF per month	For care of child under 8	Both or either parent may take leave	yes	
FRANCE	Parental leave	1977	36 months	unpaid	For care of child under 3	Both or either parent may take leave	yes	99 per cent female recipients (1995)
	Parental allowance for child-rearing	1985	36 months	low – under the minimum wage	For care of child under 3		yes	97 per cent female recipients (1995)
ITALY	Parental leave	1999	10 months		For care of child under 8	Both parents must take leave or lose one month of total	yes	Too new to know
SWEDEN	Parental leave	1974	15 months	80 per cent of salary for 360 days; flat rate for the rest	from 2 months before birth until the child is 8	Both parents must take leave or lose one month of total	yes	90 per cent leave days used by women; 50 per cent of fathers take some

ing, the Swedes tend to use the 'day' as a unit of measurement for the leaves, rather than the month or year used elsewhere.

Conditions of access to parental leaves also vary. France's paid leave (*allocation parentale d'éducation*) is certainly the most restrictive. The benefit is available only if the parent has at least two children, one of whom is under 3. In addition, she or he must have worked at least two of the five previous years. Belgians can request a Career Break for any reason, but employers must agree to replace the employee with someone on the unemployment rolls. The Swedish paid parental leave is open to many parents, yet even so, it is not absolutely universal. A parent must fulfil the employment requirement of having worked six months before birth OR at least twelve months in the previous twenty-four. Moreover, in order to receive the benefit at 80 per cent replacement rates (which is modelled on sickness insurance), the employee must have been insured for sickness benefit for at least 240 consecutive days before the birth (European Commission, 1999: 138). If these requirements are not met, parents caring for their children receive a small allowance as a substitute.[18] Italians have the easiest access to leaves. They can be taken at the birth of any child, and there are no conditions linked to employment.

The form of remuneration indicates the principles underpinning the leaves. Payment may be made at a relatively modest flat rate, or it may be calculated as a percentage of the parent's salary. France and Belgium fall into the first category. The French paid parental leave is the equivalent of about half the minimum wage, while in Belgium, those on a Career Break or parental leave receive an allowance, calculated in relation to unemployment insurance rates. In Italy and Sweden, in contrast, the payment corresponds to a percentage of the individual parent's salary. Nonetheless, the level is very different in the two countries. In Italy, the minimum amount equals 30 per cent of the mother's salary, although some collective agreements have made it higher and public sector workers receive more. In Sweden, the payment is 80 per cent of the parent's salary for the first twelve months, followed by a relatively low, flat-rate replacement for the remaining time.

There are also different long-term consequences for parents who choose to take a leave to care for a young child. In Sweden, under its insurance-based system, both parents have a guarantee that they can return to their jobs and retain their employment-related benefits. For example, taking parental leave does not mean a loss in seniority or pension rights. In France, on the other hand, guarantees of return to work are not strong, and there are important negative consequences for pension rights (Hantrais and Letablier, 1995a: 97). In Belgium, only the first year of a full-time Career Break is counted as the equivalent of employment; an extension means either that parents lose certain benefits that depend on being in the labour force or that they must make their own contributions to pension and other funds. For an employee taking a Career Break in order to care for a child under 6, however, the first three years are treated as the equivalent of a normal working year.[19]

Given the level of remuneration and the absence of negative long-term consequences, it is not surprising that parental leaves are far more popular (that is, more frequently used) in Sweden than in the other three countries and that demand for day-care spaces for infants is so low. Almost half (44 per cent) the mothers of children of less than a year took more than 271 days of leave, while one-third were on leave between 181 and 270 days. The average for mothers of children in this age cohort was 262 days of leave (Network, 1994: 36).

In all four countries, it is mainly women who take parental leave (Network, 1994: 2). Even in Sweden, where an announced objective of the parental leave program is to increase gender equality, 90 per cent of the total days of leave were taken by women in 1998 (European Network on Family and Work, 1998, 2). Nonetheless, more fathers are taking some leave. In families where children were born in 1981, 27 per cent of fathers had taken, on average, forty-eight days of leave before the child was eighteen months. In families with children born in 1990, 48 per cent of father took on average fifty-nine days of leave (Björnberg, 1994).[20] By 1998 half of fathers were taking at least some leave (table 8.4 and European Network on Family and Work, 1998, 2)

Originally, the paid parental leaves enjoyed little popularity in France, and those who did use the benefit were overwhelmingly women. The program became more popular after 1994, when leaves became available on the birth of a second child (Meunier, 1996: 61). The fall in the number of parents receiving the benefit was halted and the number of parents (almost all of whom were mothers) receiving the benefit tripled (Afsa, 1996). Unpaid parental leave is even less popular and also is very feminized. In 1992 only 95,000 workers were on unpaid parental leave (congé parental), despite there being 1 million households with two parents in the labour force and at least one child under 3 (DARES, 1993). The majority of mothers who took unpaid leave were between 30 and 40 years old, and in 40 per cent of the cases, it was for their third child. They were most often employed in the private sector; public sector workers tended to prefer to work part time.

The number of Belgian parents taking a Career Break is rising. Whereas there were merely 2,019 on this leave in 1985 (the first year of the program), by 1995 there were 50,400 (Network, 1994: 32). Approximately 90 per cent of them were women and fully 70 per cent were younger than 45, which justifies the characterization of the Career Break as the functional equivalent of parental leaves before 1998. Given the fact that only public sector employees have a *right* to this kind of leave, it is not surprising to observe that civil servants are most inclined to use it. In 1992, 56 per cent of the workers on leave were in the public sector, although they represent only 30 per cent of the total labour force. Moreover, more white-collar than blue-collar workers took a Career Break (Network, 1994: 32–3).

In Italy, there are no overall statistics on parental leaves, but experts judged them to be not very popular (Hantrais and Letablier, 1995a: 99). Research on the public sector found more mothers than fathers taking leave (Network, 1994: 32–3). In 1999 there was a major reform to the parental leave program, providing ten months in total over the first eight years of the child's life and providing an extra month available only to fathers. In other words, Italy's program design, for those eligible for leave, has been 'accelerated' and now resembles that of Sweden. Unpaid leave also has been extended substantially.

Cared for by Mothers

The third kind of private provision we will consider is that by mothers who are not on parental leave. Sometimes they are providing this care with no remuneration at all, but sometimes there is a tax advantage offered or even an allowance associated with mothers who provide their own childcare. Indeed, in all the cases we examined, other than Italy, government policies actively promoting care by mothers have been debated in a serious fashion, if not instituted.

As we saw in table 8.3, relatively few Swedish children under the age of 6 are cared for by a mother who is not in the labour force. The number is approximately one in seven. Policy-makers have been tempted to encourage such a form of childcare, however, and even briefly instituted a subsidy, as recounted in chapter 6. Despite being rescinded by the Social Democrats when they returned to office, the idea continues to have significant support. Therefore, it remains on the Swedish agenda.

In the other three countries, many children continue to be cared for by their mothers (even when they are in the paid labour force), and, at least in Belgium and France, policy-makers have tried to foster this practice with allowances for mothers who care for their own children. In Italy, as we saw in table 8.3, more than 25 per cent of children whose mothers are in the paid labour force still are cared for by them. Despite this situation – or perhaps because of it – no child-rearing allowances are available to Italian mothers. In Belgium, such a Child-Rearing Allowance (*Allocation socio-pédagogique*) was legislated and remains on the books, but without ever having been implemented. Nonetheless, 56 per cent of the under-3s in the Francophone Community and 50 per cent of the Flemish-speaking Community are looked after by their mothers (ONAFTS, 1994). This form of care is subsidized with tax credits. Thus, families with a stay-at-home parent and a child under three enjoy a significant tax deduction that was instituted quite explicitly to equalize the situation, once tax deductions for non-parental care were made available (Vielle, 1994: 95; see also chapter 3).

In France, public policies encourage mothers to provide their own childcare. The Child-Rearing Allowance (*Allocation parentale d'éduca-tion*) described above is hardly a classic parental leave. Parents may have access to it with only a limited history of labour force participation. Moreover, in its earlier incarnations, the link to employment was quite virtual. In 1990, in a detailed inquiry into family life, it was found that 54 per cent of children under 3 were cared for by their mothers. Moreover, fully 18 per cent of those whose mothers were in the labour force were still cared for by them, only 9 percentage points less than in Italy (Desplanques, 1993: 331).

In this chapter we have documented the wide variety of programs that now exist to provide for the care of young children. Any examination of these details results in an impression of diversity, not only in programs but also in policy goals and strategies. This sense that differences are great and decision-makers may choose from a wide range of possible ways of thinking about the care of young children is never a false one. Nonetheless, the appreciation of such details of the specific five trajectories should never blind us to the possibility that there are more general patterns of change underlying the variety. Through its focus on the ways in which post-war citizenship regimes have crumbled, our comparative study has also allowed us to uncover a set of general trends in the area of childcare. We see that social policy restructuring has followed some common trajectories in countries as far away in both space and policy legacies as Sweden and Italy, as different in their welfare regimes as social democratic Sweden, corporatist Belgium, and republican France. Moreover, while the European Union has pushed and prodded for change, these directions do not always correspond to its vision of 'social Europe.' The shift from a citizenship regime incorporating commitments to both gender and class inequalities has had an impact everywhere.

NOTES

1 'In this model, children are viewed not only as consumers of goods and services but also as citizens who already bear rights to care and to education' (Hantrais and Letablier, 1995b: 44).
2 We are using the definition of the European Commission's Childcare Network. The category 'under-3' refers to children from birth to 36 months old, that is to say, up to their third birthday. Therefore, 3-year-olds are not included.
3 Although the best – in fact, the only – systematic collection of information on all Member States, the Network's data are limited by the fact that all countries do not keep reliable or comparable information in this policy realm. The network itself recognized this lack of precision, invoking several reasons to account for it. Available data vary from one country to another. Different institutions within the same country may maintain their data quite differently, and there is a huge gap in the information about private childcare services. This constitutes the greatest problem: most of the time no reliable statistics exist (Network, 1996: 127–8). Therefore, we were forced to rely on the data collected in the mid-1990s by the Network on Childcare.
4 'Organized family day care' refers to a public service in which childminders are recruited, employed, and supported by a public agency or a publicly funded private organization (Network, 1996: 8).
5 These differences have deep historical roots. 'For more than a century, *écoles maternelles* have played a central role in the republican and secular French educational system,' being explicitly designed as a counterweight to the influence of the family (Schultheis, 1997: 254). In Sweden, in contrast, formal schooling for very young children has been neither provided nor considered necessary. See chapter 7 for the long and controversial history of public education for young children in Italy.

6 The day nurseries are the responsibility of the national Ministry of Health, but the regional governments, who are responsible for service development, and the local authorities who manage them often place them within the educational bureaucracy (Network, 1996: 72).

7 Where 6-year-olds do attend school, it is for only fifteen hours per week, so they must still have a place in a municipal childcare centre or family day care (Network, 1996: 110).

8 In 1990–91 the percentage of 2-year-olds in pre-primary schooling was 36. Fully 99 per cent of 3-year-olds attend school. In 1960–61 slightly less than 10 per cent of 2-year-olds were in school. The rate of increase has recently begun to stagnate (INSEE, 1992: 87).

9 Belgian political institutions are divided among three Communities: Francophone, Flemish-speaking, and German-speaking. The third is extremely small, however, and we do not treat it in our analysis. In 1993 in the German-speaking community there were merely 375 childcare places, all in family day care, providing for 13 per cent of the age cohort (Network, 1996: 29).

10 However, public financing is higher for centres than for family day care (Broberg and Hwang, 1991, 1992).

11 The variation in cost of each kind of service explains, in part, the different levels of spending. For example, in France, the CNAF estimated that in 1989 the daily cost was 245 FF per child in community day nurseries, 170 FF in family day care, 140 FF in parent cooperatives, and 195 FF in drop-in centres (INSEE, 1992: 127).

12 This tax deduction applies to publicly financed childcare services, such as those discussed in this section, and also to care provided by a childminder (*assistante maternelle agréée libre*) in her own home.

13 In this section we do not discuss maternity leaves. All countries of the EU have some provision for a woman to take leave at childbirth. It is a leave reserved to women and is based on her health needs. In Sweden, maternity leave is folded into the parental leave, but in the other three countries, it is treated as a different right and is regulated differently.

14 A 1981 recommendation from the International Labour Organization (ILO) preceded this Council of Ministers Recommendation (Vielle, 1994: 64–5).

15 In this case, however, the level of the benefit is slightly less than a Career Break taken to raise a young child.

16 Here, we present information only about the 'standard' situation. There are special provisions in the case of sickness or multiple births.

17 Paid parental leaves may be taken by both parents simultaneously, however, albeit on a part-time basis.

18 This is the case of a number of young mothers of under-3s who have precarious jobs. Those who are working less than fifteen hours per week are not counted in the labour force and as a result, they are not entitled to parental leave. Overall, this parental insurance system is a very marginal program. If unemployment continues to increase over the next few years, however, it could become an important issue in future debates.

19 In the case of a part-time Career Break, public authorities consider only actual hours worked in calculating retirement benefits. The employee who takes a Career Break is protected against dismissal, except for cause. Employers are forbidden to lay off an employee during a Career Break or during the first three months following her or his return to work.

20 Swedish fathers who take parental leave for an extended period tend to have specific characteristics. They work in the public sector, they are older, they are better educated, they work at jobs in which a high proportion of women are present, and their partner is well educated and earns a high income (Network, 1994: 37).

Chapter Nine

Citizenship in the Era of Welfare State Redesign

Jane Jenson and Mariette Sineau

In recent decades economic and political restructuring have begun to alter our notions of citizenship and citizen rights in profound ways. Promoting equality was a core value of the post-war years. While the class dimension of equality was most visible as a result of the important role played by political parties and unions representing workers, gender equality was never totally ignored. Moreover, by the mid-1960s active women's movements were pushing for rights and policies to eliminate long-standing inequalities between women and men. Among the many claims addressed to the state, one was virtually constant: women needed to achieve a basic civil right – the right to work – and economic autonomy, thereby breaking their dependence on men or the state. Non-discrimination and equal access to employment and remuneration were foundation principles for the second wave of the women's movement.

Such claims did not meet with an immediate and positive response. Traditionalists clung to a vision of the 'angel of the hearth' and the 'male breadwinner.' Nonetheless, the values of equality, fairness, and democracy could be legitimately invoked as women mounted their claims for full citizenship. The result was that by the mid-1970s many countries' citizenship regimes included enhanced commitments to gender equality as well as to solidarity across classes. In these citizenship regimes, the state was identified as the tool for change. Choices made via democratic means would counterbalance private power in markets. Citizens could hope not only for equality but also for democratic control over their futures.

In the 1980s and 1990s these commitments were threatened by the ideology of neo-liberalism that has predominated in the last two decades. The result was a redefinition of the basic terms of citizenship regimes, defined as the widely accepted ideas about the relationship between the citizen and the state and the balance of power among state, market, and community. The relationship between citizens and states has altered. Citizens have been transformed into 'consumers' of services, and states seek to satisfy their desires for 'consumer sovereignty,' that is, for choice (Phillips, 1993). Neo-liberal citizenship regimes also rebalance power, shifting it towards markets, which become the locale for making choices. Thus, even when they are spending public funds, government agencies are encouraged to engage in market behaviours, contracting with private companies, non-profit associations, and even other agencies of the state. Moreover, because theorists of the free market abhor 'monopolies,' an argument for and a drive towards decentralization of state power and reduced power for central authorities were easily built into neo-liberal citizenship regimes.

All of these shifts in representations of the proper relations among states and citizens as well as among states, markets, and communities have clear implications for the core values of these same regimes. The goal of equality – whether across classes, sexes, or regions of a country – takes second place. State policy as well as many political formations and other actors promote the liberty of choice. Collective choice, which is the kind of choice made by democratic institutions, gives way to more individualized and flexible modes of choices made by individuals and families.

Detailed attention to childcare programs provides a window into these processes of change and the recomposition of citizenship across our five cases. Childcare is located at the intersection of public and 'private,' family and community. As we have noted frequently, women's movements and their allies identified access to reliable, high-quality, and affordable childcare services as a condition for the equal participation of women in the labour force. Without it, mothers would find their labour force activity shaped by the need to choose between employment and family responsibilities or to find a job that did not interfere with their other tasks. Reliable, high-quality, and inexpensive childcare thus was placed high on any list of the social and economic rights of citizenship demanded by second-wave women's movements.

In recent decades, as neo-liberalism has taken hold, all the practices of working women, families, and employers have changed. New pressures and needs have arisen, which, in turn, have generated demands for adjustments in childcare programs. In response, policy-makers, other political actors, and parents have deployed and debated their ideas of gender relations as they pushed for specific policies. New ideas are never sufficient in themselves to account for change (Hall, 1989: introduction; Bradford, 1998: chapter 1). The fact that they do make a significant contribution to destabilizing the existing citizenship regimes and stimulating new choices, however, is one of the reasons that we have paid them so much attention in our study of patterns of policy shifts. At the same time, examination of these ideas about gender relations allows us to 'read' the modifications in the very principles underpinning the citizenship regimes of our cases. Only by such careful attention to program design – not simply to whether programs exist or how much is spent on them – can one uncover the restructuring of social citizenship that is under way.

Three steps remain to complete our analysis. The first step is to describe in a systematic and comparative way the direction that change has taken in each case, with particular attention to the consequences for women's right to employment and access to childcare. The second is to make some generalizations about the direction of change in patterns of childcare across our five cases. The final step involves using childcare policies as a window into the larger processes of welfare state redesign and their implications for citizenship. In this chapter, using the data from previous chapters, we proceed through these three steps.

Post-War Citizenship Regimes and Ideas about Women's Work

Our detailed analyses have permitted us to identify the links across policy domains, revealing that labour and family policies, particularly their childcare component, are never made in isolation. In each country as well as in the European Union, childcare has been a multi-purpose program, addressing the needs of labour market, family, poverty, child welfare, demographic, and other policies. In each case, childcare was nested inside a widely accepted political discourse about the relations of state, market, and community.

As a result, childcare services have borne a heavy representational burden. The first half of the term – that is, 'child' – led to demographic as well as child welfare concerns. Such concern for the child translated, in all cases, into guarantees for access to public or publicly subsidized care and to higher than average commitment – except in Italy – to public care for infants. The second half of the term – that is, 'care' – required attention to the provider: paid workers, mothers, parents, or others. The case studies have been focused on the model representation of employment, particularly that of mothers, so as to discern the ways in which the needs of employers, states, mothers, parents, and children were represented in the political discourse particular to each country.[1]

We now move to a synthetic comparison of these paradigms, examining their basic discursive principles and models of gender relations and women's employment. In doing so we reveal that, despite the variations in detail and the different childcare programs embedded in each paradigm, there has been throughout the post-1945 years a marked degree of commonality in timing and in practices. Our comparisons uncover common patterns and policy logics across the citizenship regimes of the Fordist years, as much as they reveal differences in each place.

The Post-War Dream: Children at Home with Their Mothers

Political economists and social policy analysts tend to mark 1945 as the 'start' of many things; it is a useful date for documenting reforms. Most countries emerged from the trauma of war and sought to set the world on a better path than that taken in either the 1940s or the 1930s. Indeed, there is a strong tendency to identify 1945 as the beginning of the post-war compromise, Fordism, and modern social policy. This convention is credible precisely because the end of the war resulted in the social and economic rights of citizenship and the equality discourses that we associate with the modern welfare state (for example, Marshall, 1963). Although during the 1940s a new consciousness of equality took hold, it did not yet extend to equality between the sexes. In none of our four countries did 1945 bring a fundamental change in the representations of women's work. The equality dimension of the citizenship regimes was confined to two of the three dimensions discussed here – class and territory – despite the presence of women's movement, which continued to press claims for gender equality.[2]

As a result, the first post-war decade was marked most by continuity with the 1930s representation of the relationship between mother and child. Indeed, if anything, the notion that children should be cared for by their mothers was reinforced. Booming economies made it possible to imagine that salaries would be sufficiently high for a male breadwinner to earn enough to care for his wife and dependent children. In turn, experts in child development were successfully promoting their theories about 'the need' for close bonding of mothers and infants (Wilson, 1980).

At the end of the war Belgium was poised to strengthen its commitment to pluralism. Since the nineteenth century, Belgian politics had been characterized by the institutionalized equilibrium among Belgium's three ideo-cultural 'worlds' of Roman Catholics, Socialists, and liberals. Citizenship rights and loyalties always were mediated by membership in one of the worlds, the relationship between the individual citizen and the state being mediated by communal institutions. Nonetheless, the Social Pact negotiated at the end of the war also marked a certain distance from traditional pluralism. It created a new set of structures, most obviously those of the Social Security system. Even if these public institutions continued to be organized along longstanding principles of representation of the three worlds, new state institutions henceforth would be involved in processes of conflict resolution and would have more direct contact with citizens. They became the forums in which diverging views about gender roles, about equality and fairness, and about public support for the family as well as other institutions would take place.

The drive to create and sustain consensus, which continued to underpin any political act in Belgium, generated a familialist model of the gender division of labour. Symbolized by a couple – the breadwinner and the housewife – the model provided the representational grounding for post-war family policy. As well as being focused on demographic concerns about the birth rate, programs favoured families with stay-at-home wives. A consensus-seeking élite did little to promote gender equality. Complementarity, rather than similarity, of the sexes was the basic principle.

It is not surprising, given the dominance of representations of an essentially private domain of family and children, that publicly financed and provided childcare was not a major item on the policy agenda. At the end of the war there were 3,500 childcare places available; in 1960 there were only an additional 500. Moreover, access to these places was never meant to be a right for the 'ordinary' Belgian citizen. They were intended only for the care of children at risk because of poverty or other social pathologies.

In France, too, despite a discourse of modernization, during the postwar years programs that reinforced the representation of mothers' responsibility for children's care and for the birth rate predominated.

Although the forces of the left had been sufficiently strong to insert equal treatment provisions with respect to women's employment in the constitution of the Fourth Republic, they were not strong enough to block the domination of family policy by Christian Democrats and the family movement. Therefore, representations of equality between the sexes existed uneasily beside traditional discourses about the gender division of labour. In addition, Catholics and the right justified family-based care in terms of their ideological opposition to republicanism. In particular, they sought to limit the role of the state and protect children from too much collectivism. To the extent that any infrastructure for childcare developed, it was lodged within the policy domain of public health, dominated by experts who sought to provide high-quality services to the children of the working class, who were considered to be at risk from poverty and lack of parenting skills (Norvez, 1990: chapter 4).

In post-war Italy, where Christian Democracy was dominant, the Communist party (PCI), were sometimes forced to trade away their own policy preferences in exchange for maintaining their place in the political game. As a result, any decision to mount policy challenges always had to be carefully calculated. In the case of family policy, the PCI might decide to go along with the Christian Democrats' preferences rather than press forward with their own visions of gender equality. The rights of women to work were the exception to this practice, and the post-war Italian constitution did guarantee equal treatment. Apart from that distinction, however, Christian Democrats were able to promote their familialism.

In this model, not only did the care of children belong to the family and within the family to women, but the state had practically no legitimate reason to intervene in this realm. This notion corresponded to the Catholic principle of subsidiarity. The essentially 'private' nature of family life justified inaction with respect to social categories – particularly the young and the old – with which other countries were already involved.

During the 1930s the first steps were taken towards the construction of the 'Swedish model.' Initially, it clearly represented the gender division of labour, which was institutionalized in employment and family policies encouraging women to modernize their work as housewives while discouraging their labour force participation. Thus, the 'modern housewife' was the model figure in Swedish social democracy of the 1950s. The principle of equality was, first and foremost, class-based. One result was that in post-war Sweden the idea of equality was not the same as that which in France and Italy had given rise to constitutional guarantees of economic equality, and therefore of equal pay, between the sexes; separate salary scales for women and men were abolished only in the 1960s. Instead, women and men could achieve equality via a recognition of their different – but equally important – responsibilities in public and 'private' life. Again, as was the case in Belgium, complementarity was the watchword.

It is not surprising that care for young children in this model was provided by the family, with only two exceptions. Child welfare concerns led charities to create day-care centres for children of poor women who were in the labour force, while child development concerns fostered kindergartens for children over three years in order to provide pre-school socialization.

We see from this rapid summary of the immediate post-1945 situation that all four citizenship regimes stressed equality. The emphasis, however, was almost exclusively on creating a certain degree of cross-class (and some cross-regional) equality. While policy realms such as employment, health, housing, and education were central to achieving such goals, childcare programs were also imprinted with this vision. To the extent that these programs existed, they were for the poorest children or those 'at risk' and in need of protection.

There was consensus in all four cases on the benefits of mothers providing their own childcare. Nonetheless, not all the justifications provided were the same. In Sweden, the task belonged to mothers simply because it always had been so; Social Democrats sought to update traditional gender relations but not to abolish them. In Italy, France, and Belgium, in contrast, the political right supplemented its traditional representations of gender relations with a familialism that was more political, an expression of anti-collectivism and, in some cases, of subsidiarity. As labour market conditions altered in the 1960s, therefore, the Swedish Social Democrats would rework their own understandings of equality to make them more gender neutral. In the other cases the political processes were more complicated. A shift in the balance of political forces had to occur before policy could fully incorporate new ideas about women's work and the gender division of labour.

Another Value Arrives: Gender Equality

In all four countries, a major shift in representations of gender relations began in the first years of the 1960s. At the same time, the Treaty of

Rome introduced a new actor onto the scene. In all of these cases, the citizenship regimes created real space for politics and then policies that were an expression of the value of gender equality. It joined class and territorial equality as one of the triplet of values underpinning these regimes.

The direction of movement in all five cases was the same, and by the late 1960s it was obvious that the situation had changed. Women's labour force participation climbed in these years along with a growing demand for employees in the service sector, both public and private. Both the parties of the left and the women's movement acquired greater influence, with the result that issues of family planning as well as the women's labour market situation became subjects of political debate in all five cases. Social movements agitated for better access to contraception and abortion. These forces also increased their influence over the design of social policy, including childcare. The number of available childcare places rose. At the same time, the forces of pro-natalism lost ground in both Belgium and France, where they had long succeeded in making familialism a pillar of family policy.

For all four countries, as well as for the European Community, representations of childcare as a family matter lost their impetus. States and the EC asserted their responsibility in this realm. Indeed, they claimed they had to intervene so as to promote gender equality. State policy would now be designed to help women to 'reconcile work and family life.'

In these years, the predominant reading of reconciliation identified the problem as one related only to women's needs, ignoring the fact that men also had children. The discourse of reconciliation emerged nonetheless, from a commitment to promoting women's equality with men. Thus, childcare slightly shifted policy realms, as labour market concerns and equal-opportunity policies began to shape it more than the traditional attention to demography and child welfare of the post-1945 years had done. Despite a similar trajectory, such claims were expressed in a wide variety of ways and justified by a range of political principles, because they had to be adapted to the terms of the specific citizenship regime, each of which was undergoing a within-regime update.

That the process was one of updating, not upheaval, was clearest in Sweden. In the 1960s and 1970s gender equality was grafted onto the Swedish Model. Under pressure from feminists organized within the Social Democratic party and the unions, the representation of gender relations was no longer one of 'different but equal.' It became one of simple equality. As women were starting to go out to work, these political forces promoted their view that gender equality required the provision of childcare. They argued that a collective commitment to redistributing the costs of care from mothers to parents and from parents to the collectivity was absolutely essential if women were not to be condemned to inequality and discrimination in the labour market. Parental leaves and public funds for childcare centres as well as expansion of family day care date from the early 1970s.

It is important to note, however, that it was not only Social Democratic Sweden that, under pressure from the women's movement and the left, opted for expanding publicly funded and provided childcare places. In France, too, the forces of modernity discovered within their discourses of modernity and republican equality reasons to promote an extension of childcare as a public service. Promises of a huge increase in places in day nurseries were made both by François Mitterrand as the candidate of the United Left and by the centrist Valéry Giscard d'Estaing in the 1974 presidential election.

In Belgium in the 1970s there were new mobilizations for gender equality, to be achieved by greater public support for childcare services. Its commitment to pluralism, however, prevented a unilinear direction of change. On the one hand, there was a new commitment to extending pre-primary schools and making new funds available for constructing a variety of day-care services. The goal of these initiatives was primarily to foster gender and class equality. On the other hand, the forces of Catholicism and tradition pressed for programs enabling mothers and families to provide their own care, via the creation of an allowance to recognize the social contribution of stay-at-home mothers. As a result, policy proceeded simultaneously in two contradictory directions. New public services were created without eliminating tax and other benefits going to families with stay-at-home mothers. Both were accommodated under the banner of choice.

By the mid-1970s the European Community also began to intervene on childcare issues. Finding its basis for action in article 119, which it and the European Court were reading as a guarantee of equal opportunities, the Community began to promote expanded childcare as a way for women to reconcile their dual roles as workers and mothers (Hoskyns, 1996). Unleashed by the decisions of the Court and the Equality Directives of the 1970s, the institutional foundations of Commission involvement were consolidated by the establishment of the Equal Opportunities Unit.

Only in Italy were the themes of gender equality muted, and no link was made between childcare and women's employment. Other issues predominated, as adjustments were made to the childcare regime. Despite the 'family' issue's being a potential spark for left–right conflict, the forces of modernization within the Christian Democratic camp as well as on the left did make a break with the principle of subsidiarity, which had underpinned the familialist model. Public pre-primary schools were instituted, even though this initiative meant that the dominance assured by the private – religious – system would be weakened. Thus, even in Italy, during these years commitment to childcare as a public service grew, although its route was different from that of the other jurisdictions.

Childcare Choices in the New Conditions

Early post-war family policy had incorporated demographic and pro-natalist goals, at least in Belgium, France, and Sweden. Although the family policy was an adjunct of social policy, it also had its own specificity. Fighting poverty and improving equality of opportunity was only one dimension of the mandate of family and childcare programs. Also important were child development and demographic goals, which gave family policy its specificity and autonomy, as well as its justification for a separate administrative identity. In the first post-war years most childcare programs gave top priority to the welfare of the child, with particular attention paid to those 'at risk' because of poverty or other social pathologies. By the mid-1960s, however, middle-class parents in Belgium, France, and Sweden, and to a lesser extent in Italy, had begun to seek collective forms of childcare as an expression of their own views on child development. They identified in the group experiences and educational focus of early childhood institutions substantial benefits of enhanced social and school readiness skills.

Moreover, by the 1970s an additional element had been added to childcare discussions. Publicly financed and provided childcare was also supposed to address the needs of employed mothers. The arrival of the egalitarian model of gender relations, following on the successes of second-wave feminism and the rapid rise in women's labour force participation, meant that childcare became an equal-opportunity matter. As this discourse gained ground, the European Community weighed into the discussion.

Two central ideas about women's employment underpinned the

programs for public provision of childcare services that developed through the 1970s. The first, which came to be universally shared, was that gender equality would be achieved through women's integration into what was conceptualized as a single labour market. If proper provision for childcare were made, women would have careers very similar to those of men: continuous over the life cycle, with only short breaks for parental leave; full time, with only short periods of part-time employment. As we will see in the next section, this assumption of full integration into a single, or the core, labour market did not survive the economic restructuring that began with the crisis of the 1970s.

The second idea was much more controversial, and no hegemonic position had yet been consolidated. On one side were those for whom reconciliation of work and family duties was women's responsibility. For them, the state would be involved in childcare in order to achieve equality between the sexes. In the 1970s the state could position itself on the side of women seeking such equality, sharing with them responsibility for childcare. This notion that managing the constraints of working time and caring time was women's task was contested, however, by those who articulated the notion that both parents should be encouraged and be given the means to assume caring responsibilities. In this view the state should ensure that caring time was more equitably shared across the sexes, as well as sharing some responsibility for providing it. Disputes over the distribution of caring work became even more complicated and controversial as economic and political restructuring brought other possibilities to the fore.

Women's Work: New or Recycled Representations?

As neo-liberal ideology and programs changed the rules of the game and as citizenship regimes rebalanced the relationship among states, markets, and communities by allowing the 'market' to predominate, several things happened. The changes went far beyond the financial issue of 'cutbacks' and downsizing government budgets. States did seek to control their financial commitment to childcare in the name of 'fiscal responsibility,' but neo-liberalism also led them to encourage market-mimicking contractual relationships. The idea of common public services gave way to a variety of forms of delivery. They also fostered employment in the third sector, in order to allow non-profit associations to address the needs of particular categories of children. 'Choice' became the value privileged above all else.

The result was policies designed concurrently to respond to the growing preference of parents for childcare à la carte, to absorb large numbers of unemployed, low-skilled, women workers and remove them from social assistance or welfare rolls, and to reduce the costs of childcare by providing indirect state subsidies rather than direct provision. At the same time, as a solution to two problems, states desperate to reduce unemployment rates identified various kinds of programs that encouraged parents – read women – to provide their own childcare. In that way they might be able to cut the unemployment rate and hold down the costs of childcare services.

The egalitarian model of gender relations has come under threat in all five of our case studies. Nonetheless, neither the amount nor the form of threat has been the same. The European Union, with its efforts to extend the concept of reconciliation to both parents was, alongside Sweden, the most systematically egalitarian of our cases. Through the 1980s and 1990s, as the other countries were deploying diverse representations of women's and men's work and were threatening to backtrack in policy, the equal opportunities machinery of the Commission, including the Childcare Network, continued to promote its progressive visions of reconciliation. Nonetheless, as shown also in chapter seven, its efforts came to grief, since the Commission, itself, has retreated in the last few years.

In Sweden, perception of threats to the hegemonic model of gender relations is just as recent. When the Social Democrats returned to office in 1994, they repealed the bourgeois government's care allowance, which would have funded stay-at-home mothers as a form of childcare. Opposition to this measure remains fragile, however, given the preference of some working-class parents – a core constituency of the Social Democrats – for private forms of care. Progressive forces in Sweden also have resisted, in the name of gender equality, the move to individualized care. Their opposition, as is true in Belgium and France, is to consolidation of a low-wage, female ghetto of caring work, as well as to the very notion of private domestic service. The Social Democratic government, however, like the bourgeois government before it, is committed to expanding the private service sector. Therefore, the 'exceptionalism' of Sweden's egalitarianism may be further diminished in the future.

In Belgium and France, commitment to an egalitarian model of gender relations was more equivocal, even through the 1970s. Older and traditional visions of women's role coexisted alongside those promoting equality of the sexes via labour force participation. This coexistence was most evident in Belgium, where, even at the height of enthusiasm for the egalitarian model, alternative representations had sufficient political clout to give rise to the legislation establishing (but not implementing) the Child-Rearing Allowance. Such forces gained new legitimacy as unemployment deepened and became intractable. Although in France the traditionalists, especially the pro-natalists, were reduced to a certain 'whining fringe group' in the 1970s, they never disappeared. Therefore, as the post-war citizenship regimes began to crumble in the 1980s, they could emerge from the shadows and, even with the Socialists in government, institute programs that reflected continuing commitment to traditional representations of the gender division of labour.

It is also important to note that in neither case were traditionalists triumphant. The commitment was much more than formal. New programs were developed that permitted (some) mothers of young children to remain in the labour force.

A major difficulty emerged when governments actually did design programs to foster reconciliation of work and family responsibilities. New uses of time were promoted. In Sweden, beginning as early as the 1970s, parents were encouraged to manage their family and work responsibilities by adjustments in time. Parental leaves and the right to part-time work allowed parents of young children to reduce hours in the workplace to care for their children. Despite contestation by feminists, who sought another time solution – the six-hour day for everyone – the Swedish decision since the 1970s has been that considerable care will be provided by parents, one at a time. Parental leaves made this parental care full time for the youngest children and part time in later years. This relatively progressive approach attempted to minimize the penalizing of women who provided their own childcare. Both because the discourse was one of parentalism and because concrete programmatic efforts were made to encourage (and then financially to induce) fathers to participate in leave-taking, some redistribution of caring work between women and men did occur. Moreover, because leaves were paid at near replacement values and part time work was protected and highly paid, the familiar disadvantages associated with taking a leave or working part time were somewhat attenuated.

This solution to the caring time / working time dilemma may not be stable. The Swedish Model is crumbling, just as the other models are.

As the state cuts back employees, in response to budgetary pressures, and as structural constraints on long hours of work in industry decline, the issue of time management may come to the fore in a different way in Sweden. The solution of mothers working part time in the state sector for high wages may no longer be available, and if men's hours on the job are extended, someone will have to pick up the caring burden.

These observations must be written in the conditional for Sweden, because it is too early to identify the longer-term consequences for representations of women's work and gender relations in the decline of the Swedish Model. Such is not the case for France and Belgium. In both these countries, the state has chosen to back employers' calls for a more flexible labour force. Mothers of young children will be treated as a labour force for part-time jobs as well as candidates for leaves. France and Belgium, in effect, have taken a decision that many women workers will no longer be encouraged to seek the same labour force status as male workers, at least while they are young. Programs designed to maximize the capacity to combine working time and family time, either simultaneously or consecutively, have been designed with little of the Swedish-style attention to attenuating gender differences in the use of time. Gaps widen between the ways that men and women mix working and caring times.

Nonetheless, in both France and Belgium, there is a clear understanding that not all women workers will accept such forms of conciliation. Although the Swedish programs, with their replacement-level benefits, are almost universal, this is not true for the French and Belgian ones. Low rates of remuneration and negative consequences for women trying to re-enter the labour force after a leave mean that the implementation of the leave program, in effect, targets the lowest-paid or least-skilled workers. Other solutions have been developed for those women who will work like their male colleagues in full-time and well-paid, probably professional, jobs. For them, the time crunch is solved by employing others if they do not find one of the limited places in a day nursery. In these two countries, in other words, the category of 'women worker' is bifurcated. There are different representations depending on class.

Italy remains the outlier in this discussion. Because its political regime fragmented so recently, long-standing competing representations of women's work and gender relations remained in place longer than in the other cases. While the left and some progressive Christian Democrats subscribed to the egalitarian model, with the result that equal opportunity and anti-discrimination measures were implemented, the right maintained its traditional position on the family and sex roles.

The Italian 'difference,' however, comes less from the fact that divergence existed. Only Sweden could be said to have experienced anything near consensus. Rather, it comes from the absence of any clear link until very recently between equality and childcare. In effect, Italy retains the most privatized of all the systems for infants and young children, as we saw in chapter 8. Families, when they do have children, are left to their own devices to distribute working time and caring time. They can appeal to family caregivers (mothers, parents, grandmothers, or other relatives). Or they can purchase care in the private market. One solution adopted by many young families in Italy is also 'private': they have decided to have no children, or perhaps only one child, and 'to cope' during the three years before she or he can enter school.

This overview of new representations of women's work makes it clear that ideas about gender relations and women's work cannot be analysed in isolation from citizenship regimes that underpin the ideas and set out the institutional responsibilities for specific childcare. These regimes reflect the prevailing division of labour between women and men and between citizens and the state. Nonetheless, as much as we have stressed the need to place the explanation for changes within the specific characteristics of each case, we have also noticed that citizenship regimes are moving in similar directions, albeit perhaps at different rates. In the last section of this chapter we will describe the common directions and patterns of change, linking them to the new characteristics of neo-liberalism's citizenship regimes.

Common Patterns of Movement in Childcare Programs

Contemporary citizenship regimes display an emerging consensus about the division of responsibility and power among states, markets, and communities. In this they display the convergence found in other policy realms by Kitschelt et al. (1999: passim, especially the conclusion). More emphasis on markets has meant less enthusiasm for the state. Democratic decision-making mechanisms give way to private choices made by individuals or to collective action in community organizations and associations. The latter may provide new locales for democratization, but the results still will have to be consolidated. At this time, our overview, based on the previous chapters, identifies a preponderant shift in the direction of privileging markets and individual citizens' market power to choose.

This generalization can be sustained by an examination of five directions of change we have identified in recent reforms of childcare programs, all shared by the five cases. They are as follows:

- less costly services, so as to fit within the lower limits established for government spending
- decentralization of service provision from the central government to local authorities
- increased diversification in programs available and access to them
- greater flexibility in the use of childcare
- individualization of choice.

In identifying these common patterns, we find that there is a significant blurring of distinctions across countries other literature has classified according to typologies of 'welfare state regimes,' (Esping-Andersen, 1990) or 'production regimes' (Kitschelt et al., 1999). All cases are moving towards less emphasis on services and more on transfers, delivery by private agencies (whether commercial or non-profit), and reliance on the tax system for state expenditures. While the specific routes by which they arrive at these points are the product of their own histories, the degree of convergence is striking.

In all five cases *the costs* of social programs, including childcare, have been a major concern. Budget cutbacks and limits on funds available have led states to seek less expensive programs and to shift funding to other policy sectors. Such cost-saving measures have meant, for example, in France, a clear preference for childminders, whether trained or nor, over the more expensive municipal day nurseries. In Sweden, the generosity of parental leaves was reduced substantially (from 90 to 75 per cent and then back to 80 per cent wage replacement), leaving families to assume the income lost when a parental leave is taken. This is a significant privatization of the costs of childcare.

In several cases – especially France and Belgium – tax credits for childcare expenditures have gained increasing popularity. In the late 1980s these two countries were already far ahead of all their European neighbours in the level of tax relief (Gornick et al., 1997: table 3, 56). Such 'invisible' expenditures, in the form of state revenue forgone, fit well with neo-liberalism's enthusiasm for seemingly lower 'state expenditures' as well as greater 'choice.' In France, payroll taxes are forgiven if a family employs a childminder. In Sweden, the bourgeois government lifted payroll taxes for those employing someone to provide personal services (maids as well as nannies). The Social Democratic government has sought an alternative formula that is less individualistic but that nonetheless relies on payroll tax reduction.

Cost factors have also meant that some programs that are on the books are not being implemented. For example, Swedish observers express concern about whether the cash-strapped municipal governments actually will be able to provide a childcare place for each child, despite the fact that the central government requires them to do so. Another example can be seen in Belgium. For budgetary reasons, the Child-Rearing Allowance was never implemented, while the budget of the institution responsible for childcare in the Francophone Community was frozen for several years.

Finally, strains on the unemployment insurance budgets have led some governments to transfer the costs of dealing with unemployment from ministries of labour to the institutions of the family sector that have experienced somewhat less financial pressure. Parental leave benefits, which encourage women to care for their own children are considered to have two positive consequences for government finances. The first is that someone taking parental leave may open up a position for a temporary replacement from among the unemployed. Indeed, Belgium requires employers to replace employees taking a Voluntary Career Break (which serves as a parental leave in that country) with someone from the unemployment rolls. Second, since parental leaves are financed out of the purses of the family institutions or by employers, pressure on unemployment funds decline.

Decentralization of childcare provision has occurred as part of the general processes of decentralization. In all cases, local authorities have gained new liabilities for service provision. First, this decentralization has taken the form of substantial transfers of financial responsibilities, so that local authorities must now find the funds for childcare within their own budgets. Second, local authorities also have gained new space for policy choices about which services to provide, and to whom and in what form they should be given. This has happened in all four cases: via federalization in Belgium, constitutional empowerment of regional governments in Italy, assignment of new powers to France's local authorities, and decentralization of budgets and administrative decisions in Sweden.

The national-level homogeneity that was promoted in the post-war years has given away to what may very well become less coherent provision. Decentralizing decision-making about childcare has therefore made a major contribution to our third direction of change, that of *diversification*.

One obvious exception to geographical diversification as well as decentralization is found in parental leaves, especially the European Union's Directive on Parental Leaves. To the extent that leaves are mandated by national legislation, they have been provided centrally. The EU's Directive continues this tradition, extending the range of coverage; the agreement is a mechanism for creating a set of common standards and rights across the Union. This counter-example aside, the trend is strongly in the direction of diversity for all services provided by caregivers other than parents.

Of course, there has always been considerable geographical variation in services available. Rural areas have rarely provided the same levels of service, and political differences in local administrations have meant wide variation in types of access. That said, geographical diversification can be expected only to increase in the future, underpinned as it is by the move to decentralization.

Other forms of diversification also have been observed. Universally accessible public service has given way to programs that permit and even foster divergence across classes. Differences in access to particular programs are one obvious type. Here, as limits on public spending – whether lower payments for leaves or lower subsidies for day nurseries – oblige parents to assume more of the financial costs of caregiving, access is increasingly determined by parental resources. For example, tax credits as a mechanism for funding childcare require that a family have an income sufficiently large to take advantage of the credit. The capacity to hire a childminder is class-based, and the quality of service purchased also varies by class.

Such diversification is often justified in terms of new *flexibility* provided to parents seeking to escape the rigidities of universal and insufficiently differentiated public services. In Sweden, some working-class critics of day-care centres complain about the middle-class standards and social values promoted in them. Some would prefer the flexibility associated with a care allowance that allows them to decide whom to pay, including themselves, for childcare. Other parents point to the greater flexibility provided by childminders rather than large day nurseries with regular hours. They can more easily fix their own hours, have part-time care, and so on. As employment policies enhance employers' flexibility throughout the EU, the need for more flexibility in childcare arrangements climbs. Variability in hours is essential, since other reforms in childcare programs encourage mothers to mix part-time work with part-time care allowances, as they do in France, Belgium, and Sweden.

The notion of flexibility has gained new resonance. It is especially popular among those who promote *choice* as the central value of citizenship, supposedly needed to counter the bureaucracies and collectivism of welfare states. In its left-wing versions the idea leads to calls for cooperative centres and greater parental involvement in deciding on the programs they want for their children. In its right-wing versions it promotes the right of parents to 'choose' to care for their children themselves or to hire someone to provide care at home. Both France and Belgium already make the second option readily available. More than the others, the Swedes have debated these alternatives, because such flexibility constitutes a major shift away from the public service model and equality around which their post-war citizenship regime was constructed. The debate is ongoing, as it is other Nordic countries.

In Belgium, the discourse of choice has been used since the 1970s to claim flexibility in childcare choices in the name of 'fair treatment' of those families who choose to provide their own care. The theme also shaped French debates and policy choices. In both countries lawmakers argued for a system that would not subsidize only those women who chose to confide the care of their children to someone else. They wanted public funds also to be given to stay-at-home mothers. In Sweden, bourgeois governments deployed the discourse of choice both to promote parental care (trying to appeal to those working-class parents who mistrusted the state system) and to appeal to upper-income families who might wish to hire their own nannies.

Indeed, it is this redefinition of individual choice and the expanded place given to the decisions of families about how to care for their children and the forms of relationship to market (both labour markets and markets for care) that stand out as the major shift in childcare. In the 1960s and 1970s the theme of choice was different; it was found in discussions of women's labour force participation. In its classic formulation, women should be free to choose whether to stay at home or to seek employment. As the egalitarian model took hold, the role of the state became to facilitate the choice of employment, without imposing it (except, perhaps, in the case of single mothers, whose capacity for choice was limited). One crucial element was the provision of high-quality, affordable childcare as a public service.

As revealed in the chapters on each country case and the EU, another meaning of choice is now being used, a neo-liberal definition that construes individuals and families less as citizens and more as consumers. Their sovereignty as consumers requires that they have choice about what kinds of services they want, how much they wish to 'invest' financially in their children's care, what mix of private provision they wish to assume, and so on.

As a result of such discussions, we observe that states are rethinking the place of childcare. It may no longer be found in the package of social citizenship rights expressing solidarity first to children and then to their mothers, who seek equality in labour market provision. Rather, to the extent that the state is still in the 'childcare business,' its role may become less one of direct provision than one of facilitating the expansion of choices. Thus, in Belgium, Italy, and France, individualized solutions are wholeheartedly promoted, a fact that accounts, in part, for the enthusiastic embrace of tax credits. These credits allow parents to purchase services personally. Even in Sweden, where the commitment to public provision remains, that provision has been redefined in marketized terms as local authorities now contract for services and as they expand the variety of services they make available.

Citizenship Rights in New Times

Our work, thus far, has been based on demonstrating that major shifts in representations of women's work and childcare programs have occurred. The move towards new models of gender relations, as well as towards new programs, required a substantial reconfiguration of the basic principles of citizenship, especially social citizenship rights, which had underpinned our five cases through the first post-war decades. By the late 1970s it had become clear to political decision-makers throughout Europe that the conditions that had generated the economic boom after 1945 and had underpinned the post-war compromise and welfare state no longer existed. Existing practices were at risk as political compromises and policy packages that had been carefully crafted in the 1950s and 1960s were reopened for debate. Sometimes it was new political actors who pushed for change. Sometimes it was existing actors who abandoned previous ideological commitments and staked out new terrain within neo-liberalism. Sometimes it was bureaucracies that reorganized themselves. Whoever the actors involved and whatever the terms of the debate, however, it is clear that both the economic and political foundations of the post-war order no longer hold. Adjustments are ongoing. Such shifts involve major alterations in institutions as well as in the vision and content of citizenship.

We have demonstrated that the citizenship regimes of the post-war years were built on the values of both class and gender equality. They also involved a commitment to territorial equality managed by national-level public institutions. Most often this meant that policy design was centralized, such that countrywide services would provide similar life chances to individuals no matter where they lived. The underlying principle was common citizenship rights. After 1945 social programs were designed and funded by central governments, which did not hesitate to override local differences in the name of national standards. While states were never completely successful in eliminating regional variations – Italy's unresolved problems of the *mezzogiorno* was only the most striking example of lack of success – consensus on the goal of promoting homogeneous citizenship rights did exist.

Recent political restructuring has meant, in contrast, that central governments everywhere have abandoned their commitments to overseeing a common citizenship in which the values of equality are embedded. Instead, the values of choice are paramount, along with other ways of thinking about the role of the state, the market, the community, and institutions. These changes are summarized in a schematic way, in table 9.1.

In Belgium and Italy, the move away from national standards and institutional reconfiguration is most pronounced, associated as it is with the constitutional empowerment of regional and other levels of government. Even in Sweden and France, however, the theme of democratic decentralization has taken precedence over commitments to minimizing regional inequities and the social differences long known to follow from regional differences.

These citizenship regimes have also experienced another kind of decentralization. As we have described above, in recent years there have been moves to privilege the market and to foster forms of private provision of what previously were public services. States have been withdrawing their commitments to spending public funds so as to promote equality. In large part, the shift has been justified in fiscal terms as the 'impossibility' of maintaining high tax burdens and the deficits incurred. None of the countries examined here nor the EU was spared

TABLE 9.1
Citizenship regimes at two points in time

	Societal paradigm of the post-war Keynesian welfare state	Principles of redesigned welfare states
Principal value	Equality: class, gender, territorial	Choice
Citizen/state relation	The citizen as the bearer of a right to a public service	The citizen as the consumer of services made available by the state
Dominant sector	State	Market
Institutional configuration	Country-wide institutions with national standards	Decentralized institutions with local standards

this budgetary crunch. The result is that all commitments to spending in order to foster the three forms of equality are somewhat, if not gravely, attenuated.

Although Italy resisted, longer than the others, the pressures to cut spending and reduce the role of the state, by the 1990s it, too, had been forced to fall into line. In France, after 1983 the forces of neo-liberalism successfully reoriented the governing Socialists' policies. In a dramatic abandonment of what was often termed the 'old-fashioned' – read post-war and Keynesian – economic program, François Mitterrand and his party turned swiftly to a strategy of budgetary restraint. In neither 1982 nor 1994 did the return to government of the Swedish Social Democrats bring a wholesale roll-back of the changes begun by the bourgeois governments. The language of fiscal restraint held sway at all levels of government in Belgium, while the limits imposed by the financial difficulties of some of the communities, particularly the Francophone, have opened a gap between the 'right' to certain programs and real access to services. The European Union's contribution to this move away from the previously paradigmatic position was not insignificant. The single market, the convergence criteria embedded in the move towards European Monetary Union, and other aspects of monetary union were significant disciplinary mechanisms, limiting state spending, including that on social policy.

The consequences of such shifting principles are important. It would be wrong to read the situation as simply one of cutbacks in spending.

In some cases public funds have been only marginally withdrawn. Sometimes new and quite expensive programs have been created, via tax credits or 'forgiving' employers' social security contributions, as part of the fight against unemployment. The shift is more in foundational principles; it is a redesign of citizenship rather than simply a retrenching or restructuring. Social programs now are hostages to fiscal policy and budgetary constraints. Calculations of their consequences for the deficit and debt take precedence over any assessment of their social benefits or effects on social equality, whether across classes, sexes, or regions.

Even more important than calculations about public finances, however, is the fact that the social policy realm has lost the autonomy from employment policy that it had in previous decades. Education, welfare, family, and even equality policies are tributaries of a more powerful policy domain, that of employment. Previously central policy goals – whether the well-being of children, pro-natalism, equality, or social justice – have lost ground to the overriding priority of preparing individuals for labour force participation.

A clear sign of this shift can be seen in the discourse of pro-natalism. Post-war policies often contained at least lingering (in the case of Sweden) and sometimes predominant (in the cases of France and Belgium) pro-natalist themes. Over the decades the baby boom mitigated these concerns, and this discourse faded. In recent decades, however, there has been a re-emergence of fears of low birth rates. As the Italian, Belgian, and European cases clearly attest, and as even the French case suggests, the issue of pro-natalism has mutated. It now reflects an intergenerational fear that there will not be sufficient workers paying into the social security system to support future demand both for retirement pensions and for other social programs. The birth rate must be stimulated now in order to meet the employment needs of the future.

Unemployment is a policy dilemma all countries and the EU have had to confront. The early 1970s were marked by soaring rates of both inflation and unemployment, although by the late 1970s the replacement of Keynesianism by monetarist macroeconomic policy had begun to put the lid on inflation. Yet unemployment continued to be a bugbear for policy-makers. It was stubbornly resistant to solutions for entire categories of workers, especially the long-term unemployed and young people. By the 1990s even Sweden had lost its immunity to unemployment and shared double-digit rates of unemployment with its European neighbours.

Also, it has become obvious that the labour market has changed profoundly. A full-time and secure job is no longer the norm. Social policymakers across a wide range of policy realms must juggle programs to fit within a restructured labour market in which unemployment, contingent employment, and part-time work loom large. They have identified as their central task, whether in family, education, or welfare administrations, to facilitate the movement of individuals back and forth between employment and either another status (leave, training, etc.) in the labour force or non-employment.

Post-war social policy was designed to give citizens the right to protection from the predictable and accidental pitfalls of life; social citizenship rights provided protection from life's risks. At a minimum, even in the least generous welfare states, social policy was described by the metaphor 'safety net.' In more generous cases it was a safe haven from the perilous effects of labour market commodification. Now, social policy might better be described as a trampoline, reflecting constant efforts to bounce individuals back into the labour force. There is no longer any expectation, however, that all will land in full-time, long-term, or protected employment. Rather, entire categories leave the trampoline with less force than others and find themselves reaching only the margins of the labour force. The policies crafted in the 1980s to address the unemployment crisis reveal backtracking from post-war commitments to equality within citizenship. Rather than seeking to guarantee everyone reasonable and equitable access to the labour market, states have begun to institutionalize, through labour market policies, a multi-track labour force.

After 1945 each country also experienced what we have described as a post-war compromise between capital and labour, an implicit trade-off related to the organization of production. This compromise has not survived the intensification of crisis and subsequent redesign. Employers demanded greater 'flexibility' in decisions about hiring, firing, and working time. They also began to appreciate the benefits of more diversity in working conditions, wages, and the status of their employees. In practical terms, this meant that the full-time, reasonably well-paid, semi-skilled, or skilled factory operative who had been the ideal-typical Fordist worker no longer was the model. He, and to a limited extent she, had been joined in the labour force by workers with a wide variety of employment status, ranging from part-time workers to young people working with under type of special labour contract that would allow them to be more effectively 'inserted' into working life and, more generally, into citizenship. Neither representations of the labour force nor policies regulating it could pretend that the post-war norm was still the standard and that equal labour force participation was the goal.

This restructuring had multiple consequences within each case, as documented in the earlier chapters. Unions and other organizations of workers have seen their power base shift, both at the point of production and within the state. Although, as in the case of France, there was a dramatic weakening of the union movement, the situation was not exactly the same everywhere. In Belgium, the practice of devolving decision-making on employment and social security to social dialogue between employers and unions has been altered as the state has become more involved. In order to make sure that its budgetary limits and calendar for agreement is respected, the state has been intervening more actively in the institutions of social dialogue, thereby usurping the decision-making authority of the social partners. Threats to the post-war 'Swedish model' took the form of employers' refusal to maintain peak-level bargaining practices and a drive for more diversity in collective bargaining. The weakening of traditional Italian industry and the flowering of the small producers and flexible production of the 'Third Italy' meant that unions lost their capacity to protect their Fordist victories.

The importance of this weakening of union power was that it allowed more room for employers and the state to set the direction of economic development. As a result, one of the major institutional protectors of an egalitarian model of social relations was made ineffective. In all four cases unions had promoted an egalitarian vision of social relations. Because of the fragmentation of existing patterns of employer-employee relations, in the new balance of political forces responsibility for promoting equality would be shifted to other institutions.

From 1975 the European Community provides a fine example of the ways in which the egalitarian model could be successfully promoted within the judicial and administrative branches of a quasi-state. The Equal Opportunities Unit could compensate for the limited involvement of unions at the European level, but in recent years its authority, too, has been dramatically reduced. The weakening of the Equal Opportunities Unit not only reduces space for promotion of an egalitarian model but also marks a shift away from Europe's previous commitment to egalitarian positions.

While one might linger over several different elements revealed by the redesign of the welfare state and its citizenship regimes, our analysis has focused on the consequences of adjustment for women's employment and childcare. We have examined the ways in which the fragmentation provoked by political and economic restructuring stimulated representations of women's work different from those present when the egalitarian model become predominant by the 1970s. In all five cases studied here, representations did change. Nonetheless, the extent of change, and its consequences for childcare, was not universal – indeed, the differences follow only indirectly from economic restructuring. They were, rather, more directly the consequence of the lines of cleavage along which each regime fragmented and of the ways that citizenship has been altered, as connections among markets, states, and communities are reconfigured.

This case study of the directions of change in childcare policies allows us to observe welfare state redesign in detail. These shifts in the values, discourses and representations embedded in the citizenship regimes of these four countries and the role played by the European Union in setting out standards for social citizenship mark a significant change. Childcare is not a minor program. It is one that provides a window on state-society relations at the precise point that concerns about public and private, state and market, family responsibility and employment intersect. Therefore, the directions of change observed here are not sui generis. Rather, they reflect and signal the broad patterns and directions of change to all citizenship regimes as we move into the new century.

NOTES

1 Recently, the second term has brought childcare into contact with other forms of care. As we saw in chapter 2, recent employment policies as well as reductions in state spending have focused attention on the caregiving work directed towards all types of care. Childcare becomes only one category of care, alongside the needs of the elderly, the sick, the handicapped, and so forth. For a discussion see Hantrais and Letablier (1995b: 123).

2 For the French case see Duchen (1996). Simone de Beauvoir's classic, *The Second Sex*, dates from 1949, and the pathbreaking work of Alma Myrdal and Viola Klein (1956) appeared in Sweden in the middle of the next decade.

Bibliography

Aballéa, François. 1995. 'Décentralisation et action sociale familiale. De quelques interprétations.' *Recherches et Prévisions*, no. 39 (March): 9–22.

Afsa, Eric. 1996. 'L'activité féminine à l'épreuve de l'allocation parentale d'éducation.' *Recherches et Prévisions*, no. 46 (December): 1–8.

– 1998. 'L'allocation parentale d'éducation: entre politique familiale et politique de l'emploi,' *Insee Première*, no. 569 (February).

Akerman, B. et al. 1983. *Vi kan, vi behövs!*

Alaluf, Mateo. 1999. 'Le modèle belge.' In P. Delwit, J.M. De Waele, and P. Magnette (eds), *Gouverner la Belgique*. Paris: PUF.

Amato, Giuliano. 1980. *Una repubblica da riformare*. Bologna: Il Mulino.

Ancelin, Jacqueline. 1985. 'L'action sociale de la branche famille.' *Droit social*, no. 5 (May): 438–47.

Andersson, B.E., et al. 1993. 'Rising Birth Rate in Sweden: A Consequence of the Welfare State and Family Policy.' *Childhood*, no. 1: 27–43.

Anxo, Dominique. 1993. 'Les années 90 ou la fin du modèle suédois ?' In Gazier (ed.), *Emploi, nouvelles donnés*. Paris: Economica.

Anxo, Dominique, and Anne-Marie Daune-Richard. 1991. 'La place relative des hommes et des femmes sur le marché du travail. Une comparaison France-Suède.' *Travail et emploi*, no. 47: 63–78.

Anxo, Dominique, and Mats Johansson. 1998. 'Les discriminations salariales en Suède.' *Les Cahiers du MAGE*, no. 2. Paris: CNRS-IRESCO.

Arcq, Etienne, and Pierre Blaise. 1999. 'Histoire politique de la Sécurité sociale en Belgique.' *Revue belge de sécurité sociale*, no. 3 (September).

Arcq, Etienne, and Bérengère Marques-Pereira. 1991. 'Néo-corporatisme et concertation sociale en Belgique.' *Politiques et Management Public*, vol. 9, 3 (September): 159–79.

Arcq, Etienne, and Pierre Reman. 1999. 'Les interlocuteurs sociaux et la modernisation de Sécurité sociale.' Bruxelles, CRISP, coll. *Courrier hebdoma-daire*, no. 1508–9.

Arve-Parès, Birgit. 1996. 'Entre travail et vie familiale: le modèle suédois.' *Lien social et Politiques, RIAC*, no. 36: 41–8.

Assemblea Costituente. 1946. Commissione per la Costituzione, Prima Sottocommissione. *Discussioni*. Rome.

– 1947. *Atti della Assemblea Costituente-Discussione*, vol. 7, Rome, September.

Auer, Peter, and Claudius Riegler. 1994. 'Suède: la fin du plein emploi.' *Info MISEP*, CEE, no. 46: 16–23.

Balbo, Laura, V. Capecchi, and C. Facchini. 1974. 'L'Università e le 150 ore.' *Inchiesta*, no. 14: 39–54.

Balbo, Laura, M.P. May, and G. Micheli. 1990. *Vincoli e strategie della vita quotidi-ana: Una ricerca in Emilia-Romagna*. Milan: Angeli.

– 1978. 'La doppia presenza.' *Inchiesta*, no. 32: 3–6.

Banting, Keith. 1995. 'The Welfare State as Statecraft: Territorial Politics and Canadian Social Policy.' In Stephan Leibfried and Paul Pierson (eds), *European Social Policy: Between Fragmentation and Integration*. Washington, DC: Brookings.

Barbier, Jean-Claude. 1990. 'Pour bien comparer les politiques familiales. Quelques problèmes de méthode.' *Revue Française des Affaires Sociales*, no. 3: 153–68.

– 1995. 'Relations emploi-famille: à propos de la comparaison européenne des catégories de chômeurs et de congés parentaux.' In L. Hantrais and M.-T. Letablier (eds), *La relation famille-emploi. Une comparaison des modes d'ajuste-ment en Europe*. Centre d'études de l'emploi: Dossier n° 6, Nouvelle série.

Baude, Annika. 1979. 'Public Policy and Changing Family Patterns in Sweden, 1930–1977.' In J. Lipman-Blumen and J. Bernard (eds), *Sex Roles and Social Policy*. London: Sage.

– (ed.). 1992. *Visionen om jämställdhet*. Stockholm: SNS.

Bawin-Legros, Bernadette. 1988. *Famille, mariage, divorce. Une sociologie des com-portements familiaux contemporains*. Liège: Mardaga.

– 1987. 'Cent ans de droit social en Belgique. Le travail des femmes.' *La Revue du Travail*. Bruxelles: Ministère de l'Emploi et du Travail, January–February.

Becchi, E., and A. Bondioliéd. 1992. 'Gli asili nido in Italia: Censimento e valutazioni della qualità.' *Bambini*, 2nd suppl.: 1–31.

Bégeot, F., and J.A. Fernandez-Gordon. 1997. 'La convergence démographique au-delà des différences nationales.' In J. Commaille and F. de Singly (eds), *La question familiale en Europe*. Paris: L'Harmattan.

Bergqvist, Christina. 1998. 'Still a Woman-Friendly Welfare State? The Case of Parental Leave and Childcare Policies in Sweden.' Paper presented at the Eleventh International Conference of Europeanists. Baltimore, MD: February.

Bimbi, Franca. 1991. 'Doppia presenza.' In Laura Balbo (ed.), *Tempi di vita. Studi e proposte per cabiarli*. Milan: Feltrinelli.

– 1993. 'Gender Gift Relationship and the Welfare State Cultures in Italy.' In J. Lewis (ed.), *Women and Social Policies in Europe: Work, Family and the State*. London: Edward Elgar.

– 1995a. 'Metafore di genere tra lavoro pagato e lavoro non pagato.' *Polis*, no. 3: 379–401.

– 1995b. 'Gender Division of Labor and Welfare State Provisions in Italy.' In Tineke Willemsen, Gerard Frinking and Ria Vogels (eds), *Work and Family in Europe: The Role of Politics*. Tillburg: Tillburg University Press.

– 1997. 'La debolezza delle politiche familiari in Italia: un caso di federalismo mancato?' in Franca Bimbi and Alisa Del Re (eds), *Genere e democrazia. La cittadinanza delle donne a cinquant'anni dal voto*. Turin: Rosemberg & Sellier.

Björklund, Anders. 1991. 'Evaluation de la politique du marché du travail en Suède.' OECD, *L'évaluation des programmes pour l'emploi et des mesures sociales*, 83–102. Paris: OECD.

Björnberg, Ulla. 1994. 'Familj mellan marknad och stat/politik. En fräga om kön, klass och makt.' *Sociolgisk forkning*, no. 2: 26–37.

– 1995 'Définir et concilier la famille et l'emploi en Suède.' In L. Hantrais and M.-T. Letablier (eds), *La relation famille-emploi. Une comparaison des modes d'ajustement en Europe*. Centre d'études de l'emploi: Dossier no. 6, Nouvelle série.

– 1997. 'Les limites culturelles d'une transformation des rôles familiaux.' In J. Commaille and F. de Singly (eds), *La question familiale en Europe*. Paris: L'Harmattan.

Blanpain, Roger, and Kris Engels. 1993. *European Labor Law*, 2nd ed. Deventer: Kluwer.

Boddendijk, Frank R. 1991. 'The Long Way to Equal Opportunities for Women and Men.' *Social Europe* (March): 94–7.

Boismenu, Gérard, and Jane Jenson. 1998. 'A Social Union or a Federal State? Intergovernmental Relations in the New Liberal Era.' In Leslie Pal (ed.), *How Ottawa Spends, 1998–99. Balancing Act: The Post-Deficit Mandate*. Ottawa: Carleton University Press.

Boissières, C. 1996. 'Les prestations famille sans conditions de ressources: au même niveau en 1995 qu'en 1968.' *Recherches et Prévisions*, no. 45: 49–56.

Borne, Dominique. 1988. *Histoire de la société française depuis 1945*. Paris: A. Colin.

Bosse-Platière, Suzon. 1999. 'Les assistantes maternelles. Mères et profession-nelles.' *Panoramiques*, no. 40: 122–3.

Boulaya, Nicole, and Bernadette Roussille. 1982. *L'enfant dans la vie. Une politique pour la petite enfance*. Rapport au secrétaire d'Etat à la Famille. Paris: La Documentation française.

270 Bibliography

Boyer, Robert. 1995. *Théorie de la régulation. L'Etat des savoirs*. Paris: La Découverte.

Bradford, Neil. 1998. *Commissioning Ideas: Canadian National Policy Innovation in Comparative Perspective*. Toronto: Oxford University Press.

Bradshaw, Jonathan et al. 1996. 'Aides aux familles: un classement des pays.' In J. Commaille and F. de Singly (eds), *'La politique familiale.' Problèmes politiques et sociaux*, no. 761. Paris: La Documentation française.

Brin, Hubert. 1991. *La politique familiale française*. Rapport présenté au nom du Conseil économique et social. Paris: Journal officiel de la République française.

Broberg, Anders, and C. Philip Hwang. 1991. 'Day Care for Young Children in Sweden.' In E.C. Melhuish and P. Moss (eds), *Day Care for Young Children*. London: Routledge.

– 1992. 'The Historical and Social Context of Child Care in Sweden.' In M.E. Lamb, K.J. Sternberg, C.P. Hwang, and A.G. Broberg (eds), *Child Care in Context*. Hillsdale, NJ: LEA.

Byre, Angela. 1992. *EC Social Policy and 1992*. Deventer: Kluwer.

Cahiers de Femmes d'Europe. 1990. *Garde d'enfants dans la Communauté européenne, 1985–1990*, no. 31.

– 1992. *La place des femmes sur le marché du travail. Tendances et évolutions dans les douze pays de la Communauté européenne, 1983–1990*, no. 36.

Calabro, A., and L. Grasso. 1985. *Dal movimento femminista al femminismo diffuso*. Milan: Angeli.

Calot, Gérard. 1984. 'La création de l'allocation parentale d'éducation. Une véritable révolution.' *Le Monde* (19 December): 2.

Camera dei Deputati. 1950. i Legislatura. *Atti Parlamentari: Discussioni*. Rome, 27 June.

– vi Legislatura. Commissioni Riunite. Rome, 18 November.

– 1995a. xii Legislatura. *Atti Parlamentari: Discussioni*. Rome, 7 February.

– 1995b. *Risoluzioni sulle politiche familiari*. Rome, 8 February.

– 1996. xiii Legislatura. *Atti Parlamentari: Commissione Affari Sociali*. Rome, 20 June.

Camera dei Deputati e Senato della Repubblica. 1992. xi Legistura. *Discussioni della Commissione Parlamentare per la Riforma Istituzionale*. Rome.

Camera dei Deputati, Gruppo Progresisti-Federativo. 1994. *Essere madre, essere padri. 7 proposte di legge per aiutare le mamme e i papà*. Rome.

Camera dei Deputati, Servizi Studi. 1995. Commissione speciale competente in materia di infanzia. *Bilancio, finanziara e collegato per il 1996*. Rome, November.

Cameron, David. 1996. 'Exchange Rate Politics in France, 1981–1993: The Regime-Defining Choices of the Mitterrand Presidency.' In A. Daley (ed.),

The Mitterrand Era: Policy Alternatives and Political Mobilization in France. New York: New York University Press.

Caravaggi, Giovanna, et al. 1976. *La donna e il diritto.* Rome: EDS.

Castel, Robert. 1995. *Les métamorphoses de la question sociale. Une chronique du salariat.* Paris: Fayard.

Cazzola, Giuliano. 1996. *Le nuove pensioni degli italiani.* Bologna: Il Mulino.

Censis. 1978. *Rapporto sulla situazione sociale del Paese.* Rome.

Chirac, Jacques. 1996a. Intervention à l'occasion de l'installation du Haut Conseil de la Population et de la Famille. Palais de l'Élysée, 12 April.

– 1996b. Allocution lors de la remise de la médaille de la famille française. Palais de l'Élysée, 3 June.

Christiansen, Hans. 1996. 'Suède. Combattre le chômage.' *L'Observateur de l'OCDE,* no. 197: 46–7.

Collins, Doreen. 1975. *The European Communities: The Social Policy of the First Phase.* London: Martin Robertson.

Commaille, Jacques. 1993. *Les stratégies des femmes. Travail, famille et politique.* Paris: La Découverte.

– 1996a. 'Les composantes du modèle français de la politique française.' In F. de Singly et al., *La Famille en questions. Etat de la recherche.* Paris: Syros.

– 1996b. *Misères de la famille. Question d'Etat.* Paris: Presses de Sciences Po.

Commaille, Jacques, and François de Singly (eds). 1996. 'La politique familiale.' *Problèmes politiques et sociaux,* no. 761. Paris: La Documentation française.

– 1997. 'Les règles de la méthode comparative dans le domaine de la famille. Le sens d'une comparaison.' In *La question familiale en Europe.* Paris: L'Harmattan.

Commission Européenne. 1995. *L'emploi en Europe.* Luxembourg: Office des publications officielles.

Conseil d'analyse économique. 1999. *Égalité entre hommes et femmes: Aspects économiques.'* Report by B. Majnoni d'Intignano. Paris: La Documentation française.

Conseil Économique et Social. 1991a. *Avis adopté sur la politique familiale française.* Paris: Journal officiel de la République française.

– 1991b. *La politique familiale française.* Rapport présenté au nom du CES par M. Hubert Brin. Paris: Journal officiel de la République française.

Conseil de l'Égalité des Chances entre Hommes et Femmes. 1996. *Le point de vue du Conseil sur la sécurité sociale.* Brussels: Ministère de l'Emploi et du Travail, May.

Corbetta, P., and A. Parisi. 1994. 'Ancor un 18 aprile: Il referendum sulla legge elettorale del Senato.' In C. Mershon and G. Pasquino (eds), *Politica in Italia: Edizione 1994.* Bologna: Il Mulino.

Dagastino, Cathy. 1995. 'La Cour d'arbitrage de Belgique.' *Les Cahiers du CRAPS*, no. 20 (June): 37–68.

Dahlström, Edmond, ed. 1962. *Kvinnors liv och arbete*. Stockholm: SNS.

DARES. 1993. 'Les salariés en congé parental.' *Premières Informations*, no. 334.

Daune-Richard, Anne-Marie. 1993. 'Activité et emploi des femmes: des constructions sociétales différentes en France, au Royaume-Uni et en Suède.' *Sociétés contemporaines*, no. 16: 125–43.

– 1995. 'L'interaction activité-emploi-famille et les politiques publiques: la signification sociétale différente du travail à temps partiel en France, au Royaume-Uni et en Suède.' In L. Hantrais and M-T. Letablier (eds), *La relation famille-emploi. Une comparaison des modes d'ajustement en Europe*. Centre d'études de l'Emploi: Dossier no. 6, Nouvelle série.

Debordeaux, Danièle. 1995. 'Introduction.' *Recherches et Prévisions*, no. 39 (March): 1–9.

Della Sala, Vincent. 1997. 'Hollowing and Hardening the State: European Integration and the Italian State.' *West European Politics*, vol. 20, 1: 14–33.

Del Re, Alisa. 1996. 'The relationship between women's paid and unpaid work.' In L. Hantrais and M-T. Letablier (eds), *Comparing Families and Family Policies in Europe*. Leicester, UK: Cross-National Research Papers.

Delsen, Lei, and Tom van Veen. 1991. 'The Swedish Model: Relevant for Other European Countries?' *British Journal of Industrial Relations*, vol. 30, 1: 83–105.

Delvaux, Joëlle. 1987. *Les mouvements longs de la politique familiale belge*. Université catholique de Louvain, Département de sociologie.

Delwit, P., and J.M. De Waele. 1999. 'Partis et systèmes de partis en Belgique.' In P. Delwit, J.M. De Waele, and P. Magnette (eds). *Gouverner la Belgique*. Paris: PUF.

Delwit, P. J.M. De Waele, and P. Magnette. 1999. 'Gouverner la Belgique: Clivages et compromis dans une société composite.' In P. Delwit, J.M. De Waele, and P. Magnette (eds). *Gouverner la Belgique*. Paris: PUF.

Dente, Bruno (ed.). 1990. *Le politiche pubbliche in Italia*. Bologna: Il Mulino.

Desideri, Carlo. 1995. 'Italian Regions in the European Community.' In B. Jones and M. Keating (eds), *The European Union and the Regions*. Oxford: Clarendon Press.

Designaux, Jacques, and Amédée Thevenet. 1982. *La garde des jeunes enfants*. Paris: PUF.

Desplanques, Guy. 1993. 'Garder les petits: organisation collective ou solidarité familiale.' In INSEE, *Données sociales*. Paris: INSEE.

Devillé, Anne, and Olivier Paye. 1995. 'La réforme des procédures de divorce.' Bruxelles: CRISP, coll. *Courrier hebdomadaire*, no. 1495.

Devillé, Anne, Marie-Sylvie Dupont-Bouchat, Philippe Gérard, and Olivier
Paye. 1995. 'Belgique – Du jeu des clivages à la politique du compromis.' In
L. Assier-Andrieu and J. Commaille (eds). *Politique des lois en Europe. La filia-
tion comme modèle de comparaison.* Paris: LGDJ.

Ditch, John, Jonathan Bradshaw, and Toni Eardley. 1996. *Evolution des politiques
familiales nationales en 1994.* Observatoire européen des politiques familiales
nationales. York, UK: Social Politics Research Unit, University of York.

Ditch, John et al. 1996. *Synthèse des politiques familiales nationales en 1994.*
Observatoire européen des politiques familiales nationales. York, UK: Social
Politics Research Unit, University of York.

Dock, Thierry, and Roland Janssen. 1996. 'Vers un modèle hollandais en
Belgique ?' *La Revue nouvelle,* no. 11 (November): 15–20.

Dubois, Alain. 1991. 'Les prestations familiales et le droit de l'enfant.' Brussels:
CRISP, coll. *Courrier hebdomadaire,* no. 1312–13.

– 1992. 'La famille: l'épicentre du social.' *La Revue nouvelle,* no. 4 (April):
54–60.

– 1993. 'Quel accueil de la petite enfance?' *La Revue nouvelle,* no. 7–8 (July–
August): 75–83.

– 1996. 'FESC: On achève bien l'écheveau!' *La Revue nouvelle,* no. 3 (March):
8–13.

Dubois, Alain, Perrine Humblet, and Fred Deven. 1994. L'accueil des enfants
de moins de trois ans. Brussels: CRISP, coll. *Courrier hebdomadaire,* no. 1463–4.

Duchen, Claire. 1994. *Women's Rights and Women's Lives in France, 1944–68.*
London: Routledge.

Duhamel, Olivier. 1988. 'Evolution et perspectives de la Vème République sous
la présidence de François Mitterrand.' In S. Hoffmann and G. Ross (eds),
L'expérience Mitterrand. Continuité et changement. Paris: PUF.

– 1995. *Le pouvoir politique en France.* Paris: Seuil, 1995.

Dumon, Wilfried. 1987. 'Gezinspolitiek in België.' *Tijdschrift voor sociologie,*
vol. 8, 2–3: 257–75.

– 1991. *Les politiques nationales des Etats membres de la Communauté européenne en
1991.* Observatoire européen des politiques familiales nationales. Bruxelles:
Commission des Communautés européennes.

– 1994. 'The European Observatory on National Family Policies.' *Social Europe*
no. 1 (January): 38–41.

– 1996. 'Les tendances générales.' In J. Commaille and F. de Singly (eds), '*La
politique familiale.*' *Problèmes politiques et sociaux,* no. 761. Paris: La Documentation française.

Dumont, Georges-Henri. 1991. *La Belgique hier et aujourd'hui.* Paris: PUF.

Dumont, Hugues. 1996. *Le pluralisme idéologique et l'autonomie culturelle en droit public belge*, 2 vols. Brussels: Bruylant et Publications des Facultés universitaires Saint-Louis.

Eduards, Maude. 1988. 'Gender Politics and Public Policies in Sweden.' Later published as 'Toward a Third Way: Women, Politics and Welfare Policies in Sweden.' *Social Research*, vol. 58, 3 (1991): 677–705.

Ellis, Evelyn. 1994. 'Recent Case Law of the Court of Justice on the Equal Treatment of Women and Men.' *Common Market Law Review*, vol. 31, 1 (February): 43–75.

Erixon, Lennart. 1995. *A Swedish Economic Policy: A Revindication of the Rehn-Meidner Model*, 2nd ed. Stockholm: Institutet för arbetslivsforskning.

Esping-Andersen, Gøsta. 1990. *The Three Worlds of Welfare Capitalism*. Princeton, NJ: Princeton University Press.

– 1999. *Social Foundations of Postindustrial Economies*. Oxford: Oxford University Press.

European Commission. 1988. *Childcare and Equality of Opportunity*. Brussels: DG V.

– 1994. *Community Social Policy. Current Status, 1 July 1994*. Luxembourg: EC.

– 1998. Progress Report from the Commission on the Follow-up of the Communication, 'Incorporating Equal Opportunities for Women and Men into all Community Policies and Activities.' Com (1998) 122 final. Brussels: EC.

– 1999. *Monitoring, Implementation and Application of Community Equality Law: General Report 1997 and 1998 of the Legal Experts' Group on Equal Treatment of Men and Women*. Brussels: D G Employment, Industrial Relations and Social Affairs.

European Network on Family and Work. 1998. *Parental Leave in European Union Countries*. Brussels: D G Employment, Industrial Relations and Social Affairs.

Eurostat. 1995a. *Les femmes et les hommes dans l'Union européenne: portrait statistique*. Luxembourg: Office des publications officielles des Communautés européennes.

– 1995b. *Enquête sur les forces de travail*. Luxembourg: Office des publications officielles des Communautés européenes.

– 1995c. *Statistiques en Bref. Population et conditions sociales*, 8. Luxembourg: Office des publications officielles des Communautés européenes.

– 1996. *Enquête sur les forces de travail. Résultats, 1995*. Luxembourg: Office des publications officielles des Communautés européenes.

Fabbrini, Sergio. 1994. *Quale Democrazia: L'Italia e gli altri*. Bari: Laterza.

– 1996. 'The End of Consensual Politics in Italy.' Paper presented to conference, 'Contesting the Boundaries of Italian Politics.' Carleton University, Ottawa, 22–23 March.

Fadiga, A.L., A.L. Zanatta, and M.L. Mirabile. 1993. *Demografia, Famiglia e Società*. Rome: Ediesse.

Fagnani, Jeanne. 1992. 'Travail et fécondité en France et en Allemagne de l'Ouest.' *Revue Française des Affaires Sociales*, no. 2.

- 1996a. 'L'allocation parentale d'éducation: contraintes et limites du choix d'une prestation.' *Lien social et Politiques, RIAC*, no. 36: 111–21.

- 1996b. 'Les politiques familiales dans la dynamique sociale européenne.' *Solidarité-Santé*, no. 1: 29–37.

- 1996c. 'Retravailler après une longue interruption. Le cas des mères ayant bénéficié de l'allocation parentale d'éducation.' *Revue Française des Affaires Sociales*, no. 3: 129–53.

- 1998. 'Lacunes, contradictions et incohérences des mesures de conciliation travail/famille. Bref bilan critique.' *Droit social*, no. 6 (June): 596–602.

Fagnani, Jeanne, and Evelyne Rassat. 1997. 'Les bénéficiaires de l'AGED: où résident-ils, quels sont leurs revenus ?' *Recherches et Prévisions*, no. 47 (March): 79–86.

Faustini, G. 1963. 'Il fabbisogno di asili nidi' *Maternita ed Infanzia*. Rivista del l'ONMI, 6,7,8, in Senato della Repubblica, IV Legislatura. *Documenti*. no. 1043 (23 February), Rome.

Fedele, M. 1988. *Autonomia politica regionale e sistema dei partiti*. Milan: Giuffre.

Ferrara, Maurizio. 1993. *Modelli di solidarietà*. Milan: Il Mulino.

- 1995. 'The Rise and Fall of Democratic Universalism: Health Care Reform in Italy, 1978–1994.' *Journal of Health Policy and Law*, vol. 20, 2: 275–302.

Fitoussi, Jean-Paul, and Pierre Rosanvallon. 1996. *Le nouvel âge des inégalités*. Paris: Seuil.

Foucauld, Jean-Baptiste de. 1994. 'Une nouvelle donne pour l'emploi.' *Problèmes économiques*, no. 2. 396–2.397 (2–9 November): 17–21.

Fourastié, Jean. 1979. *Les trente glorieuses, ou la révolution invisible de 1945 à 1975*. Paris: Fayard.

Fraisse, Geneviève. 2000. 'Democracy Confronts the New Domestic Services.' In Jane Jenson, Jacqueline Laufer, and Margaret Maruani (eds), *The Gendering of Inequalities: Women, Men and Work*. Aldershot, UK: Ashgate.

Franchi, G., B. Mapelli, and G. Liprano. 1987. *Donne a scuola*. Milan: Angeli.

Fransen, Gilberte, Nathalie Degimbe, and Jacques Ouziel. 1989. *Profil socio-économique des familles avec enfants*. Brussels: Ministère de l'Emploi et du Travail, série 'Famille et marché du travail,' June.

Fulcher, J. 1991. *Labour Movements, Employers and the State: Conflict and Cooperation in Britain and Sweden*. Oxford: Clarendon.

Gaudin, Pierre. 1995. 'Le département du Haut-Rhin à l'épreuve de la décentralisation.' *Recherches et Prévisions*, no. 39 (March): 33–6.

Gauthier, Anne Hélène. 1996. *The State and the Family. A Comparative Analysis of Family Policies in Industrialized Countries.* Oxford: Clarendon Press, 1996.

Giscard d'Estaing, Valéry. n.d. 'Une politique familiale.' Textes et déclarations de Valéry Giscard d'Estaing, Président de la République, *Actions et perspectives*, supplément du no. 306 d'*Actualités-Service*, publié par le Service d'Information et de Diffusion (SID).

– 1975. Speech made at La Bourboule, 13 July.

– 1976. Speech for the 30th anniversary of UNAF, Palais des Congrès, 12 June.

– 1977. Press conference held at the close of the Cabinet Council, 9 March.

– 1981. Speech to the Colloque national sur la démographie. In ministère du Travail et de la Participation / ministère de la Famille et de la Condition féminine, *Actes du Colloque*, 198–212. Cahiers de l'INED no. 92. Paris: PUF.

Golini, A. (ed.). 1994. *Tendenze demografiche e politiche per la populazione.* Bologna: Il Mulino.

Golini et al. *Famiglia, figli e società.* Turin: Edizioni Fondazione Agnelli, 1991.

Gornick, Janet et al. 1997. 'Supporting the Employment of Mothers: Policy Variation across Fourteen Welfare States.' *Journal of European Social Policy,* vol. 7, 1: 45–70.

Gorrieri, E. (ed.). 1983. 'Famiglia e reddito.' Ministero del lavoro e della previdenza sociale, Commissione nazionale per I problemi della famiglia. Rome: Istituto Poligrafico di Stato.

Gorrieri, E., et al. 1986. 'Rapporto sulla povertà.' *Inchiesta*, no. 73: 3–39.

Gorz, André. 1988. *Les métamorphoses du travail.* Paris: Galilée.

Haas, L., and Philip Hwang. 1993. 'Fathers and Company Culture in Sweden.' Paper presented to the AIS, Annapolis.

Hall, Peter A. (ed.). 1989. *The Political Power of Economic Ideas: Keynesianism Across Nations.* Princeton, NJ: Princeton University Press.

Hall, Peter A., and Rosemary C.R. Taylor. 1996. 'Political Science and the Three New Institutionalisms.' *Political Studies*, vol. 45: 936–57.

Hansson, S.-O., and A.L. Lodenius. 1988. *Operation högervridning.* Stockholm: Tiden.

Hantrais, Linda, and Marie-Thérèse Letablier. 1995. *Concepts et contextes dans les comparaisons internationales. Une observation sur les politiques familiales en Europe 1993–1995.* Paris: rapport CNAF, multigraphié.

Hatchuel, Georges. 1989. *Accueil de la petite enfance et activité féminine.* Paris: CREDOC, report to the CNAF.

Haut Conseil de La Population et de La Famille. 1987. *Vie professionnelle et vie familiale. De nouveaux équilibres à construire.* Paris: La Documentation française.

– 1989. *Démographie et politique familiale en Europe*. Paris: La Documentation française.

Held, David, Anthony McGrew, David Goldblatt, and Jonathan Perraton. 1999. *Global Transformations. Politics, Economics and Culture*. Cambridge: Polity.

Hellman, Stephen. 1997. 'Part V: Italy.' In M. Kesselman et al., *European Politics in Transition*, 3rd ed. Boston: Houghton-Mifflin.

Hemerijck, Anton, and Jelle Vissar. 1997. *A Dutch Miracle*. Amsterdam: University of Amsterdam Press.

Hinnfors, Jonas. 1995. *Familjepolitik, samhällsförändringar och partistrategier 1960–1990*. Stockholm: Almquist & Wiksell.

Hirdman, Yvonne. 1994. 'Social Engineering and the Woman Question: Sweden in the Thirties.' In W. Clement and R. Mahon (eds), *Swedish Social Democracy: A Model in Transition*. Toronto: Canadian Scholars Press.

Hoem, Britta. 1992. 'Hem och barn – och jobb!' *Välfärdsbulletin*, no. 2.

– 1993. 'The Compatibility of Employment and Childbearing in Contemporary Sweden.' *Acta Sociologica*, 36: 101–20.

Hooge, Liesbet, and Gary Marks. 1999. 'The Making of a Polity: The Struggle over European Integration.' In Herbert Kitschelt, Peter Lange, Gary Marks, and John D. Stephens (eds), *Continuity and Change in Contemporary Capitalism*. Cambridge: Cambridge University Press.

Hoskyns, Catherine. 1996. *Integrating Gender: Women, Law and Politics in the European Union*. London: Verso.

Huber, Evelyne, and John Stephens. 1998. 'Internationalization and the Social Democratic Model: Crisis and Future Prospects.'*Comparative Political Studies*, vol. 31, 3: 353–97.

Humblet, Perrine. 1996. 'La politique de garde de jeunes enfants en Belgique francophone: support aux mères et enjeu de socialisation du travail de reproduction.' In R. Dandurand, R. Hurtebise, and C. Le Bourdais (eds), *Enfances. Perspectives sociales et pluriculturelles*. Ste-Foy, QC: Presses de l'Université Laval.

Hwang, C. Philip, and A. Broberg. 1992. 'The Historical and Societal Context of Child Care in Sweden.' In Michael E. Lamb and Kathleen J. Sternberg (eds), *Child Care in Context*. Hillsdale, NJ: LEA.

Hwang, C. Philip, G. Elden, and C. Fransson. 1984. 'Arbetsgivares och arbetskamraters attityder till pappaledighet,' *Report n°1*, Göteborg University, Dept of Psychology.

Inchiesta. 1972. 'Il documento della Conferenza Episcopale Italiana sull'Assistenza.' *Inchiesta*, no. 7: 60–5.

INSEE. 1992. *Les enfants de moins de 6 ans*. Paris: INSEE.

– 1996. *Données sociales*. Paris: INSEE.

278   Bibliography

INSEE / Service des Droits des Femmes. 1995. *Les femmes. Contours et caractères.*
    Paris: INSEE.
Institut National de Statistique. 1995. 'Enquête sur les forces de travail.' *Statisti-*
    ques sociales. Brussels: Ministère des Affaires économiques.
ISTAT. 1986. *Sommario di statistiche storiche 1926–1985.* Rome: ISTAT.
Jacoby, A.L., and E. Näsman. 1989. *Mamma, Pappa, Jobb: Foraldrar och Barm om*
    Arbetesvilkor. Stockholm: Arbetslivcentrum.
Jahn, Detlef. 1993. *New Politics in Trade Unions: Applying Organizational Theory to*
    the Ecology Discourse on Nuclear Energy in Sweden and Germany. Aldershot,
    UK: Dartmouth.
Jenson, Jane. 1989. 'Paradigms and Political Discourse: Protective Legislation
    in France and the United States before 1914.' *Canadian Journal of Political*
    Science, vol. 22: 235–58.
–   1995. 'Extending the Boundaries of Citizenship: Women's Movements of
    Western Europe.' In Amrita Basu (ed.), *The Challenge of Local Feminisms:*
    Women's Movements in Global Perspective. Boulder, CO: Westview.
–   1997a. 'Fated to Live in Interesting Times: Canada's Changing Citzenship
    Regimes.' *Canadian Journal of Political Science*, vol. 30, 4 (December): 627–44.
–   1997b. 'Who Cares? Gender and Welfare Regimes.' *Social Politics, International*
    Studies in Gender, State and Society, vol. 4, 2: 182–7.
Jenson, Jane, and Rianne Mahon. 1993. 'Representing Solidarity: Class, Gender
    and the Crisis in Social-Democratic Sweden.' *New Left Review*, no. 201:
    76–100.
Jenson, Jane, and Susan D. Phillips. 1996. 'Regime Shift: New Citizenship
    Practices in Canada.' *International Journal of Canadian Studies*, vol. 14 (Fall):
    111–36.
Jenson, Jane, and Mariette Sineau. 1995. *Mitterrand et les Françaises. Un rendez-*
    vous manqué. Paris: Presses de la Fondation nationale des sciences politiques.
Jenson, Jane, Margaret Maruani, and Jacqueline Laufer (eds). 2000. *The Gender-*
    ing of Inequalities: Women, Men and Work. Avebury, UK: Ashgate.
Jobert, Bruno, and Bruno Théret. 1994. 'France: la consécration républicaine du
    néo-libéralisme.' In Bruno Jobert (ed.), *Le tournant néo-libéral en Europe.* Paris:
    L'Harmattan.
Join-Lambert, Marie-Thérèse et al. 1994. *Politiques sociales.* Paris: Presses de la
    Fondation nationale des sciences politiques / Dalloz.
Juelle, Delphine. 1995. 'Les communes face à la fédéralisation de la Belgique.'
    Les Cahiers du CRAPS, no. 20 (June): 69–87.
Junter-Loiseau, Annie, and Christa Tobler. 1995. *La notion de conciliation dans*
    les travaux du Forum. Forum européen, Institut Universitaire Européen,
    Florence, 23–4 June, multigraphié.

Karlsson, Gunnel. 1990. *Manssamhället till behag?* Stockholm: SSK.

Kergoat, Danièle. 1984. *Les femmes et le travail à temps partiel.* Paris: Ministère de l'Emploi et de la Formation professionnelle.

Kesselman, Mark. 1997. 'Part III: France.' In Mark Kesselman et al., *European Politics in Transition*, 3rd ed. Boston: Houghton-Mifflin.

Kesselman, Mark, et al. 1997. *European Politics in Transition*, 3rd ed. Boston: Houghton-Mifflin.

Keymolen, Denise, and Marie-Thérèse Coenen. 1991. *Pas à pas. L'histoire de l'émancipation de la femme en Belgique.* Brussels: Cabinet du Secrétaire d'Etat à l'Emancipation sociale.

– 1996. *La protection sociale en Europe 1995.* Brussels: Commission européenne, DG de l'emploi, des relations industrielles et des affaires sociales, 1996.

Kitschelt, Herbert, Peter Lange, Gary Marks, and John D. Stephens (eds). 1999. *Continuity and Change in Contemporary Capitalism.* Cambridge: Cambridge University Press.

Knibiehler, Yvonne. 1997. *La révolution maternelle. Femmes, maternité, citoyenneté depuis 1945.* Paris: Perrin.

Knocke, Wuokko. 1986. *Invandrade Kvinnor i lönearbete och fack. Forskningsrapport*, no. 53. Stockholm: Arbetslivscentrum.

Kyle, Gunhild. 1979. *Gästarbeterska i manssamhället.* Lund: Arkiv.

Kymlicka, Will, and Wayne Norman. 1995. 'Return of the Citizen: A Survey of Recent Work on Citizenship Theory.' In Ronald Beiner (ed.), *Theorizing Citizenship.* Albany, NY: SUNY Press.

Michel Lallement. 2000. 'France's New Service Sector and the Family.' In Jane Jenson, Jacqueline Laufer, and Margaret Maruani (eds), *The Gendering of Inequalities: Women, Men and Work.* Aldershot, UK: Ashgate.

Landsorganisation i Sverige (LO). 1969. *Fackföreningsrörlesen och Familjepolitiken.* Stockholm: Prisma.

– 1976. *Fackföreningsrörelsen och Familjepolitiken: Rapport till LO Kongress, 1976.* Stockholm: Prisma.

– 1988. *Arbetarkvinnorna: Längst ner på klasstrappan.* Stockholm: LO.

– 1995a. *Barnomsorg – för barnen och jämställdheten.* Stockholm: LO.

– 1995b. *Klass och kön.* Stockholm: LO.

Laroque, Pierre (ed.). 1985. *La politique familiale en France depuis 1945.* Commissariat général au Plan, Groupe de travail sur la politique familiale. Paris: La Documentation française.

Laufer, Jacqueline. 1996. 'Women's Employment and Equal Opportunities: from Equality to Reconciliation.' In L. Hantrais and M.-T. Letablier (eds), *Comparing Families and Family Policies in Europe.* Leicester, UK: Cross-National Research Papers.

Lautier, Bruno. 1996. 'Citoyenneté et politique d'ajustement.' In B. Marques-Pereira and I. Bizberg (ed.), *La citoyenneté sociale en Amérique latine*. Paris: L'Harmattan, CELA-IS.

Leibfried, Stephan, and Paul Pierson (eds). 1995. *European Social Policy: Between Fragmentation and Integration*. Washington, DC: Brookings.

Leira, Arnlaug. 1992. *Welfare States and Working Mothers: The Scandinavian Experience*. New York: Cambridge University Press.

Lentzen, Evelyne, and Xavier Mabille. 1995. 'Rythmes et changements dans la politique belge.' Brussels: CRISP, coll. *Courrier hebdomadaire*. no. 1500.

Leprince, Frédérique. 1987. 'La garde des jeunes enfants.' *Données sociales*. Paris: INSEE: 510–15.

Lero, Donna, and Irene Kyle. 1991. 'Families and Children in Ontario.' In Laura C. Johnson and Dick Barnhorst (eds), *Children, Families and Public Policy in the 90s*. Toronto: Thompson.

Les Cahiers du GRIF. 1994. *Le travail des femmes*. Brussels: Complexe.

Letablier, Marie-Thérèse. 1997. 'L'activité professionnelle des femmes en France sur fond de pénurie d'emplois.' *Lien social et Politiques, RIAC*, no. 36: 93–101.

Leton, A., and A. Miroir. 1999. *Les conflits communautaires en Belgique*. Paris: PUF.

Liaisons Sociales. 1993. Nos. 91–3 (10 September).

Livi Bacci, M. 1980. *Donna, fecondita e figli*. Bologna: Il Mulino.

Macchiato, Alfredo. 1996. *Privatizzazioni: tra economica e politica*. Rome: Douzelli.

Mahon, Rianne. 1991. 'From Solidaristic Wages to Solidaristic Work: A Post-Fordist Historic Compromise for Sweden?' *Economic and Industrial Democracy*, vol. 12, 3: 295–326.

– 1995. 'Swedish Unions in New Times: Women Workers as the Basis for Renewal?' Paper presented to the Amercican Political Science Association annual meeting, Chicago, 31 August to 3 September.

– 1996. 'Women Wage Earners and the Future of Swedish Unions.' *Economic and Industrial Democracy*, vol. 17: 545–86.

– 1999. '"Yesterday's Modern Times Are No Longer Modern." Swedish Unions Confront the Double Shift.' In Andrew Martin and George Ross (eds), *The Brave New World of European Labor: European Trade Unions at the Millennium*. New York: Berghahn Books.

Mahon, Rianne, and Rudolf Meidner. 1994. 'System Shift, or, What Future for the Swedish Model?' *Socialist Review*, vol. 24, 4: 57–78.

Maingain, Bernard. 1992. 'Prestations de sécurité sociale et ressources des familles: liberté, égalité, solidarité.' In E. Vieujean (ed.), *Les ressources de la famille*. Brussels: Story Scientia.

– 1993. *Vie familiale et vie professionnelle. Etat du droit, enjeux et perspectives.* Brussels: Larcier.

Malpas, Nicole, and Pierre-Yves Lambert. 1993. *Les Européens et la famille. Résultats d'une enquête d'opinion.* Brussels: Commission des Communautés européennes.

Marcou, Gérard, and Jean-Louis Thiebault (eds). 1996. *La décision gouvernementale en Europe (Belgique, Danemark, Pays-Bas, Royaume-Uni).* Paris: L'Harmattan.

Marques-Pereira, Bérengère. 1989. *L'avortement en Belgique. De la clandestinité au débat politique.* Brussels: Editions de l'Université de Bruxelles.

– 1990. 'La dynamique du compromis social-démocrate.' *Sociologie du Travail,* no. 1: 55–72.

Martin, Andrew. 1984. 'Trade Unions and Swedish Strategic Response to Change and Crisis.' In P. Gourevitch et. al., *Unions and Economic Crisis: Britain, West Germany and Sweden.* New York: Allen and Unwin.

Martin, Andrew, and George Ross. 1994. *Lessons from the Social Dimension of the European Union.* Report to the U.S. Department of Labor, Project B9K33554. Cambridge, MA: Harvard Center for European Studies.

Maruani, Margaret. 1995. 'Questions sur le chômage féminin en Europe.' *Regards sociologiques,* no. 9/10: 123–7.

– 2000. *Travail et emploi des femmes.* Paris: La Découverte.

Maruani, Margaret, and Emmanuelle Reynaud. 1993. *Sociologie de l'emploi.* Paris: La Découverte.

Math, Antoine. 1996. 'Non-take-up, niet-gebruik ou non recours? Comment traduire les termes de protection sociale.' *Recherches et prévisions,* no. 43: 19–22.

Math, Antoine, and Evelyne Renaudet. 1997. 'Développer l'accueil des enfants ou créer des emplois.' *Recherches et Prévisions,* no. 49 (September) 5–17.

Mény, Yves. 1993. *La politique comparée. Les démocraties: Allemagne, Etats-Unis, France, Grande-Bretagne, Italie,* 4th ed. Paris: Montchrestien.

Messu, Michel. 1999. 'Solidarism and Familialism: The Influence of Ideological Conceptions on the Formation of French Social Protection.' In Denis Bourget and Bruno Palier (eds), *Comparing Social Welfare Systems in Nordic Europe and France.* Paris: DREES.

Meulders, Danielle. 1995. *Les femmes et le taux d'emploi en Belgique: Causes et effets des variations des modalités de participation et d'emploi des femmes. Rapport final.* Brussels: DULBEA.

– 2000. 'European Policies Promoting More Flexible Labour Forces.' In Jane Jenson, Jacqueline Laufer, and Margaret Maruani (eds), *The Gendering of Inequalities: Women, Men and Work.* Aldershot, UK: Ashgate.

Meulders, Danielle, and Valérie Vander Stricht. 1995. 'Belgique: Hausse des taux d'activité et croissance de l'emploi atypique.' In R. Plasman (ed.), *Les femmes d'Europe sur le marché du travail.* Paris: L'Harmattan, coll. Logiques sociales.

Meunier, Philippe. 1996. 'Le recensement des allocataires des Caisses d'allocations familiales.' *Recherches et Prévisions,* no. 45: 57–63.

Miccoli, G. 1976. 'Chiesa, partito cattolico, società civile.' In V. Casttronuovo (ed.), *L'Italia contemporanea, 1945–1975.* Turin: Einuadi.

Minc, Alain. 1994. *La France de l'an 2000.* Paris: Odile Jacob / La Découverte.

Ministère des Affaires Sociales et de l'Emploi / Délégation à la Condition Féminine. 1988. *Les femmes An 2000.* Paris: La Documentation française.

Ministère de l'Emploi et du Travail. 1996a. *Le travail à temps partiel.* Brussels: Série 'Clés pour S,' February.

– 1996b. *Chômage en Belgique: Séries statistiques.* Brussels: Série 'Regards sur le marché de l'emploi,' March.

– 1996c. *L'interruption de carrière.* Brussels: Série 'Clés pour S,' April.

'Mitoyens ou citoyens? Pour en finir avec les piliers.' 1990. *La Revue nouvelle,* no. 10, numéro spécial (October).

Mitterrand, François. 1981. Speech to the Congress of UNAF. Palais des Congrès, 21 November.

– 1982a. Speech on the occasion of 8 March, International Women's Day. Palais de l'Elysée, 8 March.

– 1982b. Speech on the occasion of awarding the Médaille de la Famille française. Palais de l'Elysée, 7 June.

– 1983. Pronouncement at the Antoine Béclere maternity clinic. Clamart, 31 December.

– 1984. Interview with Katheline Evin. *Hommes et Libertés,* no. 3.

– 1985. Speech on the occasion of the installation of the Haut Conseil de la Population et de la Famille. Palais de l'Elysée, 25 October.

– 1994. Interview with Michèle Manceaux. *Marie-Claire* (May).

Moberg, Eva. 1961. 'Kvinnans villkorliga frigivning.' Reprinted in *Visionen om jämställdhet* (1993). Original appeared in *Unga Liberaler.* Stockholm: Borriers.

Moderata Samlingspartiet. 1993. *Det Bästa för Sverige – Handlingsprogram.* Stockholm: Moderata Samlingspartiet.

Molitor, Michel. 1992. 'Orthodoxie des piliers et conduites novatrices.' *Revue de l'Institut de sociologie* no. 7: 131–42.

Montalembert, Marc de. 1997. *La protection sociale en France.* Paris: La Documentation française.

Moss, Peter. 1988. *Child Care and Equality of Opportunity. Consolidated Report to the European Commission.* Brussels: DG V, publication no. 746/88.

– 1993. *Les hommes et la garde des enfants: Compte rendu du réseau des modes de garde d'enfants.* Brussels: CCE.

– 1994. Report on Work Undertaken in 1993. *Annual Report 1993: Employment Equality and Caring for Children.* Brussels: DG V.

Mrydal, Alva, and Viola Klein. 1956. *Women's Two Roles: Home and Work.* London: Routledge and Kegan Paul.

Nagels, J. 1999. 'Le modèle belge du capitalisme.' In P. Delwit, J.M. De Waele, and P. Magnette (eds). *Gouverner la Belgique.* Paris: PUF.

Näsman, Elisabet. 1990. 'Models of Population Policy – The Swedish Conception.' Paper presented at the conference on Population, Society and Demography: Policies for Europe, Turin.

– 1992. 'Parental Leave in Sweden. A Workplace Issue?' in Uschi Ebbing (ed.), *Aspects of Part-Time Working in Different Countries.* Arbeitspaper no. 7, SAMF, Gelsenkirchen.

Neiertz, Véronique. 1985. 'Contre-révolution.' *Le Monde*, 3 January.

Network on Childcare of the European Commission. 1994. *Leave Arrangements for Workers with Children.* Brussels: European Commission, DG V.

– 1996. *A Review of Services for Young Children in the EU, 1990–95.* Brussels: DG V.

Nicole, Chantal. 1986. 'L'amour en plus mais l'emploi en moins.' *Nouvelles questions féministes*, no. 13: 14–15.

Noël, Alain. 1987. 'Accumulation, Regulation, and Social Change: An Essay on French Political Economy.' *International Organization*, vol. 41, 2 (Spring): 303–33.

Norvez, Alain. 1990. *De la naissance à l'école. Santé, modes de garde et préscolarité dans la France contemporaine.* Paris: PUF/INED.

Observatoire européen des politiques familiales nationales. 1992. *Tendances et évolutions en 1992.* Louvain: Commission des Communautés européennes.

O'Connor, Julia. 1996. 'From Women in the Welfare State to Gendering Welfare State Regimes.' *Current Sociology*, vol. 44, 2 (Summer): 1–130.

Organization for Economic Cooperation and Development (OECD). 1968. *Labour Force Statistics, 1956–1966.* Paris: OECD.

– 1990a. *Le marché du travail: Quelles politiques pour les années 90?* Paris: OECD.

– 1990b. *Perspectives de l'emploi.* Paris: OECD.

– 1994. *Etudes économiques de l'OECD. Belgique.* Paris: OECD.

– 1995a. *Perspectives de l'emploi.* Paris: OECD.

– 1995b. *Labour Force Statistics, 1973–1993.* Paris: OECD.

– 1996. *Etudes économiques de l'OECD. Italie, 1995–1996.* Paris: OECD.

Office National d'Allocations Familiales pour Travailleurs Salariés. 1995. 'Les nouveaux besoins des familles.' In Ministère de la Prévoyance sociale, *50 ans de sécurité sociale ... et après?* vol. 3, *Affaire de familles*. Brussels: Bruylant.

Office National de l'Emploi. 1995. *L'interruption de carrière 1985–1995. Actualisation*. Brussels: Office National de l'Emploi.

Ohlander, Ann-Sofie. 1988. 'The Invisible Child? The Struggle over the Social Democratic Family.' In K. Misgeld, K. Molin, and K. Amark (eds), *Creating Social Democracy: A Century of the Social Democratic Labor Party in Sweden*. University Park: Penn State University Press.

– 1994. *Kvinnor, barn och arbete i Sverige 1850–1993*. Stockholm: SOU.

Olsson, Sven E. 1990. *Social Policy and the Welfare State in Sweden*. Stockholm: Arkiv furiag.

Orloff, Ann. 1993. 'Gender and the Social Rights of Citizenship: The Comparative Analysis of Gender Relations and Welfare States.' *American Sociological Review*, vol. 58 (June): 303–28.

Ouali, Nouria, and Andrea Rea. 1994. 'Flou institutionnel et formalisation des pratiques de l'informel: les expériences d'insertion professionnelle des jeunes à Brussels.' *Lien social et Politiques, RIAC*, no. 32: 103–14.

Pace, E. 1982, 'L'atteggiamento della Chiesa Cattolica nei confronti della poverta.' In G. Sarpellon, (ed.), *La poverta in Italia*. Milan: Angeli.

Palsterman, Paul. 1996. 'Communautarisation de la sécurité sociale: Pour un front du refus des sophismes.' *La Revue nouvelle* (11 November): 21–30.

Pauti, Anne. 1992. 'La politique familiale en Suède.' *Population*, vol. 47, 4 July–August: 961–85.

Paye, Olivier. 1997a. 'Féminisée la politique: recitoyennisation ou tribalisation? Une réponse à la lumière du débat parlementaire relatif à la loi belge de 1994.' *Sextant*, no. 7 (July): 139–62.

– 1997b. 'Qui doit nourrir le jeune enfant dont le père est absent? Le cas de la Belgique.' *Lien social et Politiques, RIAC*, no. 38: 85–98.

PCI. Sezione Femminile. 1989. *Le donne cambiano i tempi*. Rome.

Pedrazzi, L. (ed.). 1966. *Libro bianco sulla scuola materna*. Bologna: Il Mulino.

Peemans-Poullet, Hedwige. 1991. *Femmes en Belgique (XIXème–XXème)*. Brussels: Université des Femmes.

– 1994. 'Les droits des membres de la famille en sécurité sociale.' *Revue belge de sécurité sociale*, vol. 36, 1: 29–93.

– 1996. 'La justice sociale plutôt que la "modernisation."' *La Revue nouvelle*, no. 3 (March): 44–54.

Petersson, Olof. 1994a. *Government and Politics of the Nordic Countries*. Stockholm: Fritzes.

– 1994b. *Swedish Government and Politics*. Stockholm: Fritzes.

Pettersson, Thorleif, and Geyer Kalle. 1992. *Värderingsförändringar i Sverige. 1991.* Stockholm: Brevskolan.

Phillips, Angela, and Peter Moss. 1993. *Qui prend soin des enfants de l'Europe: Compte rendu du Réseau des modes de garde d'enfants.* Brussels: EC.

Phillips, Susan D. (ed.). 1993. 'Introduction,' *How Ottawa Spends, 1993–94: A More Democratic Canada ...?* Ottawa: Carleton University Press.

Piachault, Camille. 1984. *Daycare Facilities and Services for Children under the Age of 3 in the European Community.* Brussels: EC, DG V.

Pierson, Paul. 1994. *Dismantling the Welfare State? Reagan, Thatcher and the Politics of Retrenchment.* New York: Cambridge University Press.

Pinnelli, A. 1983. *La scuola materna negli anni '80.* Rome: Universita La Sapienza, Dipartimento di Scienze demografiche.

Pitrou, Agnès. 1992. *Les solidarités familiales.* Toulouse: Privat.

– 1994. *Les politiques familiales. Approches sociologiques.* Paris: Syros.

Pitrou, Agnès, and Renée B.-Dandurand. 1997. 'Présentation – Politiques familiales et vie de femmes.' *Lien social et Politiques, RIAC,* no. 36: 5–16.

Polanyi, Karl. 1944. *The Great Transformation.* New York: Rinehart.

Pollack, Mark A., and Emilie Hafer-Burton. 2000. 'Mainstreaming Gender in the European Union.' Paper presented at 11th Conference of Europeanists, Chicago, March.

Pontusson, Jonas. 1992a. 'At the End of the Road: Swedish Social Democracy in Crisis.' *Politics and Society,* vol. 20, 3: 48–69.

– 1992b. 'Part VI: Sweden.' In Mark Kesselman et al., *European Politics in Transition,* 2nd ed. Boston: Heath.

– 1994. 'Sweden: After the Golden Age.' In P. Anderson and P. Camiller (eds), *Mapping the West European Left.* London: Verso.

Poulet, Isabelle. 1994. 'Elasticité et résistance de l'informel: Les politiques partenariales de prévention en Belgique.' *Lien social et Politiques, RIAC,* no. 32: 87–102.

Presidenza del Consiglio dei Ministri. 1997a. *Commissione per l'analisi delle marco-compatibilità della spesa sociale,* Rome, 28 February.

– 1997b. Direttiva del Presidente del Consiglio dei Ministri. 'Azioni volte a promuovere l'attribuzione di poteri e responsabilità alle donne, a riconoscere e garantire liberté di scelte e qualità sociale a donne e uomini.' Rome, 8 March.

Presidenza del Consiglio dei Ministri, Dipartimento affari sociali. 1994. *Per una politica familiare in Italia.* Rome.

– 1996. 'Disposizioni per la promozione di diritti e di opportunità per l'infanzia e l'adolescenza.' *Disegno di legge del Presidente del Consiglio dei Ministri,* Rome, December.

Prost, Antoine. 1984. 'L'évolution de la politique familiale en France de 1938 à 1981.' *Le Mouvement social*, no. 129: 7–28.

Rezsohazy, Rudolf. 1991. *Les nouveaux enfants d'Adam et Eve. Les formes actuelles de couples et de familles*. Louvain-la-Neuve: Academia.

Rocaboy, Yvon. 1999. 'The Decentralisation of Welfare Policy in France: An Economic Perspective.' In Denis Bourget and Bruno Palier (eds), *Comparing Social Welfare Systems in Nordic Europe and France*. Paris: DREES: 541–60.

Rodano, M. 1976. 'Un decennio di lotte per le pensione.' *Donne e Politica*, no. 34: 10–15.

Rostgaard, Tine, and Torben Fridberg. 1998. *Caring for Children and Older People – A Comparison of European Policies and Practices*. Copenhagen: Danish National Institute of Social Research.

Ross, George. 1982. *Workers and Communists in France*. Berkeley: University of California Press.

– 1995. *Jacques Delors and European Integration*. Cambridge: Polity Press.

– 1997. 'Part VII: The European Union.' In M. Kesselman et al., *European Politics in Transition*, 3rd ed. Boston: Houghton-Mifflin.

Rubery, J., and C. Fagan (eds). 1992. *Bulletin sur les femmes et l'emploi dans la C. E.*, no. 1 (October).

Ryner, Magnus. 1994. 'Economic Policy in the 1980s: The 'Third Way,' the Swedish Model and the Transition from Fordism to Post-Fordism.' In W. Clement and R. Mahon (eds), *Swedish Social Democracy*. Toronto: Canadian Scholars Press.

Sainsbury, Diane. 1994. 'Women's and Men's Social Rights: Gendering Dimensions of Welfare States.' In Sainsbury (ed.) *Gendering Welfare States*. London: Sage.

Saraceno, Chiara. 1990. *Child Poverty and Deprivation in Italy: From the Early Fifties to the Late Eighties*. UNICEF Report. Florence: Ospedale degli Innocenti.

– 1994. 'The Ambivalent Familialism of the Italian Welfare State.' *Social Politics*, no. 1: 60–82.

Sarpellon, G. 1982. *La povertà in Itali*. Milan: Franco Angeli.

Schultheis, Franz. 1997. 'La contribution de la famille à la reproduction sociale: une affaire d'Etat.' In J. Commaille and F. de Singly (eds), *La question familiale en Europe*. Paris: L'Harmattan.

Seiler, D.L. 1999. 'Un État entre importation et implosion: consociativité, partitocratie et lotissement dans le sphère publique en Belgique.' In P. Delwit, J.M. De Waele, and P. Magnette (eds), *Gouverner la Belgique*. Paris: PUF.

Sénat français. 1994. *La politique familiale. La conciliation de la vie professionnelle et de la vie familiale*. Service des Affaires européennes, division des études de législation comparée, Paris.

Senato della Republica. 1963. IV Legislatura. Documenti 1043. *Disegno di legge d'iniziativa popolare: Istituzione del servizio sociale degli asili nidi per bambini fino a tre anni*, 23 February, Rome.

Seroni, A. 1977. *Questione femminile in Italia, 1970–1977*. Rome: Editori Riuniti.

Sgritta, G.B., and A.L. Zanatta. 1994. 'Familles et politiques familiales en Italie: contraintes et promesses.' In W. Dumon (ed.), *Evolution des politiques familiales dans les Etats membres de l'Union européenne*. Brussels, DG V / Observatoire Européen des Politiques Familiales Nationales.

Shafir, Gershon (ed.). 1998. *The Citizenship Debates: A Reader*. Minneapolis: University of Minnesota Press.

Sineau, Mariette. 1992. 'Droit et démocratie.' In Georges Duby and Michelle Perrot (eds), *Histoire des femmes*. Paris: Plon.

Singly, François de. 1991. 'La création politique des infortunes contemporaines de la femme mariée et salariée.' In F. de Singly and F. Schultheis (eds), *Affaires de famille, Affaires d'Etat*. Nancy: Editions de l'Est.

– 1993. 'Les habits neufs de la domination masculine.' *Esprit*, no. 196: 54–64.

SOU. 1989. *Arbetstid och Välfärd. Betänkandet av arbetstidskommitten*. Stockholm: Almänna Förlaget.

– 1990. *Demokrati och makt I Sverige. Maktutredning huvudrapport*. Stockholm: Almänna Förlaget.

Steck, Philippe. 1993. *Les prestations familiales*. Paris: PUF.

Stephens, John D., Evelyne Huber, and Leonard Ray. 1999. 'The Welfare State in Hard Times.' In Herbert Kitschelt, Peter Lange, Gary Marks, and John D. Stephens (eds), *Continuity and Change in Contemporary Capitalism*. Cambridge: Cambridge University Press.

Sterdyniak, Henri, et al. 1994. 'Lutter contre le chômage: des politiques macroéconomiques traditionnelles à la réduction du temps de travail.' *Problèmes économiques*, no. 2.396–2.397: 43–53.

Stevens, Barrie, and Wolfgang Michalski. 1994. 'Perspectives à long terme de l'emploi.' *Problèmes économiques*, no. 2.396–2.397: 17–21.

Strobel, Pierre. 1997. 'Les mésaventures de Monsieur Gagnepain.' In Francis Ronsin et al. *Démographie et politique*. Dijon: Editions universitaires de Dijon.

Sundström, Mariane. 1993. 'The Growth in Full-Time Work among Swedish Women in the 1980s.' *Acta Sociologica*, no. 36: 139–50.

Sundström, Mariane, and F.P. Stafford. 1992. 'Female Labour Force Participation, Fertility and Public Policy in Sweden.' *European Journal of Population*, no. 8: 199–215.

Sweden. n.d. [1995?] *Economic Restructuring and Industrial Policy in Sweden*. Stockholm: Ministry of Industry and Commerce.

Swenson, Peter. 1989. *Fair Shares: Unions, Pay and Politics in Sweden and West Germany*. Ithaca, NY: Cornell University Press.

Sylos Labini, Paolo. 1995. *La Crisi Italiana*. Bari: Latera.

TCO. 1971. *Familj och samhälle. Rapport från TCOs: familjepolitiska grupp*. Stockholm: Prisma.

Teague, Paul. 1989. *The European Community: The Social Dimension*. London: Kogan Page.

Teirlinck, Michèle. 1994. 'The European Union and the Family.' *Social Europe, Special Issue on the European Union and the Family*, (January): 115.

Thelen, Kathleen, and Sven Steinmo. 1992. 'Historical Institutionalism in Comparative Politics.' In Sven Steinmo and Kathleen Thelen, *Structuring Politics: Historical Institutionalism in Comparative Analysis*. New York: Cambridge University Press.

Therborn, Göran. 1983. 'Why Some Classes Are More Successful Than Others.' *New Left Review*, no. 138: 37–56.

– 1992. 'Swedish Social Democracy and the Transition from Industrial to Post-Industrial Politics.' In F. Fox Piven (ed.), *Labor Parties in Post-Industrial Societies*. New York: Oxford University Press.

Theunissen, Anne-Françoise. 1996. 'Emploi, chômage et inégalités.' *La Revue nouvelle* (March): 55–67.

Thirriot, Luc. 1990. 'Le plein emploi en Suède.' *Économies et Sociétés, Économie du travail*, no. 16: 103–67.

Tilly, Charles. 1984. *Big Structures, Large Processes, Huge Comparisons*. New York: Sage.

Ullman, Clare F. 1998. *The Welfare State's Other Crisis. Explaining the New Partnership between Nonprofit Organizations and the State in France*. Bloomington: Indiana University Press.

Vantemsche, Guy. 1994. *La sécurité sociale. 1994. Les origines du système belge. Le présent face à son passé*. Brussels: De Boeck.

Vielle, Pascale. 1994. *Les politiques publiques en faveur d'une meilleure conciliation de la vie familiale et de la vie professionnelle en Europe. Quelles conceptions des rapports sociaux de sexe?* Rapport pour l'Association internationale de la sécurité sociale / Fonds national suisse de la recherche scientifique. Geneva.

Visco Comandini, Vincenzo (ed.). 1992. 'Il cordinamento finanziario delle Regioni sugli enti locali: il caso degli asili nidi.' In *Istituto di Studi sulle Regioni*. Milan: Giuffre.

Vogel-Polsky, Eliane, and Jean Vogel. 1991. *L'Europe sociale 1993. Illusion, alibi ou réalité?* Brussels: Editions de l'Université de Brussels.

Weatherill, Stephen, and Paul Beaumont. 1993. *EC Law.* London: Penguin.

Wilson, Elizabeth. 1977. *Only Half-Way to Paradise. Women in Postwar Britain.* London: Tavistock.

Winkler, Celia. 1995. 'The Single Mother in the Swedish Welfare State, 1960–1975: A Study in Equality.' Paper presented at the 1995 annual meeting of the American Sociological Association, Washington, DC.

Wise, Lois Recascino. 1993. 'Whither Solidarity? Transitions in Public-Sector Pay Policy.' *British Journal of Industrial Relations*, vol. 31, no. 1: 75–95.

Contributors

Franca Bimbi is Professor of Sociology, University of Padua, Italy.

Anne-Marie Daune-Richard is a researcher in CNRS (Conseil national de recherche scientifique) and a member of LEST (Laboratoire d'Économie et de Sociologie du Travail) in Aix-en-Provence, France.

Vincent Della Sala is Professor of Political Science, Carleton University, Ottawa, Canada.

Jane Jenson is Professor of Political Science, Université de Montréal, Canada, and Director of the Family Network, Canadian Policy Research Networks, Inc., Ottawa, Canada.

Rianne Mahon is Professor of Public Administration and of Sociology, Carleton University, Ottawa, Canada.

Bérengère Marques-Pereira is Professor of Political Science and Director of Research in the Institut de Sociologie, Université libre de Bruxelles, Belgium.

Olivier Paye teaches political science at the Université libre de Bruxelles, Belgium.

George Ross is Professor of Political Science and of Sociology, Brandeis University, Waltham, Mass., U.S.A., and Senior Associate, Center for European Studies, Harvard University, Cambridge, Mass., U.S.A.

Mariette Sineau is Director of Research in CNRS (Conseil national de recherche scientifique) and a member of CEVIPOF (Centre d'étude de la vie politique française), Fondation nationale des sciences politiques, Paris, France.

Studies in Comparative Political Economy and Public Policy

Editors: Michael Howlett, David Laycock, Stephen McBride, Simon Fraser University

This series is designed to showcase innovative approaches to political economy and public policy from a comparative perspective. While originating in Canada, the series provides attractive offerings to a wide international audience, featuring studies with local, sub-national, cross-national, and international empirical bases and theoretical frameworks.

Published to date: